HOW
AMERICA
GOT
ON-LINE

HOW AMERICA GOT ON-LINE

Politics, Markets, and the Revolution in Telecommunications

ALAN STONE

M.E. Sharpe
Armonk, New York
London, England

Library of Congress Cataloging-in-Publication Data

Stone, Alan, 1931–
How America got on-line: politics, markets, and the revolution in
telecommunications / by Alan Stone.
p.   cm.
Includes bibliographical references and index.
ISBN 1-56324-576-0 (alk. paper). —
ISBN 1-56324-577-9 (pbk.: alk. paper)
1. Telecommunication—United States—History.
2. Entrepreneurship—United States—History.   3. Technological
innovations—Economic aspects—United States—History.
4. Information society—United States—History.   I. Title.
HE7775.S78   1997
384'.0973—dc21   97-7903
CIP

Printed in the United States of America

The paper used in this publication meets the minimum requirements of
American National Standard for Information Sciences—
Permanence of Paper for Printed Library Materials,
ANSI Z 39.48-1984.

BM (c)   10   9   8   7   6   5   4   3   2   1
BM (p)   10   9   8   7   6   5   4   3   2   1

TO CELESTE

Contents

Preface

The title of composer John Cage's autobiography, *How to Improve the World (You Will Only Make Matters Worse)*, captures the sentiment of many observers of the telecommunications industry about government control. Throughout the world there has been a movement toward privatization of telecommunications services and the introduction of competition. Where private monopoly prevailed, as in the United States and the most populous provinces of Canada, there has been a clear trend toward the introduction of competition at every level of service and in every equipment sector. As for public ownership, this book joins in its general rejection. The 1989 fall of the Berlin Wall signaled the dismal failure of public ownership as a system of production and distribution. In the West it is difficult to find an example of a publicly owned enterprise that is operated efficiently. The U.S. Postal Corporation is widely viewed as the American model of everything that is wrong with public ownership.

Rejecting public ownership, however, does not mean that government should play *no* role in shaping market structure or behavior. I eschew any attempt to provide a general theory distinguishing proper and improper governmental intervention throughout the complex modern economy; this book is about the telecommunications industry and its interfaces with other sectors. A historical view of that industry shows that the relationships between government intervention and market structure are complex and that the appropriate relationship has varied over time. There have been circumstances in which private monopolies subject to certain forms of government regulation or subsidy have resulted in excellent market performance. The static measures of such performance include technological progressiveness, relative efficiency of production, and the level of price relative to production costs. And, of course, these aspects can be measured over time. At times when technology is advancing slowly, the service is homogeneous (plain old telephone service), and there are clear scale economies, monopoly subject to regulation has led to excellent performance. AT&T and Bell Canada's experiences over long periods of time show that this has been the case. Indeed, taking a historical view of the telecommunications industry undermines the sweeping view that competition is *always* better.

How do we know when monopolies' moment should be over? The history of customer premises equipment manufacture in the United States illustrates the dynamic. In an open, entrepreneurial society there are always people who have entrepreneurial skills, capital, and a capacity for technological innovation. If the pecuniary rewards are sufficiently large, the three resources will be combined. The odds in favor of overturning or eroding a monopoly may initially be low, but history is replete with examples of persistent people and firms overcoming such odds. Before World War II the typical kinds of customer premises equipment were simple devices with little utility to customers. A typical question addressed to a regulatory commission was, for example, whether a local hotel might control telephone booths in its lobby. Regulators, as we will see, were unwilling to abrogate telephone company end-to-end responsibility in favor of such minor advances. Technological developments during and after World War II began to alter the tradeoffs. The development of telephone answering machines and recording devices coupled with wartime advances in electronics gradually triggered the introduction of many new products that could be plugged into the telephone network. Homogeneity was supplanted by heterogeneity, and entrepreneurs eventually persuaded regulators to allow the introduction of their products into the telephone network. In summary, technological possibilities triggered entrepreneurial activity which, in turn, led to reshaping the structure of the telecommunications industry.

At other times the convergence of technologies can lead to the reshaping of an industry. As we will see in Chapter 8, computers have an ancient lineage. Government support during World War II dramatically accelerated technological progress. Postwar progress was rapid as well, largely because of Bell Telephone Laboratories' invention of the transistor. Older firms such as IBM and newer ones as well, together with educational and governmental institutions, began the tentative steps that led to the convergence of computers and communications. If data could be transformed and stored, could it not also be transmitted? Thus, the traditional telecommunications industry was reshaped not only by new entrepreneurs but also by the expanding horizons of a vast new business. In a somewhat different way, the traditional telecommunications industry came into conflict with the television industry. Voice was by far the most important product carried through the network in the prewar era, but the dramatic growth of television in the postwar era inexorably led to the issue of who should carry video information. In more recent times, as the process of digitalization has advanced rapidly, we may be on the road to still another structural transformation. If all information—voice, video, data, fax, photo and so on—can be reduced to digital information as "0"s and "1"s, we may be entering a new era of product homogeneity whose future structural implications can now only be dimly seen. But on the other hand, the wide variety of service offerings, potential content, and transmission media could lead to a variety of networks, each offering heterogeneous sets of packages.

Technological possibility is thus the engine of entrepreneurship and industrial structure in telecommunications. But we should not enshrine the vision of a small inventor working in his or her laboratory to develop a new product or service on a relatively small budget. Clearly, as this book will show, there are many such people. But they are not the only—or even the primary—engine for bringing new technologies to market. No institution on earth has been responsible for more technological progress than the former monopolist AT&T through its Bell Telephone Laboratories (Bell Labs) Division. Much the same can be said about other large firms with dominant positions, such as IBM. Governmental and non-profit institutions can also play major roles. As we will see in Chapter 8, the Internet and its progeny, the World Wide Web, would probably have not been possible without university and government development and subsidies. Only after enormous expenditure and full-scale development of the Internet, a system that is becoming a full-scale alternative to the conventional telephone system, were its commercial opportunities exploited.

Yet the history of government enterprise is often a history of economic failure. The economic shambles that was the Soviet Union is a testament to the dangers of government overreach. Even in non-socialist countries, public enterprise has usually been badly run. Telecommunications in Europe, as we will see in Chapter 6, has been improving dramatically since the movement toward privatization that began when the British government privatized British Telecom (BT) in 1984. That company is incomparably more efficient and progressive than it was as a public monopoly. How can we reconcile the successes of government intervention with its numerous failures? First, the cases of successful government intervention have generally occurred in connection with the pursuit of values other than pecuniary ones. Defense preparations and the conduct of war triggered many of the most important telecommunications advances. Second, there can be very costly infrastructural goals that private firms are unwilling or unable to undertake. Sometimes those goals (for example, provision of a clean water supply) have clear positive external effects that would ramify through much of the society. Subsidies to private firms can be useful in such situations. Third, while there is a general presumption against government intervention, because market competition will ordinarily lead to better economic performances and provide superior incentives to individuals and firms, that presumption can be overcome. When the presumption is overcome, government intervention should be as light as possible. A private monopoly is superior to government enterprise. Regulation, when indicated (as in the case of a natural monopoly), should assign reasonable goals that private firms are expected to achieve rather than require a public authority to design the means and details of achieving such goals and interfere deeply in a company's day-to-day affairs. The reason is obvious. Those who operate daily in the marketplace have a better understanding of the innumerable details involved in operating a business than bureaucrats and legislators do, and they can adjust their activities far more flexibly and quickly than central planners can.

While I believe that these principles help to distinguish many of the cases of successful government intervention from the many failures, a final word of caution is necessary. Government intervention should be conducted under the sunset principle. That is, periodic re-investigation of the conditions that initially led to intervention are in order so that an established relationship does not become entrenched, as it has in the case of American agriculture. The rumblings of invention, innovation, and potential entrepreneurship should alert government and the attentive public to the changed conditions that call for new relationships or, more likely, the entry of competition. Technological changes and the possibility of market convergence between previously discrete sectors should send the same sort of signal as they did when communicating became an important function of computers. I do not for a moment underestimate the political efforts needed to dislodge an entrenched relationship. Nevertheless, as we will see, government actors have responded to such situations, helping the telecommunications industry to adjust to new realities.

The new realities are moving more rapidly in telecommunications today than ever before. One would be foolhardy, indeed, to predict the implications of technologies now coming to the fore. For example, what are the implications of web broadcasting, in which data are "pushed" to users at determined intervals rather than users having to "pull" information from various sources that they must contact? Again, what impact will Internet telephony have on the traditional long-distance carriers? Extranets (such as the one developed by Federal Express) that extend enterprise networks to suppliers, customers, and others are in their infancy. Their probable impact can now be only dimly seen. New, powerful, digital spread spectrum cordless phones that enhance security and sound quality, and can offer a range of eight-tenths of a mile from the phone base, will undoubtedly affect wire line firms in ways that we cannot yet fathom. And these are only a few of the newer technologies now coming on line. When one adds to the difficulty of predicting how new technologies will shape the future of telecommunications, the added uncertainties of how the F.C.C. and other regulators will respond, and the shifting structures of corporate alliances, it is evident that any *precise* prediction of the future is impossible. Nevertheless, the last chapter does attempt to make general judgments about the future of the increasingly important telecommunications sector.

Returning to the John Cage quotation with which I began this preface: mistakes have been made, and policies have changed, but, as this book intends to show, the complex and changing government-business relations in telecommunications have not made matters worse; they have improved the world.

I could fill two pages with the names of academics, consultants, attorneys, engineers, and business people who have aided my understanding of telecommunications and its relationships with other industries. The insights provided by these people in Canada, Germany, the United Kingdom, and the United States continuously challenged me to rethink, and often change, my views on many topics. I would like to single out my wife Celeste Stone, to whom this book is dedicated, for editing, typing, and most importantly, compelling me to reconsider a great deal in this book. I would also like to thank Michael Weber, Patricia Kolb, Steven Martin, Ana Erlic, and Elizabeth Granda at M. E. Sharpe for their exemplary efforts.

HOW
AMERICA
GOT
ON-LINE

1

From the Telegraph to Hypercommunications

Why Telecommunications?

Virtually every person who considers the future agrees that the world is in the process of major social and economic changes and that telecommunications is a driving force of those changes. If that is the case, the study of telecommunications is not simply the examination of one more sector, like pulp and paper, clothing, or automobiles. Nor is public policy for telecommunications just one more branch of public policy studies, like civil rights, airlines, or education. If the experts' projection of the future of telecommunications is a correct one, the sector will be *the* leading one in shaping our social, economic, and political futures. No reasonable person would attempt to predict the future with precision, but we can certainly surmise certain probable trends, and, as we will see, the nearly uniform considerations of the experts do portend a dominating future for communications—domination so extensive that we can call the sector hypercommunications.

The telephone began as a simple device in 1876, capable of transmitting over very short distances. At the outset, private lines, not an enormous switched network, were conceived as its probable use. Thus, lines between the offices and homes of physicians or burglar alarms between the police and a very few subscribers were conceived as typical uses. Over the next century, visionaries and entrepreneurs conceived more and more novel uses for the telephone. But in recent times the marriage of the telephone, television, and the computer has increased telecommunications possibilities exponentially, so that the new telecommunications now dominates vast numbers of other activities. A few of the new uses now on line or coming on line include (1) telemedicine, (2) telelaw, (3) tele-education, (4) data coordination, (5) design coordination, (6) telecontrol of factory and service

3

operations, (7) telebanking, (8) telemarketing, (9) telecommuting (allowing people to work at home), (10) teleshopping, and (11) teleconferencing (reducing the need for business travel).

In this chapter we will examine some of the consequences of telecommunications, and why choosing the correct set of public policies—or absence of public policies—is vitally important. Probably the best starting point to capture an understanding of the future that looms as a result of hypercommunications is to look at an older technological breakthrough that dramatically changed our economy and society. Probably the best example is the automobile. In 1900 there were approximately 8,000 automobile registrations in the United States. By 1920 there were approximately 8,131,500, and by 1950 about 40,339,000.[1] Another measure of the automobile's impact is its rank in the value of products of American industry: one hundred fiftieth in 1899, seventy-seventh in 1904, seventh in 1914, second in 1919, and first in 1925. These direct data do not begin to measure the epoch-making impact of the automobile. The automobile generated dramatic growth in other industries, including petroleum, glass, rubber, and steel; it stimulated the development of innumerable supplier industries, such as pistons, batteries, and car radios. Vast dealer networks were created to market cars. Gasoline stations and repair facilities sprang up in every city, town, and village to support the industry. Highway construction and the manufacture of materials, such as asphalt and concrete, took place throughout the country. The automobile was directly responsible for suburbanization and a large portion of the vast expansion of the leisure industry. And while we may bemoan today's environmental pollution, let us not forget that the automobile supplanted vast quantities of horse flop that littered every American community.[2]

In order to understand the imperialist tendencies of telecommunications—its ability to take over and control many other activities—its historical development from the modest beginnings of the telegraph to the contemporary capacities of hypercommunications to dominate virtually every activity should be set forth. The future is best understood as history. The most important dimensions to bear in mind when assessing telecommunications' impact are time and space, because advances in communications enable each of us to reduce the time required to communicate with others while also increasing the number of persons and institutions with whom we may communicate. For this reason, advances in communications also allow us to enlarge the area in which we can conduct social and business transactions. Thus, you can make a long-distance telephone call or write an electronic mail (E-mail) message to nearly any location in the world. Such communications are almost instantaneous. Therefore, as a practical matter your ability to conduct transactions over a wide area is increased. For the same reason the world economy has recently seen a change to what sociologist Daniel Bell terms "distributed manufacturing," in which "most firms in retailing (such as Reebok or The Gap) have production in more than forty different countries so as to be able to respond rapidly to style changes and point of sale marketing information."[3]

While the foregoing examples suggest the power of communications to coordinate activity, it also enhances one's opportunity to control activities. The control may be exercised not only over persons but over things, such as machines, as well. Communications expert James R. Beniger has pioneered work in the area of control. He defines control as "purposive influence toward a predetermined goal" consisting of "two essential elements: *influence* of one agent over another, meaning that the former causes changes in the behavior of the latter; and *purpose,* in the sense that that influence is directed toward some prior goal of the controlling agent. . . . Control encompasses the entire range from absolute control to the weakest . . . form."[4]

Modern communications, as an example, allows McDonald's Corporation from its headquarters in Oak Brook, Illinois, to "control" the management of about fourteen thousand restaurants and the production of millions of hamburgers throughout the world. Without modern telecommunications, McDonald's would have to rely on hiring only persons whose trustworthiness, veracity, and competence would be beyond question. The investigative costs to do this in the case of any large enterprise are virtually prohibitive. For this reason in the era before modern communications, merchants tended to hire, whenever possible, members of their own families for distant transactions; only they could be reasonably trusted.[5] Given the speed with which information can now be transmitted and the accuracy with which it can be measured, a person exercising control can afford to take greater personnel risks. If a mistake is made, the ability to recover using modern communications is much greater than without it.

This introduces three other aspects of modern communications: dialectic, feedback, and accuracy. Before looking at these concepts, consider that the cost of obtaining information is a component of almost every activity. Information costs are those costs incurred in obtaining information about the prospective use of resources. Thus, when a pharmaceutical company expends millions of dollars to develop information about a product's safety, effectiveness, and side effects, it has incurred information costs. To take another example, the United States government expends millions of dollars each year to learn about the actions and potential actions of foreign nations. And, of course, entire industries, such as advertising and book publishing, sell information.[6] If we next assume that a great deal of human behavior, notably market behavior, involves a quest to be more efficient rather than less efficient, it follows that this consideration applies to information costs, just as it does to production or acquisition costs. Telecommunications can obviously be a factor in reducing information costs and, hence, total costs.

Let us now return to dialectic, feedback, and accuracy. Dialectic is the process of dispute or debate with other persons. Obviously, almost all situations involve degrees of uncertainty or risk. Discussions with people whose assessments and information differ from one's own can lead to a higher synthesis. The larger the network of discussants is and the more interactive the discussion is, the more likely it is that one can reach a better and more efficient solution. Modern telecommunications is the instrument to accomplish these goals. And the dialectic possibilities of telecommunications continue to increase as costs for services (such as fax, long distance, and video) fall, technological progress continues, and new services (such as the Internet) develop. Feedback consists of communicating the results of actions taken to see how closely the actual results correspond to the anticipated ones. Obviously, the opportunity to correct as quickly as possible when things are going wrong is enormously advantageous in adjusting both ends and means. Again, it is clear that this advantage of modern telecommunications ramifies throughout the economy and society. The net result of the dialectic and feedback processes is to facilitate the likelihood of greater control by controllers over persons and things to do what the controller desires—the essence of accuracy.

It is easier to conceive the power of telecommunications by looking at the past rather than contemplating the future. Consider the telegraph. Less than twenty-five years after Samuel F.B. Morse invented a practical telegraph in 1837, there were 32,000 miles of pole line transmitting approximately five million messages per year. Coast-to-coast transmission began in 1861, and in 1866 the second Atlantic cable opened, permitting rapid communication between North America and Europe. Samuel F.B. Morse, a devoutly religious man, exclaimed about his invention, "What hath God wrought!" And at least part of the answer is that it contributed in a major way to extraordinary transformations in economic and social life. Geographical markets were expanded and integrated, capital flows were greatly facilitated, information and transaction costs were dramatically reduced for all businesses ready to use the new technology, the time required to enter into transactions dramatically diminished, while the number of transactions increased substantially. New businesses, such as credit reporting, commodity exchanges, a national securities market, and wire services developed. Socially, personal communications between people located far apart took place more rapidly than anyone had dreamed possible before the telegraph's invention.[7]

Of course, one must be careful not to overstate the telegraph's contribution to the transformation of life that occurred from its invention in 1837 until the telephone's invention in 1876. It was a major contributor, not the dominant factor, in the transformation during that period. Certainly the railroad played a more important role, as did extraordinary changes in industrial technologies. Even in communications we can easily forget about such important developments during that period as ink pens with steel nibs, the lead pencil, mass-produced envelopes, and, most importantly, the typewriter.[8] The era of hypercommunications was far off, but even in its infancy, telecommunications had crucial impacts in the business and social worlds. With each successive phase in telecommunications history, the sector became increasingly important.

The Plan of the Book

There are many ways in which telecommunications can be studied. It can be examined as a history of invention and technological breakthroughs, starting with Morse's telegraph through such recent innovations as digital cellular telephony, fiber optics, and asynchronous transfer mode (ATM) switching. This book will not be a telecommunications engineering text. Nevertheless, it will be attentive to technological developments because the behavior of government and private-sector actors cannot be understood without considering their responses to technological breakthroughs and opportunities. Nor will the book be a social history of telecommunications, although attention must be paid to the impact of the telephone and other telecommunications devices on our social lives and the entrepreneurial and marketing decisions that triggered new uses and their consequences. Nor will this book be a business history of the corporate organizations, most importantly AT&T and its predecessors, that have been the major players in the dramatic changes that have occurred since the invention of the telephone to the present day. Nor will this book be a legal history of the administrative and court decisions that have been crucial in shaping modern telecommunications. Nor will this book be a political study of the important actors and forces that have shaped the pertinent communications statutes, such as the Communications Act of 1934.

Rather, a book on telecommunications must be interdisciplinary, incorporating a study of all of these facets. The interface of business and government in telecommunications must embrace all of these topics, for in the real world, engineers, businesspersons, and governmental actors incorporate all of these disciplines in arriving at strategies and policies. Consider a single historical example that illustrates the point. Until the 1940s, the basic path of an intercity telephone conversation was through wire pairs. After that time, wire pairs were gradually supplanted by microwave transmission and coaxial cable. While the cost and technological considerations of wire pairs led regulators to believe that the industry was a natural monopoly (an industry in which production is carried out most efficiently by a single firm), the later technological developments and associated cost considerations led them to change their minds in favor of regulated competition.[9] In more recent times fiber optics have significantly supplanted microwave and coaxial cable, and this has led some analysts to believe that the basic transmission of intercity telecommunications would once again be undertaken by a single provider if fierce competition prevailed.[10] At this juncture it is not important to evaluate the various economic, technological, or policy claims. It is only necessary to illustrate that issues in telecommunications cannot be neatly subdivided into discrete segments. The field is inherently interdisciplinary and is treated that way by those who are actively involved as well as those who study it. The state of technology at any time is the starting point, however.

This book is, then, an interdisciplinary look at telecommunications from its early period to the present time. It will examine the impact of each major new development from the earliest crude telephones through the most modern digital devices. We will see how the vision of telecommunications moved from private lines to local loops, long distance to today's global networks. But uncertainty and incorrect analysis have also played roles with an important policy message. Policymakers should be cautious and government intervention incorporating uncertainty will fare better than that which embraces rigid planning. A brief story about the microprocessor, one of the most important contributors to hypercommunications, illustrates the importance of uncertainty and the difficulty of incorporating all of the relevant variables that lead to a correct decision. In 1971 Marcian E. (Ted) Hoff, an engineer at the then three-year-old Intel Corporation, invented the microprocessor, a new kind of chip. The microprocessor placed most of the transistors (a device invented earlier by AT&T) that constitute a computer's logic circuits on a single chip and made the chip programmable—controllable by software. By 1975 Intel thought that its microprocessors were too slow and limited to be used for anything but specialized controllers for applications like traffic lights. In that year Bill Gates, not yet twenty, showed that BASIC, an important computer programming language, could operate on a microprocessor. By 1980 Intel was able to place 30,000 transistors on a chip that ran far more rapidly than the original microprocessor. In that period IBM, which had dominated the mainframe computer industry, had decided to enter the personal computer (PC) business and was casting about for a supplier of microprocessors and another supplier of an operating system. It chose, respectively, Intel and Microsoft. IBM was confident that it would dominate the PC business as it had the mainframe business, a judgment shared by virtually every knowledgeable observer and journalist. Accordingly, IBM made an enormous business mistake. It failed to obtain exclusive rights to either Intel's microprocessor line or Microsoft's operating system.[11]

IBM's decision allowed Intel and Microsoft to supply hundreds of so-called clones that soon deluged the PC market, reducing IBM to a lesser role. The PC, in turn, boosted the power of telecommunications as no device had since the invention of the telephone. Electronic mail, the Internet, and a whole host of equipment and services based on the PC were either not conceived or dimly surmised at the time Ted Hoff had his stroke of genius. The point of the story is that even the highly intelligent and knowledgeable actors associated with the genesis of the PC could not accurately glimpse future developments. There are simply too many variables in the social world for even the most extraordinary mind to incorporate. The story, rather, illustrates once again what Friedrich A. Hayek, the Nobel Prize–winning economist, terms the "synoptic delusion": The utilization of knowledge "is and remains widely dispersed among individuals . . . and in the case of very complex phenomena the powers of science are . . . limited by the practical impossibility of ascertaining all the particular facts which we would have to know if its theories were to give us the power of predicting specific events."[12]

This perceptive conclusion is not an invitation to paralysis; neither markets nor government can operate that way. Rather, it leads, first, to the adoption of mechanisms that allow flexible adjustment, of which free markets are the most obvious example. When government actors intervene in this process by stimulating one technology at the expense of others, the synoptic delusion is bound to occur. Indeed, government is more likely to do so than people engaged in the day-to-day workings of a complex activity that is disciplined by a market. But as we will see in this book, there are times when government must act because nonmarket values are involved or the market is not performing or is doing so unsatisfactorily. This leads to the second important conclusion that follows from Hayek's synoptic delusion hypothesis. When government is constrained to act, it should do so modestly. Lighter regulation in which reasonable performance goals are set for private monopolists (such as the old AT&T) is far superior to rigid government planning of goals, specific design standards, and inflexible timetables. Again, agencies with continuous regulatory authority over *specific* industries are superior instruments than oversight and legislation through generalist institutions, such as Congress or state legislatures. These and similar themes will be seen throughout this book.

The third conclusion that follows from Hayek's synoptic delusion concept concerns what has been termed public philosophy. Walter Lippmann, the great American political theorist, coined the phrase "public philosophy" to apply to the most central features of a society, including such values as free speech and religion. These underlying values tend not be questioned and form the bases for specific actions. The phrase public philosophy, thus, describes underlying axioms and the unquestioned bases of policymaking.[13] The same conception can apply to economic ideologies, such as "socialism," "free markets," "welfare state," and so on. Different public philosophies employ important conceptual terms that guide policymakers' decision making to a presumably sound solution. For example, in recent times the word "privatization" has entered the vocabulary of policymakers. It essentially means selling off government property to private investors. The term, widely used in contemporary public discourse, would have little political importance in earlier eras when the idea of selling off state property played no role in government thinking about policymaking. In 1933, for example, when Franklin D. Roosevelt became president of the United States, a strong statist trend was in evidence throughout the major nations, and competition—indeed, the whole business enterprise system—was in disrepute. Business firms had to be guided by "wise" government officials and the strong arm of the state. This conception applied to telecommunications as it did to other important sectors. Once such a public philosophy becomes established—sometimes over vigorous opposition—policies are made incrementally. I do not suggest that policies are made mechanistically in the way one follows a recipe. There can be difficulties and uncertainties, to be sure. Nevertheless, a public philosophy reduces the amount of information that must be considered in solving public problems and the amount of effort required in reaching decisions, since it guides patterns of thought to a policy conclusion.[14]

A point is reached, however, when even modifications of a prevailing public philosophy no longer achieve desirable results or are unable to reasonably approximate expected outcomes. The synoptic delusion, in short, has struck with hurricane force. When this occurs, policymakers search for a new public philosophy. Economist John Maynard Keynes prophetically wrote that "Practical men who believe themselves to be quite exempt from any intellectual influences are usually the slaves of some defunct economist. Madmen in authority, who hear voices in the air, are usually distilling their frenzy from some academic scribbler of a few years back."[15] In recent times, the intellectual repute of public ownership and close governmental regulation has symbolically crumbled just as the actual crumbling of the Berlin Wall symbolized the political damage and economic stagnation associated with regimes that embraced the dead hand of state ownership. These developments occurred at the same time as an unprecedented rate of technological progress in the West and Japan in such areas as telecommunications, computers, microprocessors, optoelectronics, robotics, and biotechnology. These and other progressive fields were associated with private-sector firms and entrepreneurship. Philosopher of science Thomas S. Kuhn perceptively wrote that "Political revolutions are inaugurated by a growing sense . . . that existing institutions have ceased adequately to meet the problems posed by an environment that they have created."[16] Gradually (but associated with Margaret Thatcher's ascendancy to the British prime ministership in 1979) a new public philosophy came to prevail in which vigorous competition, privatization of public enterprises, a market economy, and technological progress through entrepreneurship were cornerstones.[17]

Reform of the telecommunications sector became a vital component of the new public philosophy because of the importance of that sector. The speed with which information can move around the globe is the most important facet of the world economy. Control and coordination can occur almost simultaneously everywhere. A factory in Malaysia or a financial center in Germany can be readily directed from New York or Tokyo. Nations, even regions, can no longer be viewed as isolated but are, rather, part of the world economy. In turn then, every nation's (and firm's) competitiveness requires that full attention be paid to cost reduction and quality control. Not only does the telecommunications revolution closely affect the competitiveness of nations and firms, but its efficient application is one of the key elements in the path to superior competitiveness.[18] One of the most important inquiries in this book will be to see how and why the public philosophy concerning American telecommunications has changed several times—why yesterday's conventional wisdom has become, in contemporary eyes, fallacious theory.

Once a new public philosophy has become established—often after a struggle—it moves to the background. It becomes invisible politics, so to speak, until it is frontally challenged. Visible politics usually becomes the clash of interests, interest groups, and governmental actors who make their arguments in terms of appealing to the dominant public philosophy. Of course, there are times that interests cannot attain their goals under a public philosophy and, therefore, must call for either its modification or its overthrow. The safest course *usually,* however, is for an interest group to attempt to persuade political decision makers that its self-interest is the public interest. As we will see, MCI in its struggle against AT&T followed such a gradualist strategy until it was ready to directly challenge the existing public philosophy. The major reason that attorneys are the principal actors in carrying out these strategies no matter what the forums are—courts, legislatures, administrative agencies—is that their art consists of attempting to converge their clients' self-interest with the reigning conception of the public interest. They are adept at using the short hard phrases, such as "competition" or "public service," that purport to capture the essential goals of the public philosophy. Crude lobbying, mobilizing public opinion, perhaps even bribery may occasionally be employed by the actors in telecommunications policy. But, as we will see, the old-fashioned art of persuasion is the most important resource that the actors can bring to bear.

The private-sector actors in telecommunications policy are usually individual firms (or would-be firms) and are almost never larger than industry segments that enter into temporary alliances. In the United States, for example, MCI and AT&T have usually been at each other's throats, fighting bitterly before administrative agencies, courts, and Congress. Yet occasionally they have joined together to seek a common end against other rivals, such as the local operating companies or cable firms. As we will see, nothing could be further from the truth than that there is a "big business" interest. Large firms in the industry are rarely unified over long time periods about anything other than that they would pay less rather than more taxes. And it should be noted at the outset that AT&T, the largest firm in telecommunications, has lost most of the major battles before public forums since 1968, although it won most before that date. These results are consistent because AT&T was able to persuade political actors that its self-interest accorded with the public interest before 1968. But in the changed environment after that date, AT&T was less and less able to persuade political decision makers that its self-interest accorded with the public interest. For that reason, we will see, AT&T lost more and more of its battles.

Politics, Technology, and Markets

Ultimately, changes in public policy toward telecommunications can be traced to technological or marketing innovations. But the linkages are not direct. Technological issues are usually intermixed with other ones and are usually framed in terms of a prevailing public philosophy, although the implications of new technologies can also help to reshape public philosophies. Relationships between politics, technology, and markets in telecommunications cannot be reduced to a set of simple statements; they are complex. Nevertheless, an attempt will be made to sort out the relationships as they apply to telecommunications.

We start with the observation that new inventions or discoveries do not automatically lead to an understanding of what markets or submarkets they can exploit commercially. Technological possibilities are not self-executing; rather, entrepreneurs or would-be entrepreneurs must conceive of what markets to attempt to reach and how to reach them. Further, adjustments must be continuously made as market signals are received. Consider, for example, the videocassette recorder (VCR). Ampex, an American firm, was the original VCR innovator but failed to make any impact on the market. Sony, one of the most successful consumer electronics firms, launched its Betamax format in 1975 and failed to gain much market acceptance. Philips Electronics, the giant Dutch firm, saw the opportunities but failed to bring its product to market in a reasonable time. The winner was JVC, which introduced its VHS format in 1976 and generally made the correct marketing and production decisions.[19]

Technological and marketing innovations can be just as critical in established industries. Consider the automobile. "In 1958, Alfred P. Sloan, the architect of General Motors highly successful product strategy ... and justly famous management system ... had just retired from the chairmanship after almost 40 years. The company he left behind dominated its industry. ... Imports were then a minor part of the market. Volkswagen was a curiosity; Nissan and Toyota engineers were busily trying to figure out why their first exports were falling apart on the Los Angeles freeway; and Honda was producing motorcycles."[20] Within a few years the marketing and technological innovations of the principal Japanese producers responding to the possibilities raised by energy shortages, new production methods, the application of electronics to automobiles, and the like had radically transformed the American automobile industry.

Entrepreneurship is the starting point in understanding the relationships between politics, technology, and markets, not just in such industries as VCRs and automobiles but in such traditionally heavily regulated industries as telecommunications as well. But what exactly is entrepreneurship? The classic exposition is provided by economist Joseph Schumpeter.

> The function of entrepreneurs is to reform or revolutionize the pattern of production by exploiting an invention or, more generally, an untried technological possibility for producing a new commodity or producing an old one in a new way, by opening up a new source of supply of materials or a new outlet for products, by reorganizing an industry and so on. ... To undertake such new things is difficult and constitutes a distinct economic function, first, because they lie outside the routine tasks which everyone understands, and, secondly, because the environment resists in many ways. ... This function does not essentially consist in either inventing anything or otherwise creating the conditions which the enterprise exploits. It consists in getting things done.[21]

Innovation appears in both large firms, such as AT&T or IBM, as well as upstarts who face initial difficulty in obtaining venture capital; nowhere is this more the case than in telecommunications, where the telephone, invented in 1876, was first conceived as a supplement to the telegraph. Its *initial* uses were thought to be as a toy for the rich and a vital instrument for physicians, as well as a device that could be employed as a burglar alarm. Within short order, new uses were seen largely due to the foresight of Theodore J. Vail, one of the greatest managers in American business history. Telecommunications from its outset to the present day has frequently innovated in all the ways that Schumpeter described. Entrepreneurship has appeared in old and new firms and companies of every size.

Innovation and entrepreneurship in telecommunications differ from those in many other industries in a crucial way that shapes the politics of that sector. In many other industries, a firm may enter without the necessity of obtaining the approval of a governmental authority. Telecommunications has traditionally been characterized by entry controls. Thus, any person or company may decide to open and operate a steel mill or a microchip foundry, but entry into cable television or the operation of cellular telephones is restricted by government controls. Subject to the laws of bankruptcy, a firm may similarly exit from an industry or switch to another activity as it wishes. But in telecommunications the firms granted operating franchises must obtain governmental permission to exit from the field or to enter a different business field. While firms in every industry are subject to a variety of regulatory controls, such as complying with environmental or civil rights rules, they are free to exercise independent judgment about most matters, such as prices, design, advertising campaigns, and so on. Without minimizing the regulatory burden on such firms, the behavior of firms in so-called public utilities, of which telecommunications is a prime example, is regulated in a qualitatively higher degree. Rates, for example, are closely regulated in public utilities. Until the 1990s, one could not move into a new territory or enter even a related field without securing government approval. IBM, for example, moved from the manufacture of tabulators and electric typewriters to computers. Such a transition in a regulated industry had been unlawful without government approval. And to complicate the matter further, telecommunications (like most every other sector) is also subject to the rules of the Sherman Antitrust Act governing competition.

In telecommunications, then, technological and economic concerns are closely intertwined with political issues. Business firms can seek a variety of goals relating to profits and sales. And while I will not discuss the complex problems concerning the goals of business firms, it is safe to say that they ordinarily prefer more to less profit. Accordingly, they will adopt not only economic strategies but strategies that will attempt to persuade government agencies that the firm's economic interests accord with the broader conception of the public interest. If the prevailing public philosophy will fit the bill, the firm utilizes its persuasiveness to show that its desired plans best satisfy it. But if the prevailing public philosophy is not congenial to a firm's goals, it begins the process of undermining that philosophy or carving out an exception to it. The forums chosen in which to undertake these efforts include regulatory agencies, courts, and legislatures at both the state and federal levels.

Not only is the politics of telecommunications intimately connected with technological and economic considerations, it is largely a politics in which individual firms are the fundamental private-sector actors. Firms may enter into alliances with other firms or governmental actors (which, as we will see, can sometimes adopt different perspectives), but these alliances tend to be temporary. MCI and AT&T have struggled in every conceivable forum, but there have been some post-1984 issues in which the two firms were on the same side. Until the AT&T's divestiture in 1984, its long-distance arm and the various local operating companies, such as Southwestern Bell, were part of the same organization in which differences were settled internally. Since the 1984 breakup, the separate firms have often clashed over issues.

Many of the past and present political battles between firms and their allies have concerned boundary issues. These include such questions as what activities a particular firm or sector should be permitted to undertake. For example, should cable television firms be permitted to provide telephone service? Should long-distance companies be permitted to provide local service, and vice versa? Should companies that distribute information also be permitted to produce content? Should firms that distribute information be permitted to supply customer premises equipment or manufacture switches and transmission equipment? In largely unregulated industries cost and quality analysis in the market is the mechanism by which companies determine whether to organize particular activities internally or through the market employing the price mechanism.[22] For example, automobile manufacturers determine whether to manufacture engines internally or to contract with a supplier. But in sectors that are highly regulated, such as telecommunications, courts, regulatory agencies, and legislatures often make such boundary decisions. Frequently we will see that boundary issues have been extremely important in telecommunications from early days through the Telecommunications Act of 1996.

The second set of political issues, closely related to the boundary issue, concerns entry and the structure of an industry. A preliminary question is how we define a market. For example, are metal food containers and glass food containers part of the same market even though their physical compositions are different? Economists as well as courts that consider such questions use the concept of cross elasticity of demand to answer the question. Under that concept the focus is on the extent to which consumers will switch from one product or service to another if the price or quality of one changes while the other remains constant.[23] It is obvious that since all customers have limited resources, the sale of any product or service affects the sale of every other product or service to some degree. But when consumer switching leads to high cross elasticity of demand, we can say that two products or services form part of the same product market.

Because of the deep government involvement in telecommunications, the cross elasticity of demand arises in a peculiar way. Government rules may impose artificial entry barriers when, in fact, full-scale competition is technologically feasible. For example, cable companies and local telephone operating companies might be able to deliver the same kinds of information and, therefore, have high cross elasticities of demand. But government policies have kept these industries in their respective niches. The political ramification of new technological possibilities is that some firms, industry segments, and government actors seek to break down these artificial barriers, while others seek to preserve them. At times bargaining can occur so that each firm or sector enters each other's field with government officials acting as arbiters. Sometimes, too, a would-be entrant adopts the strategy of initially attempting to enter a small market niche and then gradually enter into other parts until it is a full-scale competitor. As we will see, this was the strategy that MCI adopted when it undertook to end AT&T's long-distance monopoly and make the industry a somewhat competitive one.

The third set of issues with which policymakers have been involved concerns allocation. We conventionally think of land and personal property in terms of allocation and use legal conceptions, most importantly contract and property, to determine such questions as who owns what, and why. The philosopher David Hume's formulation is still the best one: "Some method must be shown by which we may distinguish what particular goods are to be assigned to each particular person, while the rest of mankind are excluded from their possession and enjoyment."[24] While the principle of property allocation is widely accepted in the cases of land and personal property, many people do not think of the concept in important segments of telecommunications, especially wireless transmission. Yet, as economist R.H. Coase argued, the same principles apply. The electromagnetic spectrum available for the transmission of information is a scarce resource in exactly the same way that the number of Rembrandt paintings is even more limited. Therefore, contract and property rules can be applied to spectra.[25]

Precisely the same point can be made about transmission through satellites in the sky and wire under or above the ground.

These observations raise a number of issues in telecommunications politics. The threshold one is whether the free market, government rules, or some hybrid of the two should be the principal allocation mechanism. If the unregulated market is the mechanism and government plays no role in the allocation process, the traditional rules governing ownership, transfer, and obligation for automobiles or commercial real estate apply. But that has been the rare case in telecommunications transmission; government has almost always played a significant role. Accordingly, governmental players devise rules that competing firms and other actors bitterly contest. But while such allocation issues have led to heated contests, one should not get the misconception that the electromagnetic spectrum capable of exploitation is inherently limited and cannot be expanded. Just as the Netherlands reclaims land from the sea, innovators have continuously discovered ways of utilizing hitherto unused spectra or utilizing spectra in new ways. Some of the most contentious battles have occurred when new spectra can be utilized or when frequencies already in use can be used in novel ways. The same principles apply to the other transmission media, including satellites and wires. Keeping rivals out can be just as important a strategy as enlarging capacity utilization in some cases.

The Network

The biggest antitrust case in history was *United States v. AT&T,* which resulted in the breakup of that giant company in 1984. The principal focus of that case was on one of the thorniest issues in telecommunications: whether it is sound policy to allow a single company to dominate too many of the component parts of a network. AT&T, in its defense of controlling local telephone service, long distance, equipment manufacture, and research, argued, "If a toaster is defective, it may blow a fuse, but it cannot affect the electrical service of others. By contrast, an improperly designed or maintained telephone, when put into operation, can distort the electric current flowing to it from the central office in such a way as to cause return signals that interfere with the quality of service not only for that customer, but for his neighbor as well. . . . Indeed, a malfunctioning device or a blockage in a local switching center in New York can have a direct impact on a caller as far away as California."[26] While AT&T had an obvious vested interest in strongly arguing that the complementarity of the components of the telecommunications network required common ownership of all the parts, it is nevertheless true that such a network has distinct characteristics.

In any event, the theme has been very important in American telecommunications policy and compels us to look closely at the network idea and the components of a network.

Until the 1970s, telecommunications and broadcasting were conceived as being distinctive networks. Simon Nora and Alain Minc, who were among the first to notice that the markets were converging, wrote: "Designed like a star with a single point of emission, the television network is unidirectional, broadcasting from the center toward all of the receivers. On the other hand, telecommunications networks handle the traffic between two points, a transmitter and receiver; furthermore, telecommunication can occur in each direction, while the television receiver is condemned to remain totally voiceless."[27] Convergence of the two previously disparate sectors has been based, in part, on digitalization and the development of encryption/decryption technologies so that broadcasting signals can be properly received only by those persons for whom they are intended. At the same time, the capabilities of the separate cable television and telephone networks have been increasingly becoming identical. Thus, the idea that broadcasting and telecommunications constitute distinct networks, although largely useful at one time, is increasingly less so.

The convergence of traditional broadcasting and telecommunications is joined by another important convergence with immense implications—the marriage of telecommunications and the computer networks. Once, one carried voice and the other carried data. Among the important implications of the convergence is the conceptualization of information as a large, inclusive category of services once comprehended as discrete. The idea of an "information society" was conceived by economist Fritz Machlup in the early 1960s, when he grouped together the various industries and services, the primary purposes of which were the generation, transformation, and provision of information.[28] It was during that same period of the early 1960s that digital communication was first introduced into telephone networks. The ability to use a series of binary codes (zeros and ones) to represent information meant that the type of information conveyed became of secondary importance to the ability to represent it digitally. Moreover, it also followed that it would be possible to transmit information from machines to machines, machines to persons, and persons to machines, just as persons had traditionally communicated to persons.

Based on the intellectual effort begun by Machlup and the implications of digitalization, the concept of "information" was developed. The kind of information became secondary to the question of how it can be reduced to zeros and ones—a task still under way. There are several important implications. First, information can be in the form of speech, music, motion videos, still pictures, data, text, graphics, and signals (such as those used in pagers). It is not far-fetched to agree with James R. Beniger that "eventually tastes, odors and possibly even sensations, all might one day be stored, processed and communicated in the same digital form."[29] Second, because of the diverse kinds of information, telecommunications is no longer a homogeneous distribution system transmitting only voice information in a constricted information range. Because customers can desire various mixes and quantities of different kinds of information, distribution can become a heterogeneous system in which different distribution firms provide a variety of information packages, almost simultaneously or at different times. Third, because of digitalization a wide variety of digital devices, such as CD-ROMs, digital cameras, game consoles, and so on can be plugged into the telecommunications distribution system.

Information content requires a transmission device to begin its travels through the network. The traditional device is, of course, the plain old telephone. But in recent times it has been joined by the computer (often through a modem), fax machine, pager, videophone, wireless transmitter, cellular telephone, and so on. The same devices are in use at the reception end, but antennae and multimedia receivers (capable of receiving different kinds of information almost simultaneously) supplement them. Early in the telephone's life, however, the same instrument became capable of transmitting and receiving, and this has been the usual model since. These instruments are grouped in the category of customer premises equipment (CPE). The transmission medium is the next component of the network and is usually composed of twisted copper wires, fiber-optic lines, coaxial cable, satellites, and various wireless frequencies. Although they have an ancient lineage, storage and forwarding devices—the next component of the network—have only recently come into common use. They include answering machines, tape recorders, instructed microchips, telephone services, computer devices, and video on demand. The heart of a network is switching, which allows each subscriber to communicate with a large number of other persons through different transmission paths. For this purpose switching and transmission equipment, often of exceptional complexity, are necessary. Transmission paths are divided into local service and long distance, each with differing economic characteristics. Finally, networks require signaling devices that facilitate the establishment, supervision, and disconnection of communication as well as billing. Signaling equipment is contained not only in transmitters and receivers, but in central offices as well. All of these activities must share common standards and must function harmoniously.

Until the late 1960s, AT&T persuaded governmental actors that the network required centralized control and coordination. Experience bolstered its monopoly position by showing that the costs of intervention into the network exceeded the benefits. Accordingly, even government actors ordinarily hostile to monopoly went along with AT&T's network domination. After the late 1960s, technological and entrepreneurial innovation began to erode AT&T's position, and government regulators gradually opened each part of the network to other firms. Although the positions are superficially inconsistent, the response of regulators and legislators correctly served a higher interest—the public interest.[30]

There can, of course, be a variety of networks, including the telephone network, Internet, cable television, and so on. These independent networks may or may not be interconnected. When one considers the complexity of networks, it may be surprising, until one learns the reasons, that until 1984 American telecommunications was dominated in every facet by a single firm—AT&T and its predecessor companies. Indeed, it is no exaggeration to state that from the invention of the telephone until 1984, the story of American telecommunications was largely the story of a single firm and its relationships with government agencies and (with the single exception of Western Union for a short time) much smaller rivals. Even since 1984 the single most important firm in American telecommunications has been AT&T. It is to that company and its development that we now turn.

2

The Rise of AT&T

The Invention of the Telephone

On December 31, 1983, the day before AT&T was broken up, it was the largest corporation in the world. It dominated the four major markets in telephony: long distance, local service (or local loops), customer premises equipment manufacture, and switching and transmission gear manufacture. Based on its technological leadership, AT&T could probably have been a major factor in a variety of other industries, such as motion picture equipment, radio and television broadcasting, and consumer electronics. But the restrictions imposed by various government decisions on the company precluded AT&T from becoming an even larger company. Yet its beginnings were quite modest.

Alexander Graham Bell was a teacher of the deaf and an experimenter who consciously became interested in the development of a "speaking telephone." Bell was in competition with Elisha Gray, another brilliant inventor, to see who would be the first to develop a speaking telephone. Both men had strong financial backing and encouragement from scientists. Many other inventors were also engaged in the pursuit of developing a voice-grade telephone, and after Bell's victory some of them claimed that his patents were invalid because their inventions preceded his.[1]

On February 14, 1876, Bell filed his basic patent application for a telephone transmitter employing a magnetized reed attached to a membrane diaphragm—an apparatus capable of transmitting sounds and changes of pitch, but not speech. Nevertheless, the patent application, like others drafted by skilled patent lawyers, was sufficiently broad to cover other apparatuses for transmitting speech. Only several hours later, Elisha Gray arrived at the Patent Office and filed a caveat (notice of pending patent application) for a method of transmitting and receiving speech, but there is considerable doubt whether Gray's instruments would have conveyed speech. In any event, it was not until March 1876–almost a month after the filing of the patent application—that Bell was able to convey the famous words over a telephone to his assistant: "Mr. Watson, come here; I want you."

The events surrounding the filings on the same day and the suspicion that Bell might have unlawfully seen Gray's caveat to amend his original application together with the claims of many others that they had invented the telephone led to much litigation. Nevertheless, the 1876 basic process patent (and Bell's 1877 basic receiver patent) withstood approximately six hundred lawsuits and patent interference proceedings, including a suit brought by the United States for patent cancellation.[2] In 1887 a divided Supreme Court upheld Bell's claim against five challengers. While doubts about the circumstances will always remain and one may quarrel with the patent laws, the weight of evidence and authority supports Bell's claim. However, AT&T's enemies continued to claim that the patents were unlawfully obtained and upheld by a conspiracy embracing a majority of the Supreme Court, patent examiners, and numerous circuit court judges. The furor is understandable considering that the basic telephone patents were the most valuable in history.

The First Era of Telephone Competition

Prior to his patent filing and invention of the telephone Bell and his partners, Boston businessmen Gardiner Hubbard and Thomas Sanders, formed the first predecessor enterprise to AT&T on February 27, 1875. Under the Bell Patent Association's agreement, Hubbard and Sanders would supply the capital and all would share equally in any patents Bell might obtain. Hubbard offered to sell for $100,000 the 1876 patent to Western Union shortly after it was filed, but was turned down because Western Union's management believed that the telephone was impractical. By November 1877 Western Union recognized that it had blundered and organized a subsidiary called the American Speaking Telephone Company. Western Union, then far superior in resources to the Bell enterprises, acquired several telephone patents (including Gray's) and employed Thomas A. Edison, already recognized as a brilliant inventor, to develop telephonic inventions. Thus, the first era of competition in the telephone industry had begun.

Not only was Western Union armed with a deep pocket that would allow it to easily undercut Bell rates but, moreover, most of Western Union's equipment and technology was at the time superior to Bell's. Accordingly, the Bell interests could do battle in two ways: They could develop or buy superior technology, and they could bring a patent infringement suit. The suit was brought before a court in September 1878 and was settled in November 1879. Under the terms of the settlement, Western Union agreed to withdraw from the telephone business, in exchange for which it would be paid a royalty of 20 percent on all telephones used in the United States. Western Union also agreed to assign existing and future telephone patents to National Bell, then the Bell interests' company. The agreement was to end at the expiration of the basic Bell patents in 1893–94. The first era of telephone competition ended shortly after it began.

Why had it ended so abruptly? First, contrary to one myth, Western Union clearly was not hoodwinked, for four days after the settlement, National Bell's shares were sold at $955.50—an increase of $505 above the September market price. It strains credulity to suppose that Western Union's management was not privy to the clear sentiment of the investment community. Bell had won a victory and Western Union knew it. The evidence indicates that Western Union settled for several reasons. First, financier Jay Gould had organized a new telegraph rival in May 1879 with a capitalization of $10 million. Moreover, Gould threatened an alliance with the Bell interests and promised to bankroll the infringement suit. Rather than fight on two fronts, according to this view, Western Union made peace on the telephone front in order to wage war more effectively on the telegraph front.

However, this two-front factor cannot alone explain Western Union's behavior. The telephone's commercial importance at the time was trivial in comparison to the telegraph's. Western Union's contest with the Bell interests was more a skirmish than a battle. Western Union could have fought on relatively cheaply if it believed that it could have won the patent battle in the courts. But Western Union agreed to a settlement precisely because its attorneys and other officials became convinced that the Bell interests would fight and ultimately prevail. George Gifford, Western Union's lawyer, became convinced that Alexander Graham Bell had invented the telephone and that Western Union was an infringer. Accordingly, he urged his client to settle.[3]

The patent wars and the Western Union competition would impress Bell interests in an important way. Patents would become a critical component of telecommunications and, with it, research. The basic transmitter and the basic receiver were only the beginning. When the fundamental patents expired in 1893 and 1894, the Bell interests sought to be well ahead of their adversaries, which entailed obtaining more advanced patents either through internal development or from independent inventors. The latter alternative was at first more desirable when individual inventors working in their own shops could make continuous and significant contributions to telephonic advance. But when telephonic research became sufficiently complex to require large capital investment, substantial group effort, and advanced mathematical techniques, a major research laboratory was required. In this sense the patent battles and the Western Union competition ultimately led to the creation of that extraordinary facility, Bell Telephone Laboratories (Bell Labs).

The Business of Communications

Early telephone service and equipment were rudimentary by contemporary standards. Yet even in its earliest phases the Bell interests were compelled to devise policies based on the peculiar characteristics of telephone communication. The single most important characteristic is the interactivity of the network; that is, a weakness in any part of the system reduces the ability of the other parts to operate to full potential. A bad transmitter, for example, will be reflected in inferior sound flowing to the receiver. Early on, the Bell policymakers realized that weaknesses in any part of the system can retard the expansion of the network, lower its quality, or otherwise impede its more widespread acceptance and use, with a resulting negative impact on revenues. For this reason, the Bell policymakers sought control over each piece of equipment and service that the network comprised. This, in turn, raised the issue of whether such control should be exercised under a system of ownership or under a system of licensing according to standards set by Bell. Since licensing entails a considerably smaller capital outlay, it is not surprising that the Bell interests first chose that path so that the system would grow much more rapidly, since others would incur the costs for local systems, equipment supply, and so forth.

Another peculiar characteristic of the telephone business that the Bell policymakers came to understand was that the value of telephone service to any subscriber depends on the number of persons with whom he or she can communicate. The greater the number is, the more valuable the service is. This consideration compelled the Bell policymakers to focus attention to switching. Without a central switch, forty-five lines are needed to connect ten nodes, whereas with one central switch, only ten lines are required. Gradually the idea of a network evolved, consisting of switching centers distant from each other but connected by trunk lines, and hierarchies of switches. As the network grew, the company was impelled to invest resources not only in the engineering problems but in basic research as well. For in many cases the basic science and mathematics upon which the complex switching would be based was yet to be discovered.

When one combines the interactivity of the network with the ever increasing complexity that results from expanding it, the theoretical justification for direct ownership of each part of an integrated network—local loops, long distance, CPE (customer premises equipment), and switching and transmission gear—is clear. Economic and technological considerations led to the integration of research, planning, engineering, design, manufacturing, and operating capability within one firm. Thus the theory of the firm discussed in Chapter 1 shows why the Bell interests organized much of their activity internally rather than through the market employing the price mechanism.[4]

The Bell system followed this dynamic. The more complex and changing a product or service is, the greater the costs incurred in instructing others who are responsible for component parts; the less the tolerance for deviation, the larger the costs will be for the failure to fulfill one's part in an overall interactive system. When complementarity is critical, yet at the same time the component sectors of an industry progress at uneven rates, the costs of discoordination can be very high. If licensees or independent sellers would have an incentive not to cooperate with the Bell interests in implementing or developing a new technology quickly or meeting a Bell target or rising standard of service, the effects would be felt throughout the network, and would be costly. The transaction costs in telephony are very high, so negotiation and changes and discussions of scientific and technological matters are more common than in many other industries. To the Bell interests transaction costs would be reduced if a single firm had the authority to enforce its will upon all segments of an industry.

Of course, it does not follow that only a single firm monopolizing all parts of the system was possible. But it does follow that a dominant, vertically integrated firm that could enforce its will on reluctant independents—the network manager role that AT&T undertook—was the direction in which telephone technology impelled the Bell interests, sometimes against their will.

The Foundations of AT&T

The predivestiture structure that we knew as AT&T, a holding company embracing operating companies and divisions in all phases of the telephone business, came into existence at the end of December 1899. Although much has changed over the years, it is remarkable how many AT&T policies in effect at the 1984 breakup (such as the one that insisted on leasing and not selling telephones) were in place on New Year's Day, 1900. AT&T, which had existed as a long-distance company since 1885, took over the property of the American Bell Telephone Company, its parent, and from that point until January 1, 1984, performed several functions in the Bell system.

First, AT&T operated the Bell system's long-distance service through the Long Lines Department. Second, it operated as a high command, making decisions for and coordinating the system as a whole. Third, it owned controlling shares in Western Electric, its principal supply and manufacturing company, and in the local operating companies. Over the years AT&T's shares in operating companies tended to increase. For example, AT&T had acquired 50.1 percent of Pacific Telephone and Telegraph's shares by 1905. By 1980 the figure had jumped to 90.18 percent. In two cases—Southern New England Telephone (SNET) and Cincinnati Bell—AT&T always owned less than 30 percent of the shares. AT&T's shares in these two firms were not affected by the divestiture, but they were sold nonetheless.

Bell Telephone Laboratories (Bell Labs), the last important component of the basic predivestiture structure, was incorporated in 1924. Almost at the outset it became one of the preeminent research organizations in the world. It was jointly owned by Western Electric and AT&T and was formed in order to better coordinate research and development, which had previously been undertaken by Western Electric Research Laboratories and various AT&T research and engineering departments. It is not uncommon for large corporations to have sizable research departments, but such research is almost always of an applied nature. In contrast, Bell Labs made enormous contributions not only in applied research but in pure science and mathematics as well. In large part the Bell system's early commitment to science and technology stemmed from the fact that many of Bell's technical problems could not be solved before advances were made in these fields.[5]

The complex structure of the Bell system evolved gradually from the invention of the telephone. Not until July 9, 1877, did the three original partners supersede their original partnership agreement when they formed a Massachusetts trust (a business form then popular) entitled the "Bell Telephone Company, Gardiner G. Hubbard, trustee." By February 1878 the time had come to finance expansion of the business. Accordingly, the next stage was the New England Telephone Company, capitalized at $200,000. This company, which was restricted to New England, appointed agents to develop exclusive territories and compensated them with commissions on telephone and call bell (ringer) rentals. The markets opened up by the development of switching and other new services, the fight with Western Union, and other factors continued to impose an enormous financial burden on the Bell interests that the New England Telephone Company structure only partly alleviated. Accordingly, Hubbard and Sanders incorporated the Bell Telephone Company (a corporation, not a Massachusetts trust) in July 1878. But as they sought and obtained new investors, Sanders and Hubbard saw control begin to slip away. The new company, capitalized at $450,000, attracted as general manager Theodore J. Vail, a man who combined exceptional managerial abilities and a keen political sense. Vail had established a system of fast mail delivery for the Post Office. Beginning as a lowly mail clerk for the Union Pacific Railroad, Vail's ability and energy in transportation services led to a meteoric rise. At the age of thirty in 1876, he was appointed general superintendent of the Railway Mail Service. Dissatisfied with economizing measures by Congress, he joined the Bell interests with the promise of the New York City franchise.[6]

Few large institutions have ever borne the imprint of one person as thoroughly as Vail's on AT&T and its predecessors. He settled the Western Union suit and assertively moved to enlarge the use of the telephone. Among his first moves were expansion of the central switchboard exchanges, telephone fire alarm systems, and long distance (or toll lines), which, though modest by contemporary standards, were pathbreaking at the time. These ambitious projects led to further financial strain and the creation of a new company in March 1879, the National Bell Telephone Company, capitalized at $850,000. At this point the original partners were no longer able to control the fortunes of the telephone. After the Western Union settlement, under which the Bell telephone interests were required to purchase Western Union and American Speaking Telephone's equipment, the need for additional capital led to still another transformation. The American Bell Telephone Company was incorporated on April 17, 1880, and capitalized at $7,350,000.

AT&T owes its creation to Vail's dream of long distance. Even though the technology was incapable of carrying conversations very far in the 1880s, Vail was committed to the promise of allowing every subscriber to converse with every other one. Because American Bell met with little success in interesting its local licensees to jointly engage in long distance to and from their territories, it incorporated American Telephone & Telegraph (AT&T) as a long-distance subsidiary in February 1885. Interestingly, the certificate of incorporation contemplated a network that would extend throughout the United States, Canada, and Mexico. Under Vail's leadership, by 1888 the new company was already confident that long distance would be a success.[7]

Ambitious plans entail substantial risks. Typical of such large-scale projects undertaken for the first time, the costs of creating a long-distance network were greater than initially seen. In 1888 AT&T was compelled to float a $2 million debenture issue to finance long-distance expansion. This bond issue and later public stock and bond offerings—a common feature in AT&T history—have acted as long-term incentives for the firm to be efficient in its operations. In its frequent resort to capital markets, especially in its sales of debentures, notes, and bonds, AT&T has had to appeal not to potential customers of its telephones but to investors who are ordinarily indifferent to the product or service in which they are investing. To them, return matters. Investors focus on risk, yield, and other financial variables. Any company seeking to sell debt instruments or stock in financial markets is reasonably expected to know that it must deal with sophisticated investors who will compare the seller's performance (and probable performance) to those of other such firms, including those in highly competitive industries. If a company such as AT&T wishes, then, to sell stocks and bonds on favorable terms, its performance and probable performance must measure up to that of its rivals in competitive industries. The discipline imposed by the financial markets acts upon the firm as a surrogate for competition. Of course, this does not necessarily guarantee that such a firm will be efficient any more than competition necessarily assures that a firm will be efficient. But in both cases a strong incentive to be efficient is provided. Thus, the commitment that AT&T made to long distance had important consequences for the firm's efficiency.

The Bell interests' spur toward increased capitalization met with resistance by the Massachusetts legislature, which led the leaders of AT&T and American Bell to reach an important decision in 1899. In contrast to Massachusetts, New York, where AT&T was incorporated, was far more generous on the issue of increasing corporate capitalization. For that reason in late December 1899 AT&T became the parent company and corporate headquarters were moved from Boston to New York.

When 1900 dawned, AT&T was on its way to forming a comprehensive vertical structure. Western Electric, already an electrical equipment manufacturer, had been acquired in a gradual process that began on July 5, 1881. The need to keep up with an expanding demand for telephone equipment coupled with dissatisfaction with prior arrangements because of delays, shortfalls, imprecision, and so on led to the decision to begin the acquisition process of a major manufacturing facility. Hence, the Western Electric acquisition was a specific example of the empirical findings of economic historians Harold Livesay and Patrick Porter. Firms engage in backward vertical mergers "by a desire to rationalize flows by . . . assuring needed raw materials rather than from a desire to add profits of the manufacturer to that of those downstream in the business."[8]

Similar rational considerations governed the license relationship for local operating companies. After a number of experiments that proved unsatisfactory, American Bell in the early 1880s solved the problem of how best to exploit local markets. It would offer licensees permanent licenses in exchange for stock, thus becoming a partner in the local-loop business. This allowed American Bell to conserve capital for long distance and other phases of the telephone business and at the same time maintain considerable influence so as to assure that licensees took a long-run view of the business.

Thus, American Bell assumed, even at this early stage, the role of network manager that would guarantee the overall performance of an interactive system. It could further assure that as new technological innovations came about the licensees would not resist deploying them.

Gradually the local licensees consolidated into larger territories for several reasons, including economies in centralized management, lower transaction costs in larger exchanges, the high capital costs of some newer technologies, and increased coordination requirements. The final step was AT&T's increased equity holdings in most licensees, which was more than 90 percent by the mid-1930s. The causes were the profitability of local-loop operations and AT&T's dissatisfaction with minority ownership. AT&T officials had found that some of their licensees were not cooperating in the development of long distance and were resisting closer uniformity in good telephone practice. Moreover, under the system of minority share ownership some local managers were performing inadequately, impelling AT&T to incur higher supervision costs than would be the case with majority control. Consequently, AT&T purchased licensees' stocks whenever it could.[9]

The basic predivestiture structure of AT&T was thus complete. As this review shows, sound business reasons existed for the integration of each component into the Bell system that died on the last day of 1983. As we shall see, sound reasons also existed for AT&T's dominant status as regulated network manager and the structure of local and long-distance monopolies.

Regulated Monopoly and Public Service

At 7 A.M. on September 17, 1945, the fuses in the offices of the Keystone Telephone Company were pulled, marking the close of the second era of competitive telephony. Forty years earlier, the Bell system faced competition in many local markets and long distance. AT&T's ability to survive the competitive onslaught as well as attacks by prominent legislators and the Justice Department is another tribute to Theodore J. Vail's genius. For, at a critical time in the company's history, he recognized the benefits of close public utility regulation through regulatory commissions, in exchange for which AT&T and its licensees obligated themselves to attain such goals as universal service and technological progressiveness. AT&T, in a word, had a private agenda wrapped in a public philosophy. It sought to show that its private interest was identical with the public interest.

The second competitive era began inauspiciously for AT&T. Antimonopoly sentiment was rampant in the 1890s, and telephone competition was expected to lower prices and spur progressiveness. Yet by 1920 the belief in competition as the best public policy in telephony was dead; nor

was it revived until the late 1960s. The overwhelming sentiment that competition was not the answer in telephony is summarized in a 1919 Missouri
Public Service Commission report: "Competition between public service
corporations was in vogue for many years as the proper method of securing
the best results for the public. . . . The consensus of modern opinion, however,
is that competition has failed to bring the result desired."[10]

The principal reason that telephone competition fell into disfavor was
AT&T's advocacy of a public philosophy that persuaded virtually every
important actor—eventually even its rivals—that the public interest would
be best served under a regime in which public service commissions regulated telephone monopolies. American Bell (and AT&T) did not come to
this position all at once but, rather, gradually and, once again, under the
leadership of Vail. After the basic patents expired in 1893 and 1894, AT&T
first sought to buy up sufficient patents to keep ahead of rivals. Because of
adverse court decisions, that strategy failed. Competition began to develop
gradually, and by about 1900 and for a few years thereafter more than five
hundred independent telephone companies were established annually.
Moreover, AT&T was singularly unsuccessful in preventing municipalities
from granting franchises to rivals.[11] At the same time that competition
provided a threat, so did nationalization. Manitoba in 1907 and England in
1911 had nationalized most of their respective telephone services.

After the turn of the century, progressivism, one of the tenets of which
was firm government control of large business enterprise, had become the
dominant public philosophy. One of the critical moves that AT&T undertook, especially after Vail's return to the company in 1907, was to seize
upon progressive sentiment and turn it to the Bell system's advantage. To
do this AT&T first embraced the theory of natural monopoly that had
become fashionable in academic circles at the turn of the century. Although
today an industry is considered a natural monopoly if production is done
most efficiently by a single firm as output increases, the term had a somewhat different meaning in the Progressive Era. Based on the wave of bankruptcies and deteriorated service that had occurred in the traditional public
service industries when multiple franchises were granted, the earlier view
held that service to the public is best undertaken by a single franchisee or a
"natural monopoly." It is important to note the distinction between that
conception and the later economic one. *Better* and more comprehensive
service based on empirical observation is different from a theoretical conception that purports to predict what is *most* efficient. AT&T sought to
clothe itself in the older natural-monopoly conception, the better to portray
itself as the bearer of the public interest.

When Vail rejoined AT&T as president in 1907, he realized that one of his most important tasks was the elaboration of how an AT&T-dominated telecommunications industry would best accord with progressivism. Prior to his return the AT&T leadership was split about what its best strategy should be. Annual reports, therefore, avoided the important issue of the company's attitude toward close regulation. In the 1907 *Annual Report,* the first written since Vail's return, the company spelled out a refined theory of regulation that delineated the proper roles of private company and governmental supervisor: "It is not believed that there is any objection to [public control] provided it is independent, intelligent, considerate, thorough and just, recognizing, as does the Interstate Commerce Commission . . . that capital is entitled to fair return and good management or enterprise to its reward."[12]

The 1910 *Annual Report* even more enthusiastically endorsed public regulation, adding that it should assure that plant and services is of the highest possible standard, efficient, and that service should be extended as far as possible—the universal service standard. Telephone companies are public service institutions and should be compelled by regulators to attain such standards. But regulators should stop short of attempting to manage the business. The following is the critical argument Vail made in favor of monopoly:

> If there is to be State control and regulation, there should also be State protection—protection to a corporation striving to serve the whole community (some part of whose service must necessarily be unprofitable) from aggressive competition which covers only that part which is profitable. . . . That competition should be suppressed which arises out of the promotion of unnecessary duplication, which gives no additional facilities or service. . . . State control and regulation, to be effective at all, should be of such a character that the results from the operation of any one enterprise would not warrant the expenditure or investment necessary for mere duplication and straight competition. . . . Two local telephone exchanges in the same community are regarded as competing exchanges, and the public tolerates this dual service only in the fast disappearing idea that through competition in the telephone service, some benefit may be obtained. . . . Two exchange systems in the same place offering identically the same list of subscribers . . . are as useless as a duplicate system of highways or streets not connecting with each other.[13]

The 1910 *Annual Report* then established the quid pro quo that would replace competition. AT&T and its affiliates would willingly submit to commission regulation that would be committed to guaranteeing an efficient and progressive telephone service. Further, the commissions would be expected to prod the telephone system to attain high standards and expand the system. AT&T committed itself to be a network manager of the Bell operating companies and noncompeting independents. AT&T rejected, however, interconnection with independent companies that competed with either a Bell licensee or an affiliated independent on the ground that such interconnection was redundant. AT&T promised to unremittingly improve equipment and operating procedures and to continue expansion into uneconomic, sparsely settled and difficult-to-reach territories. Most importantly, AT&T committed itself to ultimately attain universal service so that virtually everyone who desired a telephone could have one and could communicate with everyone else. Obviously, the public utility commissions (PUCs) would be expected to regulate telephone pricing so that the subsidy flows would allow these goals to be achieved.

It should be noted too that Vail held out the olive branch to independents—a shrewd political strategy. AT&T did not advocate that it become the sole provider of telephone service but rather the network manager of a vast network that included Bell companies, Bell licensees, and noncompeting independents. Politically this was important because independents often had strong ties to local elites. Merchants and other businesses increasingly relying on the telephone approved the regulatory commission idea that promised stable and reasonable rates as well as a high grade of service. They usually disapproved of competing service because nonconnecting systems prevented them from communicating with some suppliers and customers.[14] Thus, those independents who favored competition and rejected the independent regulatory commission idea were increasingly isolated both politically and in terms of the goal of attaining a vast network in which any person could converse with any other.

Notwithstanding some conduct that was sharply criticized, a major antitrust investigation, as well as the threat of nationalization, AT&T had successfully wrapped itself in the mantle of the dominant public philosophy when Vail retired in 1919. By the early 1920s AT&T and the surviving independents were close allies.

The Public-Private Partnership

At the end of 1920 all but three of the forty-eight states had PUCs with the power to regulate telephones. Since most telephone matters concerned local rates or local service, the PUCs were the core of the system of regulation. Notwithstanding the differing public philosophies that prevailed in the 1920s and 1930s, the idea that privately owned firms in public utility industries should be closely regulated was widely accepted.

At the federal level telephones first became subject to rate regulation (by the Interstate Commerce Commission) under the 1910 Mann-Elkins Act. Under an agreement (known as the Kingsbury Commitment) into which the Justice Department and AT&T entered in 1913, the company agreed not to acquire any competitors and to furnish interconnection to noncompeting independents into the Bell network. And in 1921 Congress enacted the Willis-Graham Act, extending ICC jurisdiction over telephone mergers and acquisitions, thereby effectively abrogating the portion of the Kingsbury Commitment prohibiting AT&T acquisitions. By this time earlier controversies had subsided and every major actor had come to agree with Vail's 1908 formulation: "One policy, one System, Universal Service."

In the thirteen years between Willis-Graham's enactment and creation of the Federal Communications Commission in 1934, the ICC considered at least 274 merger and acquisition cases, certifying 271. State PUCs that could regulate telephone mergers generally approved them, as well. The ICC's activities served to rationalize the industry. The leading study of ICC telephone regulation concluded that acquisitions usually occurred "because the smaller system lacked capital, credit and revenues to extend or even maintain its plant or because the owners of the small enterprise desire to withdraw from the telephone business."[15]

Although the F.C.C. supplanted the ICC in 1934 and gained greater powers, it is nevertheless true that until the major changes that began after World War II, the bulk of regulation occurred at the state PUC level, and the regulatory system worked well. Even a cursory look at the American telephone industry from 1920 to 1968 shows its remarkable progress under the regulated network manager system. Telephone company profits were reasonable and far from monopoly levels in large part because they were rigorously controlled by public utility regulators. Of course, trends in communications, like trends in other sectors, are dependent in no small degree on general economic trends. Thus, a downturn during parts of the Great Depression as well as substantial growth during the boom that followed World War II are to be expected. Nevertheless, while GNP increased approximately fivefold between 1920 and 1970 (from about $140 billion to approximately $722 billion, in 1958 dollars), telephones increased almost ninefold (from 13 million to 120 million) during the same time period. Even more remarkable, while 35 percent of households had telephones in 1920, the comparable percentage in the larger 1970 population was 90.5 percent. And, of course, since interconnection of telephones was virtually completed by 1970, the value of the telephone to each subscriber was incomparably greater in 1970 than in 1920.

These considerations do not begin to exhaust the long-run achievements of the regulated network manager system. The telephone in America had achieved the status of a necessity for both business and residential users; the structures of commerce, entertainment (through radio and television), and social intercourse became completely dependent on the telephone system.

Americans needed to work fewer hours per year to obtain telephone service than residents of other developed nations. A 1971 Department of Commerce study, for example, showed that the average American needed to work twenty-six hours per year to obtain basic telephone service, whereas the average French citizen required 179 hours. The number of Americans on waiting lists to obtain telephone service was lower than that of any other country with a large system. Finally, we must consider the extraordinary research and development record of Bell Labs, the benefits from which have extended far beyond telecommunications.[16]

PUCs have often been attacked. They have been charged with corruption, incompetence, or simply disregard for the public. But considering the large number of cases that they have handled, there have been very few cases of proved corruption or blatant disregard for the laws they are charged with enforcing. PUC critics usually are satisfied with naked allegations of the agencies being "captured" by the regulated firms. And, of course, some demagogues, claiming to represent "the consumers' interest," oppose all rate increases. But these sweeping claims are nothing more, as R.H. Coase has said, than presumptions of what the consumer interest *should* be.[17]

The PUCs are compelled to exercise continual—long-term and short-term—authority over the industries they regulate. They must consider both the consumers' interests and the producers' interests, for unless the producer can make a reasonable profit and attract capital for expansion, the consumer cannot be effectively served. PUCs cannot avoid blame for performance deficiencies; they cannot even blame the regulated companies for deficiencies because their own lack of foresight or inadequate supervision of the industry is viewed as the primary source of failure. In short, PUCs should be obligation oriented and collaborative with regulated firms. Although collaboration is inconsistent with a strictly adversarial attitude, it is not inconsistent with one in which the PUC does not act on or grant a company's request unless the company's showing is clear and convincing.

What compels PUCs to behave in this fashion? PUCs are constrained in many ways. Courts, the executive branch, and legislatures exercise considerable supervision—and, more importantly, power—over PUCs through hearings, legislation, appropriations, oversight, and enforcement. Information about alleged transgressions on the part of PUCs or the firms they regulate is readily available from a variety of sources, many of which have strong incentives to exercise considerable scrutiny. There are many eyes on the results of PUC regulation as well as on the ways in which the results are achieved. All decisions, including regulatory ones, allocate resources so that there are winners and losers. For example, if our utility rates increase and our service does not improve, we know it; if we experience a brownout, we know it. Criticism of this kind is often used by political actors willing to exploit it as an issue. In addition, others are deeply involved in most regulatory decisions, either as close watchers or as participants. Interests concerned about PUC telephone proceedings include (1) residential subscribers, (2) consumer organizations, (3) business users, (4) trade associations, (5) equipment suppliers and potential suppliers, (6) competing carriers, (7) large telephone companies, (8) independent telephone companies, (9) rural cooperative telephone companies, (10) telephone company trade associations, (11) companies involved in other markets or technologies on which PUC decisions may impinge, and (12) government purchasers of telecommunications services, such as the Department of Defense.

This, of course, does not suggest that all of these economic interests are represented in every proceeding. Rather, they do hire lawyers and lobbyists to scrutinize what PUCs and the F.C.C. are doing or plan to do, so that any economic interest that may be affected by a proceeding usually has the opportunity to intervene. Further, a variety of governmental institutions claim to represent not their own interests but the public interest, often with varying and divergent views of what constitutes the public interest. These "guardians" of the public interest include (1) other state PUCs, (2) NARUC (the association of regulatory commissioners whose predecessor dates from 1889), (3) local governments, (4) other state and local government agencies, (5) state attorneys general, (6) local prosecutors, (7) the Justice Department, (8) the Department of Commerce and various divisions of it concerned with telecommunications, (9) the Office of Management and Budget and parallel state agencies, (10) various watchdog agencies (such as the General Accounting Office and its state parallels), (11) legislators who are attentive to public utility and telecommunications issues, (12) legislative committees, (13) other agencies (such as agriculture departments in rural telecommunications matters and the Department of State in international matters), and, of course, (14) the courts. Always present, too, is the threat of a special committee appointed to examine the performance of PUCs or regulatory agencies in general. Finally, there have been numerous instances of agency staff, concluding that a PUC has taken a wrong turn, leaking information to the media, legislators, and others.

There are also many private guardians of the public interest. Muckrakers such as Ralph Nader have existed even before public utility commissions. Although these would-be guardians of the public interest are often biased or simplistic or have failed to investigate an issue reasonably well, they do serve a useful purpose. The threat of investigation provides regulators with an added incentive to defend their actions and to show that the alternatives were less attractive. These "political entrepreneurs," as James Q. Wilson calls them, are adept at mobilizing latent public sentiment by revealing a scandal or capitalizing on a crisis.[18] In their endeavors, the private guardians of the public interest are often surreptitiously aided in obtaining information from PUC insiders. They are also adept at leaking what they have learned to sympathetic media reporters.

Legislative appropriations and oversight hearings, executive-branch reviews, adverse publicity, the threat of forced resignations, and even criminal prosecution provide PUCs strong supplementary incentives to follow paths dictated by statutory goals. PUCs do make mistakes and can differ among themselves, but, like courts, they establish principles that are developed over the years and that are based on experience, daily contact with concerned actors, and continuous supervision of regulated firms. Decisions are articulated in written opinions based on facts and reasoned to conclusions that regulators hope will withstand the scrutiny of courts, legislators, executive-branch officials, and the attentive public. And, they have usually withstood this scrutiny.

By 1920 PUCs concluded, in the words of the California agency: "After a number of years of experience with two telephone systems in these communities, the subscribers almost unanimously demand a consolidation into one system."[19] Thus, the PUCs had accepted as the public interest the basic vision outlined by Vail. That is, in exchange for monopoly privileges, telephone companies became stewards charged with rendering cheap, efficient service of high and improving quality. Telephone companies were held to the standard of end-to-end responsibility in which they were continuously charged with maintaining the quality, safety, and effectiveness of each component of the network. Since the telephone companies were charged with end-to-end responsibility and the network's overall quality was adversely affected by the quality of the worst component of the system, PUCs required telephone companies to lease equipment. If subscribers supplied their own equipment, according to PUCs, quality could not be assured.[20] Finally, PUCs devised many quantitative standards governing such things as switchboard capacity, promptness in handling calls, and conversion time to higher levels of service.

Ultimately, the regulated network manager system must be judged by performance criteria. Did the system work? In general we can say that the system worked well, and although there were some rough spots and downturns, it improved in the long run. Consider one example: Before World War II, the time required to establish a long-distance telephone call was approximately three minutes; in the 1960s, it was one and one-half minutes; and by 1973, it was further reduced to under forty seconds. The same progress applies to other measures of telephone company performance as well, all of which occurred under conditions of reasonable, and often declining, rates. According to the Department of Labor, the Bell system's productivity gains between 1972 and 1977 exceeded those of all but one of the sixty-three industries that reported such data. Moreover, fifty-one of these industries had labor productivity growth less than one-half of the Bell system's. In the overall inflationary period from 1947 to 1977, the telephone industry's rate of price increase was about one-half that of all industries combined. Between 1960 and 1973, the consumer price index (CPI) increased 44.4 percentage points, but the residential telephone component increased only 14.6 percentage points. Further, during the highly inflationary period of 1973 to 1979, the CPI increased 84.3 percentage points and the telephone component only 16 percentage points. Between 1965 and 1977 more than 240 of the 264 items in the CPI showed rates of price increases greater than telephone rate increases.

Both the postwar and prewar record, we should recall, occurred as AT&T continuously engaged in extensive research and development to assure progressiveness and the attainment of universal service. And this occurred when rates were made in such a way that Bell profits were always reasonable.[21]

The First Boundary Problem: Radio and Telephones

We noted in Chapter 1 that political disputes in telecommunications frequently arise in connection with boundary problems when entrepreneurs see the commercial opportunities for a new technology. When the older and newer technologies may compete for the same markets, a clash is almost inevitable. If the older technology is a heavily regulated one, the crucial issues include what kind of public policy regime should govern the new technology—competition or public utility status, or some mix of both. A second set of issues concerns whether firms in the older industry should be allowed to enter the new one, and whether firms in the newer one should be allowed to compete with those in the older, heavily regulated one.

Even as AT&T and the telephone independents were settling their controversies, a new one based on the boundary problem and AT&T's technological prowess was brewing. The radio controversy unleashed considerable resentment against AT&T that would carry over into the anti-big-business 1930s. The Bell system's successes in developing other novel technologies, such as television and sound motion pictures, would contribute importantly to an extremely hostile F.C.C. investigation in the 1930s and to the 1949 antitrust suit against the company.

When World War I ended few people saw that the most dramatic application of radio would be in broadcasting, not point-to-point communication. AT&T envisoned radio's potential in extending long-distance telephony. Accordingly, it invested its efforts in radio development and acquired patents of others. Its overall attitude before the radio boom was that radio telephony could never replace wire service but could be a valuable supplement to reach relatively inaccessible places.[22]

Unregulated firms such as General Electric, Westinghouse, and United Fruit became involved in radio research for their own reasons. General Electric and AT&T contested twenty radio-related patent interferences between 1912 and 1926, and each firm could block the exploitation of the other's patents. That is, each could not effectively use its patents without infringing upon patents held by another firm. Because these events occurred in the period around World War I, the United States government (principally through the Navy's Bureau of Steam Engineering) sought to resolve the patent tangle and, at the same time, assure that control of the new technology and its development was in American hands. The net result was the formation in 1919 of the Radio Corporation of America (RCA), closely linked with General Electric, and the creation in 1920 of a patent pool embracing General Electric, AT&T, and other firms that allocated exclusive and nonexclusive fields in virtually every phase of communications, including broadcasting.[23]

Even though the patent pool agreements were carefully crafted, bitter disputes between AT&T and a coalition led by General Electric erupted, largely because of ambiguities in the clauses concerning broadcasting. At the time the agreements were signed none of the parties foresaw how rapidly the broadcasting boom would occur. Although they envisioned many uses for radio, they did not anticipate its importance as a medium of entertainment and information. The broadcasting boom began in 1920, a few months after the patent pool was formed. When Westinghouse erected a powerful transmitter in the Pittsburgh area and developed a regular schedule for the station to broadcast nightly, AT&T and the other members of the patent pool then appreciated the lucrative opportunities in the new field of broadcasting. By 1925—only five years after Westinghouse's KDKA had begun—2,750,000 households had radio sets. And this figure barely touched the vast market of families that would want radios.

The inevitable disputes were fought not only in the realm of interpreting the patent pool agreements, but in the political area of defining the public interest in broadcasting as well. AT&T sought to include broadcasting on its side of the boundary through a concept it called "toll broadcasting." On January 6, 1922, AT&T issued a public announcement stating that it would operate a radio station. AT&T "will provide no program of its own, but provide the channels through which anyone with whom it makes a contract can send out their own programs. Just as the company leases its long distance wire facilities for the use of newspapers, banks and other concerns so it will lease its radio telephone facilities and will not provide the matter which is sent out from this station."[24]

AT&T, in a word, had devised a plan in which there would be a complete divorce between the production of programs and their distribution to the public. Unlike the system that prevails today in which the networks and cable companies determine which programs will be distributed, the toll broadcasting idea envisioned the distributor as nothing more than the conveyor of material over which it had no control. Just as the telephone company has no control over the conversations of its subscribers, radio transmitting companies would simply sell blocks of time to programmers.

But AT&T's attempt to employ public service principles in broadcasting soon collapsed. Although toll broadcasting does not necessarily imply monopoly in distributing programming, AT&T was attacked on the ground that it was seeking to extend its telephone monopoly. Further, the decision of the arbitrator appointed to decide whether AT&T could enter broadcasting under the patent pool agreement was adverse to the telephone company's position. The effort of RCA and its allies to exclude AT&T from broadcasting was reinforced by AT&T's assertion of its patent rights against radio stations infringing on its broadcasting transmitter patents. Even though AT&T was legally entitled to protect these patents, the adverse publicity reinforced the public fear that the company was attempting to enlarge its monopoly. Legislative and executive attacks on the telephone "monopoly" intensified, and at the same time some government officials expressed displeasure over certain news commentary on an AT&T station. All of these factors led to AT&T's withdrawal from broadcasting in 1926 and its decision to sell its existing stations to RCA. The toll broadcasting experiment ended, demonstrating how difficult it would be to embrace novel technologies within the public service ambit.

The Creation of the Federal Communications Commission

At the most obvious level, the F.C.C. was created in 1934 to combine the radio regulatory functions of the Federal Radio Commission (FRC—created in 1927 to grant, renew, or revoke station licenses) and the telephone regulatory functions of the ICC into a unified agency.[25] AT&T had opposed the creation of a unified agency when it was first proposed in 1929, but with the advent of the New Deal in 1933 and the climate of anti-big-business feelings focused on public utility holding companies, AT&T expressed even more apprehension. Even though the major governmental reports advocating the creation of a unified agency emphasized that significant changes in existing law would not take place, AT&T had reason to be apprehensive. The House Report envisioned a future report by the new agency on such topics as whether AT&T ought to be compelled to engage in competitive bidding for equipment instead of relying on Western Electric.

Nevertheless, the Communications Act of 1934 was intended to be largely a matter of administrative consolidation. But it was also expected to be the prelude to much more drastic regulation and legislation that would follow an F.C.C. investigation of telephone company practices. Certainly the New Deal's first one hundred days justified AT&T's apprehension, in which it was joined by the independent telephone companies. Among the statutes that then sailed through Congress were those that divorced commercial banking from investment banking; established federal control over new securities issues; and, most controversially, created the National Recovery Administration to establish federal supervision over virtually every facet of activity in almost every industry. From AT&T's perspective the federal government had marched beyond the boundaries between private management and regulation under the old public philosophy and was on the road to establishing a new one in which government would dictate how a company ran its affairs on a daily basis.

The forces favoring the new agency, however, were successful precisely because they identified the public interest with administrative consolidation and a full-scale investigation. With these arguments the proponents of the new agency did not need to find particular examples of AT&T wrongdoing. Vague accusations and calls for an investigation were employed as secondary arguments. The forceful statement of ICC commissioner Joseph B. Eastman, the most highly respected regulator in the nation, that the ICC was doing a satisfactory job of telephone regulation, as well as declining interstate rates, were insufficient to overcome the chorus calling for a new agency. The new F.C.C. was created in 1934. The chain of events that eventually transformed American telecommunications can be traced to its origin.

3

The Assault Begins

The Beginnings

The beginnings of the massive breakup of the Bell system in 1984 can be traced to the creation of the Federal Communications Commission (F.C.C.) in the early New Deal. The Communications Act of 1934 consolidated the radio functions of the Federal Radio Commission and the telephone functions of the Interstate Commerce Commission (ICC) into a new independent regulatory commission that was to regulate interstate and foreign communications by wire and radio in the public interest. Like other independent regulatory commissions, the F.C.C. could act both like a court in adjudicatory proceedings and like a legislature in rule-making proceedings. The F.C.C.'s work in foreign and interstate communications was to be complemented by the regulatory jurisdiction of the various state and local public utility commissions. One should recall that in 1934—and for many years afterward—the bulk of telephone traffic was local, not long distance, and therefore largely supervised by the state and local agencies.

The F.C.C.'s powers over interstate and foreign telecommunications under the 1934 statute were broad. The agency's fundamental goals were enumerated in Section 1: "To make available, so far as possible, to all the people of the United States a rapid, efficient, nation-wide and world-wide wire and radio communication service with adequate facilities at reasonable charges."[1] While the framers of the legislation accepted the regulated network manager system and AT&T's leadership of it, they were nevertheless hostile to the company, suspicious that its rates and rate base were excessively high. This was in keeping with the New Dealers' public philosophy, which was sharply critical of big business. The bigger the firm was, the more antagonistic the New Dealers were. Their public philosophy blamed the alleged greed of big business for the Great Depression that began in 1929. Indeed, the failure of the New Deal to lift the nation out of the Great

Depression only confirmed in their minds that the predatory behavior of big business was responsible for sabotaging the recovery.[2]

A persistent theme in congressional debates on telecommunications was that the new agency should investigate AT&T's structure, rates, and practices. Between 1934 and 1939 the F.C.C. conducted a telephone investigation that, after findings and a report, was expected to be the basis for additional legislation. The staff investigation is important in that its influence and the hostility it generated toward AT&T persisted after the end of World War II. More than any other factor, it led to the 1949 suit against AT&T—the *United States v. Western Electric* case—which was in large part based on the findings of the investigation, especially those relating to the suspicion of excess profits resulting from the ties between Western Electric, on the one hand, and AT&T and the operating companies on the other. The evidence that Western Electric's profits were reasonable for an industrial corporation and that it operated efficiently was beside the point to the investigators.[3]

The driving force behind the F.C.C.'s hostility toward AT&T was Commissioner Paul A. Walker, described in *Business Week* as a person who "cherishes some private hate against the Bell System."[4] Ironically, the company's extraordinary technological advances in radio, telephotography, television transmission, stereophonic sound, and talking motion pictures only confirmed the fear of Walker and other New Dealers that AT&T would expand its telephone monopoly to many other areas. AT&T's political response to new markets during this era was to back away from all fields other than its basic telephone business.

Prelude to the *Western Electric* Case

While World War II did not entirely suspend partisan politics, most administrative actions were postponed until after the Allied victory. Nevertheless, even during the war, planners fashioned a new public philosophy to deal with the postwar situation. The underlying assumption of most thoughtful persons was that a boom based on pent up wartime savings would be followed by a new depression, much like the 1929–39 episode; few thoughtful people expected the extraordinary sustained growth that characterized the post–World War II era. Accordingly, much theorizing was expended on how to prevent or, at least, moderate the inevitable downturn. Many policymakers looked to Keynesian fiscal policy in the macroeconomic area joined with antitrust policy at the industrial level. Belief in the public philosophy that dominated the Harry Truman presidency was shaped by the sharp economic downturn of 1937. Many observers close to the administration sought to place paramount blame for that recession on big business. Essentially they theorized that big business, exercising monopoly power, had instituted arbitrary price increases. When consumers were unable to purchase goods at these excessively high prices, big business did not lower prices; rather, it laid off workers, reduced output, and postponed investments.[5] Thus, the key to preventing another depression in the postwar era was vigorous antitrust action.

Notwithstanding some Republican opposition, to be against monopolies in the immediate post–World War II era was not only politically popular but economically popular as well, in that the theory addressed some of the major economic problems facing the nation at the time. President Truman, an advocate of vigorous antitrust action, vetoed the Reed-Bulwinkle Act in 1948, which granted antitrust exemption to railroad common carriers for jointly formulating rate and other agreements. (Congress overrode the veto.) Truman also vetoed a 1950 bill, this time successfully, that would have allowed certain basing point pricing practices on the ground that the bill would encourage industrywide uniform prices. In both cases, Truman stated his strong support for the antitrust laws. However, antitrust is not primarily a matter of enacting statutes or of vetoing them. The Sherman Act is sufficiently broad to allow the Antitrust Division of the Justice Department to challenge a wide variety of practices. In short, antitrust is primarily a matter of executive-branch enforcement. Therefore, it is in the activities of the Justice Department and the Federal Trade Commission, which is also responsible for antitrust enforcement, that we must look to ascertain the administration's principles on antitrust.

The Truman Antitrust Division was one of the most vigorous since the enactment of the Sherman law in 1890. Aside from bringing the *Western Electric* case, consider its other activities in 1949 alone. The Truman administration pursued old and new cases vigorously, largely eschewing compromise in the form of negotiated settlements. A New Jersey court upheld the Antitrust Division's contention that General Electric unlawfully monopolized basic tungsten filament incandescent lamp patents. A suit was filed to break up the Great Atlantic and Pacific Tea Company, then the nation's largest food retailer. A major monopoly case was brought against the large tobacco companies, and another was brought to sever the stock and management relationships among Du Pont, General Motors, and U.S. Rubber. American Can Company, the nation's largest manufacturer of tin cans, was charged with monopolizing. Other major pending cases, in some of which the government sought drastic restructuring remedies, involved Bausch and Lomb Optical Company, the four largest meat packers, major dairies, the three largest farm machinery manufacturers, seventeen investment banking firms, Eastman Kodak, Timken Roller Bearing Company, United Shoe Machinery Corporation, U.S. Alkali Export Association, and the Yellow Cab Company. Meanwhile, the Federal Trade Commission was prosecuting some of the biggest cases it had ever undertaken—its targets included major steel manufacturers and cement producers. Thus, AT&T was in good company when the Antitrust Division brought its action, the major purpose of which was to divorce Western Electric from AT&T and to create three separate corporations from Western.

Large size alone is insufficient to bring an antitrust case; there had to be other factors present before action could be taken. One of the most important factors involved the extension of market power from one market into others. The Supreme Court's favorable disposition in the 1948 Paramount decision to the divorces of motion picture production and distribution from exhibition constituted an open invitation to attack vertical integration when associated with substantial market power. But from the perspective of antitrust law, the case that provided the closest parallels to the AT&T–Western Electric situation involved the Pullman Company. When a district court decided the *United States v. Pullman Company* case in 1943, and it was upheld by the Supreme Court, the decision was viewed as a major breakthrough.[6] Pullman had provided sleeping car service to the railroads since 1900, achieving dominance of such service through long-term contracts. It used the leverage of its service business to achieve an almost complete monopoly of sleeping car manufacture for a subsidiary that made the cars, effectively preventing others from any sales in the industry. The district court held that it was not necessary for the government to show abusive conduct or intent; benevolent monopoly is monopoly nonetheless. The monopolistic effects of Pullman's arrangements with the railroads were sufficient to prove a violation of the Sherman Act, even though all the defendant's customers were satisfied and Pullman's business was run in an efficient, even exemplary, manner. As a result of the violation, the court ordered the separation of the two components of Pullman's business. The resemblance between the Pullman and Western Electric situations was readily apparent and might result in AT&T divesting Western Electric even if vertical integration was efficient and reasonable.[7]

The *United States v. Western Electric* Case

Why did the Justice Department bring its 1949 antitrust suit against AT&T and the Bell system? Unlike the 1974 case, it was not triggered by the complaints of competitors; there were no complaints about AT&T's performance. Indeed, the company's wartime effort was uniformly viewed as exemplary, and its peacetime plans were visionary.[8] Rather, the suit stemmed from the Truman administration's public philosophy and complemented the many other antitrust cases brought during that era. The first media mention of the pending case occurred in mid-December 1948 when *Business Week* reported that the Antitrust Division was preparing a "Pullman case" against AT&T to divorce Western Electric from the parent company.[9] Less than one month later the Justice Department brought its antitrust suit against the company. In contrast to most large-scale antitrust matters, the FBI had not conducted a wide-ranging investigation prior to the suit. The reason was that the case was based almost entirely on the F.C.C.'s hostile investigation in the 1930s. The complaint, consisting of seventy-three pages, described events in AT&T's history that went back to the turn of the century, and it proposed a divorce of Western Electric from AT&T and a division of Western's plants into three competing, independent equipment manufacturers. In a statement accompanying the complaint, Attorney General Tom Clark stated that the purpose of the suit was to

> restore competition in the manufacture and sale of telephone equipment. . . . This in turn will lower the cost of such equipment and create a situation under which state and federal regulatory commissions will be afforded an opportunity to reduce telephone rates to subscribers. Absence of competition in the manufacture and sale of telephone equipment has tended to defeat effective public regulation of rates charged subscribers for telephone service.[10]

The complaint was, of course, not prepared by the attorney general but by Holmes Baldridge, an Antitrust Division attorney who had been a leading staff participant in the F.C.C.'s investigation and later a lead attorney in the Pullman case. The government's prayer for relief called for not only the divestiture of Western Electric but also for (1) AT&T to acquire all of its equipment by competitive bidding, (2) Western Electric to sell its 50 percent share in Bell Labs to AT&T, and (3) AT&T and Western Electric's successors to license all patents to all applicants on a nondiscriminatory and reasonable royalty basis[11] (even though AT&T had already voluntarily instituted an extremely liberal patent-licensing policy).

AT&T's April 24, 1949, answer to the complaint consisted of a general denial of the Justice Department's allegations, several technical legal arguments, and a recitation of the advantages of an integrated telephone system carefully regulated by government agencies. The heart of the defense to the government's call for drastic relief claimed that the costs of a vertically integrated system were lower than they would be with arm's-length market transactions between independent manufacturers and the operating companies. "Since all the operating units of the System have common problems there are many things that can be done better and more economically in their behalf by a central organization. The American Company has undertaken to do these things either directly or through its subsidiaries."[12] These included (1) developing and recommending technical standards and operating methods and (2) providing the research and development results of Bell Labs and the manufacturing and supply facilities of Western Electric. Some installations for operating companies were custom-made with considerable give and take among AT&T, Western Electric, and the local operating companies. The lawsuit was, thus, fundamentally about the relative benefits and costs of vertical integration.

The Settlement of 1956

On January 24, 1956, about seven years after the antitrust suit was filed, AT&T and the Justice Department entered into a consent decree and final judgment in the *Western Electric* case. Although a long lapse of time between the filing of a complaint and its resolution is not unusual in complex antitrust cases, the *Western Electric* case was unusual in that so few formal proceedings had transpired in the interim. While one view holds that the Republican administration that came to power in 1953 capitulated to AT&T, it does not explain the lack of action between 1949 and 1953 when the Democratic Truman administration that brought the case was in power.

While trial courts play a major role in handling cases before them, it is nevertheless clear that an important shift in public philosophy was taking place. The postwar return to depression did not occur; to the contrary, the American economy had embarked on a sharp upward trend from 1948 to 1956. Gross national product increased an annual average of 4.7 percent (in constant dollars) during those years, while personal disposable income (in constant dollars) increased at an annual average of 4.6 percent, notwithstanding two minor recessions. The unemployment rate averaged only 4.3 percent—a sharp decline from the 1938 rate of 19 percent.[13] Events had severely undermined the argument in favor of the antitrust philosophy. At the same time, the United States had become locked in a cold war with the Soviet Union, its most formidable rival since the war of independence. Firms with important research and production facilities were now not just large companies but also national resources, so that any drastic restructuring would weaken not only the companies but would undermine national survival as well. The new public philosophy based on rising affluence and national survival was on the ascendant in 1956, while the older antitrust one—although far from dormant—was in decline. For these reasons the Eisenhower administration was anxious to terminate its major cases against IBM and AT&T.

When we combine these changes with the showing that AT&T made to Justice Department attorneys undermining the foundations of the case, and the support given to AT&T by the Department of Defense, we can readily understand the consent decree of January 1956. The most important aspects of the settlement concerned what it did *not* do; that is, it did not require AT&T to divest Western Electric and it did not impair the relationship of Bell Labs and the other components of the Bell system. In short, the settlement left the structure of AT&T largely unchanged, except that Western Electric was required to sell the Westrex Corporation, a subsidiary that manufactured sound recording equipment for the movie industry. However, it had become clear as early as 1950, when AT&T announced that Western Electric would no longer manufacture radio broadcasting transmitting equipment or television station apparatus, that the company would withdraw from businesses unrelated to point-to-point telecommunications. Although Western Electric's endeavors in these fields were promising in the 1950s, AT&T had learned through experience that any activity in non-telephonic fields would be politically troublesome. Thus, AT&T agreed in the settlement that Western Electric would not manufacture products not required by the operating companies and AT&T, except for certain products like the artificial larynx and those manufactured for the United States government, most importantly the Department of Defense. Further, AT&T and its operating subsidiaries agreed not to engage in unregulated, non-public-service activities with the exceptions of working for the federal government, doing experimental work, providing circuits, giving advice and assistance to other communications common carriers, and directory advertising. In summary, AT&T and its component parts agreed to limit themselves to communications activities, defense-related work, and the network manager role.

One of the most important elements in the 1956 settlement was that all past and future Bell system patents were made subject to compulsory license at reasonable royalty rates to all applicants not controlled by foreign interests without regard to prospective use. When one considers that Bell Labs had invented the junction transistor—the basis of all modern electronics—and much else, one can begin to appreciate the value to other firms of this crucial provision. Nevertheless, the settlement was viewed with deep suspicion by adherents of the old antitrust philosophy, many of whom held positions of influence in the Democratic Party. One of the most important of these people was Representative Emmanuel Celler, chairman of the House antitrust subcommittee. In 1958, Celler began searching for evidence that would support charges of a "sellout." The subsequent hearings would be useful as an attack on the Republican administration as well as a vindication of Celler's view that only a venal conspiracy consisting of AT&T, top administration officials, and the Department of Defense could have led to such a weak settlement. The Celler committee's report does not reflect a careful evaluation of the testimony and documents collected in the hearings.[14] Nevertheless, suspicion lingered, and AT&T's later opponents would use the Celler report to argue that the 1956 agreement insufficiently constrained AT&T and that other remedies against the company were necessary. There is a thread, then, that goes from the F.C.C.'s 1930s investigation through the 1956 settlement to the later government actions restructuring American telecommunications.

The Assault in Telecommunications: Interconnection

While the *Western Electric* episode constituted an assault on the basic structure of AT&T, the F.C.C. and the state public utility commissions were also quietly confronting issues concerning the company and its place in postwar telecommunications. Most of the challenges have their roots in technological changes that began to occur even before World War II but that were accelerated during the war. These changes generated entrepreneurial activity as old and new firms sought to seize opportunities to use telecommunications in novel ways. This, in turn, raised three new issues: (1) what interconnection rights into the Bell network should be granted to the entrepreneurs, (2) how the newly available portions of the expanded radio spectrum should be allocated (spectrum, like land, is a scarce resource), and (3) how regulators could solve the problem of drawing the boundary between regulated public service activity and unregulated competitive activity. AT&T's reactions to these issues and the responses of federal and state regulators constituted a major controversy in the 1974 suit. During the first postwar decade, the regulatory agencies, most importantly the F.C.C., attempted to resolve the new problems within a traditional public service context. But even then, there were those who advocated a new framework that would grant a larger role to competition. The early postwar events concerning answering and recording devices in the customer premises equipment (CPE) market and intercity television transmission in long-distance transmission constitute the first phase of the erosion of the public service conception. The second phase, culminating in a direct attack on interconnection restrictions, began in 1956.

The most important initial contentions concerned the Bell system's long-standing interconnection restrictions that prohibited customer-provided interconnection (with few exceptions) into the AT&T-dominated network. AT&T provided CPE and switching and transmission gear, usually of its own manufacture, as well as long-distance transmission. Although its operating companies were joined by many independent local companies, the interfaces between local loops and the national network were controlled or supervised by AT&T. Such controls were exercised over all communications products, including voice, video, data, facsimile, and so forth. AT&T's interconnection policy was embodied in the company's related tariffs and had deep historic roots. The interconnection restrictions were uniformly upheld from their beginnings and applied both to instruments that were substituted for Bell equipment as well as those that were added on, such as answering machines.

At a superficial level these interconnection restrictions can be viewed as a naked attempt by AT&T to enlarge its monopoly from those segments of telecommunications in which monopoly was lawfully granted to other product markets in which monopoly was not lawfully granted. Under most circumstances, such tie-in arrangements of a lawful monopoly product or service with another product or service constitutes a violation of the Sherman Antitrust Act.[15] Nevertheless, sound justifications can overcome the presumption of illegality. The AT&T argument began by observing that almost from its beginnings the telephone industry has had inventors who developed what are called foreign attachments that supplement or substitute for the components supplied by telephone companies. As early as 1884 the Bell system adopted a policy rejecting such interconnection on the ground that they were injurious to transmitters.

As telephone use grew in the early 1890s and the expiration of the Bell patents neared, the number of foreign attachments that could be made easily and attached to the basic instruments proliferated.[16] Some of these devices were found to impair the intelligibility of communications or the quality of the signal, such as an "ear pad for Telephone Receivers."[17] Still other devices during the late nineteenth and early twentieth centuries preyed on public fears, implying that the telephone mouthpiece was a health hazard. For example, a flyer for the Improved Antiseptic Nickel Mouthpiece Attachment claimed that "the scrapings from many telephone mouthpieces were subjected to the microscope by Prof. Kauffman of the Board of Health and great numbers of bacteria germs were found . . . which shows that great danger actually exists in inhaling these germs in the mouth and nostrils."[18] Still another advertisement for a mouthpiece warned that telephones "may be infected with the most dreadful contagious diseases" because people touched the mouthpiece with sore lips.[19] Such flagrant claims, needless to say, angered Bell officials.[20] Other attachments sold to consumers did not work, and in almost all cases there was some degree of transmission loss that resulted from interconnecting the device into the telephone network.[21]

Because of the interactive nature of the telephone network, telephone companies and regulators responsible for the overall quality of the network could not adopt a casual attitude toward such devices. Those adversely affected by foreign attachments that malfunctioned or reduced the quality of conversation included not only those using them but parties to conversations and other subscribers using Bell equipment as well. The proliferation of foreign attachments and the difficulty of locating and testing them before their introduction into the network might cause such engineering and technical problems as hazardous voltages, line imbalance, attenuation, other forms of quality deterioration, and substantial costs. Bell licensees and the telephone companies incurred high transaction and information costs resulting from (1) discovering such attachments, preferably before harm might occur, (2) testing the devices, (3) negotiating with their manufacturers and sellers, (4) proposing modifications and policing the manufacturers' adherence to the new standards, (5) retesting the devices, (6) installing them or supervising their installation, (7) instructing subscribers in the correct use and maintenance of devices so that the network would not be impaired, and (8) repairing them.

For these reasons the Bell system adopted a policy uniformly approved by the state public service commissions known as end-to-end responsibility. Taking responsibility for the entire network made sound economic sense not only for the telephone company but for the subscribers as well, since it assured lower telephone company costs. For these same reasons, independent companies that were not integrated backward like AT&T also imposed interconnection restrictions. The ICC, PUCs, and the F.C.C. uniformly upheld these provisions as reasonable restrictions.[22] Indeed, they often compelled telephone companies to adopt the provisions. However, the tariffs did not bar all interconnection; rather, customer interconnection was prohibited unless a good reason to override the prohibition could be provided. Hence, information and transaction costs were largely shifted to the customer seeking the exception and were not imposed on other subscribers. Those granted exceptions tended to be reliable customers who could be trusted not to impair the network. For example, the United States Army had well-trained telephone personnel and for security reasons maintained control over CPE. Mining and railroad companies also were permitted to provide and maintain certain CPE because of the hazards telephone company employees would face in maintaining the equipment.[23]

AT&T's interconnection policies were, then, clearly defined and settled as the postwar era began in 1946. But several factors conspired in the policy's undermining, among which, ironically, was AT&T's business and technological successes. From 1946 to 1970, per capita GNP in constant dollars more than doubled, but the number of telephones almost quadrupled. In that period the percentage of households with telephone service increased from 51.4 percent to 90.5 percent. At the same time, telephone rate increases consistently trailed the rate of inflation. To a considerable extent, AT&T achieved these results because of its technological prowess. Coaxial cable, microwave transmission, the transistor and electronic switching, for all of which AT&T was significantly responsible, revolutionized telecommunications technology within a very short time. Increased capacity, lower costs, increased demand, and the general economic boom stimulated telecommunications in this period. No one firm—not even one as large as AT&T—could possibly seize all of the opportunities as rapidly as they could be realized. At the same time, prospective lucrative markets inevitably attracted entrepreneurs seeking to plug into the network through new CPE or private systems that could become more valuable through interconnecting into the public switched network.[24]

AT&T's initial postwar responses to the first proceedings, involving recording or answering machines, was to either bar interconnection or to permit interconnection under conditions it carefully controlled, and, in general, the F.C.C. and state regulatory bodies upheld AT&T's responses with some modification.[25] But in a major proceeding known as the *Hush-A-Phone* case, things began to change. Like so many events that lead to the establishment of important principles, the *Hush-A-Phone* case had its origins in a relatively small and simple matter. The Hush-A-Phone device, consisting of a simple cuplike attachment that could be snapped onto the telephone handset, was intended to assure relative privacy. It was entirely acoustic and did not involve any electrical or inductive connection into the network. As such, the Hush-A-Phone—unlike most prior interconnection devices—did not raise the issues of physical harm, network safety, or technical compatibility.[26]

AT&T and its affiliates objected to the Hush-A-Phone principally because it reduced the intelligibility of communication. Because the quality of telephone conversations between users and other parties was lessened by the Hush-A-Phone attachment, the Bell system determined that the device degraded the network. In keeping with its tariff provisions generally prohibiting interconnection, the Bell system notified several Hush-A-Phone customers (most of them department stores) that the attachment was illegal and should be removed. As a result, the Hush-A-Phone company brought action against the Bell system in 1948, requesting the F.C.C. to change the interconnection provisions of AT&T's tariffs to permit the use of the device. In response, the Bell system claimed that the Hush-A-Phone was ineffective in that it impaired the intelligibility of telephone service and did not afford any significant increase in privacy. Telephone engineers, including some not employed by telephone companies, also complained that the Hush-A-Phone raised the transmitters of certain telephones above their cradles when the instruments were hung up, which tied up central-office lines and delayed incoming calls. It was also noted that the California PUC's policy was to deny interconnection rights if a device *might* impair the network because the administrative costs of policing such devices would be too high.[27]

In February 1951, in an initial decision, the F.C.C. unanimously agreed to dismiss Hush-A-Phone's complaint, but stated that each foreign attachment must be considered separately based upon potential impairment or quality reduction of the network. In 1955 an almost entirely different group of commissioners upheld the initial decision, 6–0, ruling that the device impaired intelligibility, naturalness, and voice recognition.[28] Hush-A-Phone Corporation was not about to give up, notwithstanding the long line of precedent against its position, and appealed the F.C.C.'s decision to the Court of Appeals for the District of Columbia Circuit. To the surprise of most observers, the court's November 1956 decision reversed the F.C.C., upholding Hush-A-Phone's contentions.[29] Since there was no federal judicial precedent in the area of interconnection, the court was relatively free to vent its views on the subject without constraint. Accordingly, it ignored the network concept and every reason that the PUCs and F.C.C. had provided to support interconnection restrictions. The court disregarded the facts that regulatory agencies have an interest in the quality of transmission and that statutes (including the 1934 Communications Act) direct them to consider quality and promote improvements in the network. In effect, the court held that if an interconnecting device does not physically impair any of the facilities of the telephone company, any commission restriction on interconnection is an "unwarranted interference with the telephone subscriber's *right* reasonably to use his telephone in ways which are privately beneficial without being publicly detrimental" (emphasis added).[30]

Notwithstanding the surprising result in the *Hush-A-Phone* appeal, it is important to appreciate what the court's decision did not do. Although the court's comment, "privately beneficial without being publicly detrimental," would open the door to the introduction of more such devices, the court did not command the F.C.C. to deregulate CPE interconnection or to promote competition, and it certainly did not warrant any substitution for Bell-provided equipment. Accordingly, the F.C.C., upon remand, directed AT&T to amend its tariffs so as to distinguish between harmful and harmless interconnecting devices. Thus, at this juncture, the company could not prohibit devices that did not injure or impair the system or its operation. The amended AT&T tariffs were filed in April 1957, in accordance with the decisions, but in an accompanying statement AT&T made it clear that liberalized interconnection did not apply to electrical devices because these did create a safety hazard.

Control over Television Transmission

During the early post–World War II period, in which AT&T's position on interconnection was being undermined, an equally important threat was mounted in the realm of spectrum allocation. We noted in Chapter 1 that entry, industry structure, and allocation issues have been crucial in telecommunications policy. Theoretically, a monopolist should fight against technological innovations that enlarge market capacity beyond its ability to dominate it. AT&T's response to the most important new transmission technologies with enormous potential to enlarge markets was far more complex than the simple theoretical model would have predicted. The television boom that was promised before World War II, but postponed until after the Allied victory, illustrates the complex response.

In order to understand the issues, a short technical digression is necessary. After World War II the dominant medium for distributing television programs was not yet clear. What was known from the outset of experimental telecasting was that the twisted pair of wires used to carry telephonic transmission was inadequate to carry television signals over long distances. The range of frequencies to be carried in video transmission was simply too broad for both ordinary copper wires and cable. The two principal contenders for the lucrative television transmission market were microwave relay and coaxial cable. While coaxial cable bore a clear resemblance to ordinary copper wire or cable, we cannot assume that AT&T necessarily favored coaxial cable to microwave relay. That AT&T had a strong historical commitment to coaxial cable is evident, as it was in large part developed by AT&T precisely to transmit television signals. During the 1930s, AT&T had been encouraged in this endeavor by RCA, which would become the largest customer of television program distribution. Coaxial cable, consisting of a special cable in which one conductor is completely surrounded by a second one, greatly reduced attenuation and distortion and dramatically reduced power losses at high frequencies. Additionally, the increase in transmission paths compared with traditional two-way voice channels was dramatic. Thus, coaxial cable would permit AT&T to experience a great increase in telephone capacity and at the same time allow it to accommodate the anticipated television boom.

However, at the end of World War II, microwave relay loomed as an alternative for both long-distance voice and television transmission, although it was not necessarily conceived of as a competitor to coaxial cable. While it was entirely possible that one of the two technologies might be the sole survivor for economic or technological reasons, AT&T then contemplated that each would serve its purpose in the television and telephone long-distance markets, and that distance, terrain, and other variables would determine which would be the most economic between any two points. In AT&T's view, both technologies had to be considered in transmission of voice and television, and as such they were within the jurisdiction of regulators and public service companies.

Nevertheless, in that period, coaxial cable was a more reliable technology. In microwave relay, the microwaves travel only slightly above the horizon and are subject to fading because of atmospheric conditions, and must be retransmitted at towers approximately twenty-five to thirty-five miles apart. A comprehensive microwave system requires the design of (1) repeater circuits; (2) antennae with high gain, good directional qualities, and a low capacity for distortion; (3) filters that can connect a number of different radio channels to a common antenna (thus reducing the quantity of antennae otherwise needed); and (4) repeater amplifiers to compensate for transmission loss in the previous path.[31] But the complete microwave system is more than a sum of its parts; indeed, the larger the system became, the greater were the questions of transmission quality, flexibility, dependability, and economy.

A conflict was virtually inevitable between AT&T and the television networks over who would dominate the nationwide transmission of television programming. By February 1948 the television networks' plans were greater than AT&T's combined coaxial-microwave system could handle. Accordingly, the Television Broadcasters Association (TBA) urged the F.C.C. to provide frequency space for a private intercity television microwave operation because AT&T and other common carriers could not adequately meet the needs of the television networks. The controversy heated up considerably when AT&T refused to transmit an NBC video program between New York and Boston because the program had been transmitted previously from Philadelphia to New York over the lines of a television network, rather than AT&T's.[32] The controversy, which the F.C.C. ultimately resolved, further undermined AT&T's transmission monopoly by allowing other firms to distribute intercity video traffic where AT&T and the other telephone and telegraph companies were unable to do so. The agency also rejected any AT&T tariff that refused to transmit television transmission at reasonable rates.[33]

Spectrum as a Scarce Resource

The controversy between AT&T and the television networks was only the first of several interconnection and spectrum allocation battles that erupted between the telecommunications giants and large users in the postwar era. In contrast to the prewar era in which corporate users saw telecommunications as an incidental cost of doing business, important users began to see telecommunications as a crucial resource in transacting business. In particular, the petroleum industry—an important actor in both the *Above 890 Mc* and the *Carterfone* proceedings—typified the burgeoning interest of many industrial and commercial sectors in the enormous possibilities of telecommunications. In October 1947, the American Petroleum Institute (API) created its Central Committee on Radio Facilities; oceangoing-vessel-to-shore communications, petroleum pipelines, and geophysical exploration were only the beginnings of its newfound interests in telecommunications. The head of the API committee projected that "Practically every division or branch of the petroleum industry can well be served by one or more adaptations of radio to effect economies in operation, increase safety or raise efficiency. Radio may, perhaps, provide new methods of processing oil to supplement or even replace the present catalytic refining processes."[34]

Many other industries gradually discovered what the petroleum industry did early in the postwar era—telecommunications was a valuable resource. This realization raised for industry representatives a host of issues, including whether they should have the choice of a private system or telephone-company-provided service, interconnection rights, and, of course, frequency allocation. The crosscutting conflicts meant that industrial and commercial microwave users could have interests in conflict not only with telephone companies but with each other as well. For example, API and the theater television interests clashed in 1952 over the allocation of certain microwave frequencies. The political battle over microwave frequencies came to resemble a barroom brawl, but with one difference: virtually every interest took a position in conflict with AT&T's. In 1953, the Radio-Electronics Television Manufacturers Association (RETMA), desiring a degree of predictability on how to plan the manufacture of sets in the future, requested that the F.C.C. conduct an overall study and promulgate microwave rules in accordance with current and future requirements.[35] As the F.C.C. prepared to act, a dozen user organizations, including railroads, motor carriers, and forest industries, banded together in 1954 as the Microwave Users Council.

In May 1957 the F.C.C. began its protracted *Above 890 Mc* hearings to decide the fate of the microwave portion of the radio frequency spectrum. For the first time in an F.C.C. proceeding, virtually all big business—led by the petroleum industry—contended that it needed privately provided micro-wave to serve its unique requirements, thus potentially foreclosing AT&T and other common carriers from a large volume of communications traffic. The F.C.C.'s 1959 decision went much further in weakening AT&T's control over telecommunications than it had in the 1949 television matter, in which the agency conceived non-common-carrier transmission of television as a temporary and supplementary phenomenon. In *Above 890 Mc,* it found that a frequency shortage did not then exist and that a shortage was not likely to develop in the future. Second, the F.C.C. projected that there would be few private microwave users. Therefore, the intense demand of a few private-line users (demonstrated by their vigorous participation in the hearings) and a projected small overall private-line demand were the key reasons the F.C.C. agreed to permit private microwave. Because the agency viewed private microwave as an exception to common-carrier control of intercity communications, the issue was treated much like a military or police service, for which there is little or no need to discuss boundary questions between public and nonpublic services.[36]

Thus, AT&T and the other public service companies suffered a major defeat. Clearly the agency was impressed by the intensity expressed by large users of private microwave and felt obligated to accommodate their interests. Of course, the petroleum industry was pleased with the outcome. And, not surprisingly, when the commission reconsidered *Above 890 Mc* in 1960, it upheld its original decision, largely on the grounds initially set forth.[37] Although the door for competition was not yet opened wide, it certainly opened considerably more as a result of the *Above 890 Mc* case. Nevertheless, if the F.C.C. presumed that the new competition between private and common carriage would reduce its supervisory role, the decision had precisely the opposite effect. AT&T's tariff responses (usually called TELPAK) were invariably challenged before the agency, which became more deeply involved in AT&T's corporate affairs than ever before.[38] The challenges to AT&T, however, were just beginning.

Space Communications

The unique history of the American space program was responsible for the distinctive economic structure of the communications-satellite industry as well as for AT&T's strong, but not dominant, position within it. While the story of satellites began before the Soviet Union's launch of Sputnik I on October 4, 1957, certainly that event had great impact on the structure of the industry. The United States suffered a serious blow to its prestige in science and technology, which, in turn, led to a strong American commitment under government guidance to space technology. Thus, communications satellites became not just a business; they became intertwined with national prestige and a substantial commitment of government resources. At the very least, patents developed under the government's auspices as well as its exclusive control over satellite launching would inevitably lead to cries of blatant favoritism if only existing common carriers were allowed to deploy communications satellites. Nevertheless, the Eisenhower administration made it clear that it had "achieved communications facilities second to none among the nations of the world. Accordingly, the Government should encourage private enterprise in the establishment and operation of satellite relays for revenue producing purposes."[39] Yet the government's commitment to "private enterprise," a policy endorsed by the Kennedy administration over the objection of several liberals in Congress, did not specify the future structure of the satellite communications industry. It did not address such issues as whether the industry would be dominated by AT&T, whether a number of common carriers would jointly operate satellites, or the roles of the aerospace companies and television networks. Moreover, even if government operation of the industry was ruled out, the government could still play a major role by participating in joint ventures.

AT&T's plan for satellite communications was based in part on the argument that public service principles should prevail in telecommunications regardless of the transmission means—satellites, wire, or microwave. Because AT&T anticipated the charge that it sought to monopolize satellite communications, its plan specified that all U.S. international common carriers should have full access to the satellite system and to ownership participation. The corporation that was finally formed represented a compromise among the various interests and was far from the type of structure that AT&T sought. The 1962 Communications Satellite Act established the Communications Satellite Corporation (Comsat), which would operate satellites for international communication. Although communications common carriers could hold stock in the new corporation, their ownership and voting participation was sharply limited; only six of the fifteen directors could be chosen by the carriers and no single carrier could vote for more than three directors. In short, the statute established a structure in which Comsat would be free of dominance by the existing international common carriers. And, since the suppliers of telecommunications equipment now included aerospace companies, a new carrier's entry into international satellite communications would, in turn, raise the hopes of those seeking to enter domestic satellite communications when that became technologically feasible.

The successful launch of Hughes Aircraft's *Early Bird* satellite in 1965 led the ABC television network to request the F.C.C. to allow it a private satellite that would link its network. This precipitated the F.C.C. to institute its domestic satellite inquiry to investigate general domestic satellite problems. By 1966, the battle had grown as AT&T opposed privately operated satellites on technical grounds (for instance, interference with microwave facilities) and argued that prohibitive costs limited the system's usefulness. The networks, with the support of the Ford Foundation, argued that a satellite system could relay programs for considerably less cost than what was paid to the public service companies. Since the Ford Foundation expressed no interest in operating a domestic satellite system, AT&T was in the unenviable position of attacking the proposals of an organization that had no financial interest in the outcome. By 1969, AT&T announced that it would end its opposition to the television networks' operation of private satellite systems[40]—but by then, the company was in full-scale retreat on many fronts. The *Carterfone* case would be crucial in undermining AT&T's position.

Carterfone

As early as 1966, the House Small Business Subcommittee on Regulatory Agencies heard testimony from antique telephone dealers complaining of the CPE interconnection restrictions, even though the Bell system and other telephone companies had gone far in accommodating customer demand for antique and decorator telephone housing. However, the problem extended beyond antique and decorator telephones as numerous business interests sought interconnection rights. For example, the large National Retail Merchants Association stated that its inability to interconnect privately owned systems into the public switched network was a major impediment to its full use of private microwave systems. But AT&T and the other telephone companies felt justified in maintaining interconnection restrictions. Yet the difficulty of supervising CPE worsened because of the postwar proliferation of such devices. Moreover, the F.C.C.'s final word on the issue in the *Above 890 Mc* decision (1959) approved tariff regulations that limited interconnection, while *Hush-A-Phone* was treated as a narrow exception to the general rule.[41] Finally, during the period immediately preceding the F.C.C.'s 1968 *Carterfone* decision, state commissions largely upheld the interconnection restrictions.[42] Thus, prior to the *Carterfone* decision, AT&T and the other telephone companies were provided with a clear decision rule: the interconnection restriction in tariffs would be upheld against devices that might harm any component of the network, *except* if there was widespread public demand for a device and a simple telephone company adjustment could alleviate the safety or quality problem.

The Carterfone, the device that changed telecommunications regulation, was invented by Thomas F. Carter in 1959. Carter, who had been involved in two-way radio, office intercoms, and other communications systems since 1946, discovered in the mid-1950s that his customers with two-way-radio-equipped vehicles sought to connect with telephone users for various reasons. Reminiscing in 1985, Carter said, "The men in the field decided they wanted to talk directly to the supply house to eliminate third party errors. I started designing a little item that would allow these people to do that." The Carterfone device, an equivalent of which was not offered by the Bell system, permitted direct voice communication between persons using the telephone network and those located at remote mobile radio terminals. When attached to a telephone, the Carterfone allowed communication to take place between the mobile radio user and those using the telephone network without the need for a base station operator to relay messages manually. The instrument worked by having the mobile station base operator place the telephone receiver on a cradle in the Carterfone to effect an inductive and acoustic connection between the telephone line and the mobile radio channel. Not surprisingly, then, the Carterfone met with considerable demand. Carter Electronics's Texas location probably helped bring the device to the attention of oil companies. Although not the only customers of Carter's corporation, they were among the most important and provided strong support during the F.C.C. hearings. Because offshore drilling became an important activity of the petroleum industry during the 1960s, the American Petroleum Institute strongly endorsed the Carterfone's value in this area at the F.C.C. hearings. Yet offshore drilling was only one of many uses that petroleum companies found for the device. Other endorsements for the Carterfone and Carter's position came from utilities, the United States Air Force, the National Aeronautics and Space Agency, the Antitrust Division, the National Retail Merchants Association, and, within the F.C.C., the Common Carrier Bureau. Thus, the Carterfone benefited from much support.[43]

In a March 1965 letter to F.C.C. chairman E. William Henry, Carter requested legal clarification of how the interconnection restriction applied to the Carterfone instrument. Told that the restrictions prohibit interconnection "except as specifically provided in the tariffs" and of his right to lodge a formal complaint with the F.C.C., Carter instead filed a private antitrust suit against AT&T, Southwestern Bell, and General Telephone of the Southwest, charging violations of the Sherman Act. The district court then referred the case to the F.C.C. on the ground that the agency had primary jurisdiction. In the fall of 1966, the F.C.C. began its action on the interconnection issues, and on August 30, 1967, the hearing examiner issued an initial decision, finding against AT&T, Southwestern Bell, and General Telephone of the Southwest in almost every particular. He found that (1) users (notably, oil companies) were satisfied with the Carterfone, (2) a substantial unfilled demand existed for the device, and (3) it did not impair the safety or quality of the network.[44]

The F.C.C., in its decision, went much further than the hearing examiner, using its *Carterfone* decision as a vehicle to establish new equipment-interconnection principles. The F.C.C. held that there was "no material distinction between a foreign attachment such as the Hush-A-Phone and an interconnection device such as the Carterfone so far as the present problem is concerned."[45] The new rule advanced by the agency held "that a customer desiring to use an interconnecting device to improve the utility to him of both the telephone system and a private radio system should be able to do so, so long as the interconnection does not adversely affect the telephone company's operations or the telephone system's utility for others."[46]

After telephone company legal maneuvers had failed to move the F.C.C. to change its position, the companies revised their interconnection tariffs in August 1968. The new, liberal provisions permitted the direct electrical connection and interface of customer-provided CPE, other terminal equipment (such as computers), and customer-provided microwave systems into the network, subject to several restrictions. The most important restriction specified that some devices (such as computers) would be connected into the telephone network through a telephone-company-provided control device. The provision was, of course, an invitation to raise the issue of why only telephone companies could provide these devices.

After *Carterfone*, AT&T was clearly on the defensive in the equipment area, and a new era had been ushered in. The revival of the microwave battle, as we will see in the next chapter, reshaped the long-distance component of the industry as well.

4

MCI and the
Long-Distance Challenge

Little Strokes Fell Great Oaks

"Little strokes fell great oaks" was the aphorism Benjamin Franklin devised to describe the way in which gradual changes lead to dramatic transformations. His aphorism accurately portrays the way in which Microwave Communications Inc. (MCI), a small upstart firm, helped to transform the telecommunications landscape, leading to the breakup of AT&T in 1984, and moved the old public philosophy to a new one in which a form of competition would play a significant role. MCI's gradually unfolding strategy is instructive. It did not all at once batter the old public service philosophy in which AT&T acted as the dominating network manager dedicated to fulfilling the goal of universal access at reasonable rates. Rather, MCI's strategy was to carve out exception after exception to the old public philosophy over the opposition of AT&T. Eventually the old public philosophy became untenable and a new one, based on carefully controlled competition and the breakup of AT&T, came to prevail.

How MCI gradually changed public policy in American telecommunications by portraying its self-interest as the public interest is, thus, a critical part of this story. As in the case of CPE, a demand for immediate full-scale competition in long distance would have been rebuffed by the F.C.C. and PUCs. The political dynamic in the case of long distance was similar to and complementary to that in CPE. MCI and others did not at first challenge AT&T's monopoly of long-distance service; rather, they initially made the reasonable request to be allowed to serve markets not being served by the Bell system. Although peripheral competition with AT&T might exist, the main thrust of the new entrants would be to enter new markets. In the 1960s, the extraordinary potential of the computer, particularly in data transmission, provided the principal arguments for the new firms seeking entry. That is, neither AT&T nor any other single firm could be reasonably expected to serve fully the enormous markets that would be opened up by data transmission. Consequently, the public interest demanded that new specialized firms be permitted to enter carefully delineated segments of the new markets.

Once MCI and other new firms successfully portrayed themselves as representing the public interest, the F.C.C. was virtually committed to their survival. Because it usually takes time for firms in new services and industries to become profitable, the F.C.C. adopted a protective stance toward the young firms. In fact, MCI used a political strategy to exploit the F.C.C.'s commitment: be aggressive toward AT&T and the independent telephone companies. Demand and litigate. In this way, the F.C.C. and the courts would be further encouraged to preserve MCI. Forgotten in the particular battles between MCI and other new entrants, on the one hand, and AT&T on the other, would be the original reason for MCI's license—to develop new markets innovatively, especially in data communications. They never did.

It is important to appreciate that the transformation that MCI's moves ushered in did not come about because AT&T's record was a bad one; the newcomer simply promised to serve markets left unattended. Indeed, as the following summary shows, AT&T's record was exemplary. In 1965, an already high 85 percent of households had telephone service; by 1975, the figure had risen to 93 percent. During the same period, the total number of telephones in use (including company, service, and private) had risen from 82 million to 130 million. The Bell system accounted for most of the totals as well as the increases,[1] and it achieved these results at high levels of productivity. According to a study conducted by the Department of Labor, in the period between 1972 and 1977 the Bell system's labor productivity growth exceeded that of all industries but one (hosiery). AT&T's price performance was also found to be exemplary—from 1947 to 1977, the telephone service industry's average price increases were about half that of all other industries combined. Whereas the CPI between 1960 and 1973 increased by 44.4 percent, the residential telephone component of the index increased by only 14.6 percent.[2] Further, from December 1964 to May 1974, the CPI rose 55.6 percent, food prices increased 72.1 percent, housing 56.5 percent, and medical care 67.3 percent, whereas rates for telephone service rose only 18.5 percent.[3] Thus, AT&T's overall economic performance was undoubtedly high. Its technological and scientific progress between 1969 and 1973 were equally impressive, laying the groundwork for future improvement. For example, in 1969 alone Bell Labs developed the UNIX operating system for minicomputers, the spin-flip RAMAN laser (the first tunable high-power laser in the infrared region), superconducting alloys, and a computer program that produced artificial speech from printed English words and sentences. In the realm of customer services during these years, AT&T had unveiled a telephone that allowed customers to dial emergency numbers (such as 911) without initially depositing a coin, major breakthroughs in dataphone service, the Touch-tone dial, conference telephones, higher capacity PBXs,* and the 698A Code Com set, which provided communication capability for the deaf and blind through combinations of flashing lamps, vibrating finger pads, and sending keys. Comparable progress was made in central-office equipment, especially in the realm of data switching. During the same period, great improvements were made even in such traditional components as cable and connectors.[4] Moreover, AT&T's plans for the future were not limited to short-term goals. The 1971 Bell Labs *Annual Report* described research in areas that would not be fully developed for some time. For example, the report devoted considerable space to the development of fiber optics—a technology that would not begin to come on line until the late 1970s and early 1980s.[5] In addition, the report described scientific work in such diverse areas as superconductivity, lasers and holograms, glassy metals, radio astronomy, and econometrics.[6]

The Rise of MCI

MCI, or more accurately one of the companies called MCI, began its regulatory life on the last day of 1963 when it filed a Communications Act Section 214 application with the F.C.C. for authorization to construct and operate a point-to-point microwave common-carrier system from Chicago to St. Louis and intermediate points. Its proposed service would be both intrastate and interstate. Section 214 requires interstate carriers to obtain from the F.C.C. a certificate that present or future public convenience and necessity will require the construction and operation of the line. Further, the F.C.C. is required to notify the governor or designated agency of the states in which the construction will take place and to hear complaints about the application, which, in turn, entails a state hearing (usually conducted by the PUC). Section 214 was "designed to prevent *useless duplication* of facilities with consequent higher charges upon the users of the service (emphasis added).[7]

Thus, to set the stage for one of the most protracted and complex series of events in the history of telecommunications policy, the burden of proving

---

*A private branch exchange (PBX) is a switching system belonging to a single organization, usually located on the organization's premises, that provides private telecommunications services within each of the organization's premises and between its various premises as well as access into the public switched network.

the necessity for a new or supplemental service was clearly on MCI. Although the statute presumed that monopoly service was desirable, the presumption was rebuttable. Moreover, MCI had to satisfy not only the F.C.C. but also the Illinois regulators in regard to the intrastate traffic it proposed to carry. A 1968 Illinois Supreme Court decision succinctly restated the state's long-standing principle on public utility competition:

> The method of regulating public utilities in Illinois is based upon the theory of regulated monopoly rather than competition. Before one utility is permitted to take the business of another already in the field, it must be shown that the existing one is rendering unsatisfactory service and is unable or unwilling to provide adequate facilities. . . . Where additional or extended service is required in the interest of the public and a utility in the field makes known its willingness and ability to furnish the required service, the commerce commission is not justified in granting a certificate of convenience and necessity to a competing utility until the utility in the field has had an opportunity to demonstrate its ability to give the required service.[8]

Accordingly, MCI argued that its new service was unique and not offered by the Bell system. Its principal selling point was flexibility. MCI's amended application stated that it proposed a microwave system that would provide users with "the bandwidth they wanted and [that they could] increase or decrease these bandwidths at any time to handle any changes in their communication load, or type of equipment."[9] MCI claimed that for the first time small-demand users would have private-line service available through a common carrier and that the rates along the Chicago–St. Louis route would be substantially lower than those offered by Bell.

In February 1964, AT&T and Illinois Bell petitioned the F.C.C. to deny MCI's application. AT&T claimed that (1) it and the other common carriers had fulfilled every public need for which MCI had applied, and (2) MCI's proposal was an attempt to attract only a more profitable segment of the total communications market—a cream-skimming arrangement that would impose an economic burden on other Bell customers. Cream-skimming, as the term implies, consists in taking away customers who can be served at a profit, leaving to AT&T and the other utilities the customers who are far more costly to serve or can only be served at a loss. According to AT&T's view, MCI could undercut its rates because MCI did not incur AT&T's universal service obligations. A statement prepared for AT&T by Alfred Kahn, William Baumol, and Otto Eckstein—three of the nation's most distinguished economists—argued that "nationwide rate uniformity and the entry of substantial numbers of competitors are incompatible. . . . The greater the degree of competition, the less the likelihood of Bell's being able to continue uniformity, supplying their sparse routes at their present prices which are relatively low in relation to costs. It will be unable to make up its losses among the denser routes because competition will render that impossible."[10] Thus, only AT&T's rate averaging allowed MCI to cream-skim.

Complex procedural battles and filing errors committed by MCI delayed the F.C.C. hearing examiner's initial decision until October 1967. In essence, the hearing examiner was sympathetic to MCI's claim, and the decision came down to nothing more than a plea to give the newcomers a chance, even though he conceded that MCI's offerings were not novel or unavailable from AT&T and Illinois Bell.[11] The appeal to the full commission occurred in 1968, shortly after the F.C.C. heard the *Carterfone* case. During this period, William McGowan joined MCI, even though he had no previous experience in telecommunications. However, he was an expert in finance, an area in which MCI needed help. Like most experts in financial deals, McGowan had to work closely with lawyers, and it was from one of his lawyer contacts that McGowan met MCI's John Goeken. In August 1968, while the F.C.C. was deciding the MCI case, McGowan and colleagues established a new company—Microwave Communications of America (Micom)—that would function to sponsor prospective MCI operating companies in other markets. Further, McGowan, Goeken, and Micom would each receive 25 percent of the shares of each operating company and the remaining shares would be divided among private investors.[12]

It thus became clear that MCI's Illinois venture was the prelude to many others in which it would compete with AT&T. AT&T's initial competitive response was the Series 11000 tariff offering for private-line users. Series 11000 tariffs were for discrete high-capacity channels dedicated to single customers or joint users. Instead of directly combating AT&T's competition in the marketplace, MCI began what became a consistent strategy from that time forward of using administrative, political, and judicial processes to prevent AT&T from offering its service. MCI's consistent strategy and its acceptance by the F.C.C. is why observers have labeled the competitive process in telecommunications as "contrived competition."[13] Or as Peter Huber, Michael Kellogg, and John Thorne, three prominent telecommunications analysts, succinctly put it in 1992: "AT&T, MCI and Sprint all recognize that gloves-off competition would quickly produce two bankruptcies, one re-regulated monopoly and then a deluge of antitrust suits by the bankrupts against the monopolist."[14] Characteristically, AT&T had greater regulatory burdens than its competitors, and its responses had been delayed in protracted proceedings while competitors were free to make flexible and rapid changes. For these reasons the response to Series 11000 tariffs typified the nature of long-distance "competition" from MCI's beginnings.

Although Series 11000 was discontinued in 1972 because it did not meet sales projections, its anticipated introduction while the commission's MCI decision was pending made clear MCI's peculiar views on competition. MCI sought outright rejection or suspension of the tariff (even though it was priced well above cost) on the ground that telephone companies should not be allowed to depart from rate-averaging principles in individual competitive services. In spite of detailed Bell data that showed Series 11000 rates were priced about 20 percent above costs, MCI also charged that AT&T's offering was based on noncompensatory rates.[15] Thus, MCI's views on competition as well as a major component of its strategy were revealed in the Series 11000 episode; that is, competition meant that AT&T should not be permitted to provide offerings that conflicted with MCI's, even if AT&T's rates were fully compensatory. MCI claimed that it could provide its "unique" private-line service if AT&T did not offer competitive services. To achieve this result, MCI had to persuade the F.C.C. that the Communications Act should be interpreted as adopting this version of competition. Under McGowan's leadership, MCI adopted a political-legal strategy; as an admirer of McGowan's admitted, "McGowan spent the summer and fall of 1968 lobbying the government to grant MCI's license for Chicago to St. Louis. That consisted mainly of talking with people at the F.C.C. and Congress."[16] This strategy would consist first of gaining legislative sympathy and publicity through congressional hearings aimed at AT&T. Since this was a time characterized by anti-big-business sentiment, it was not difficult for MCI to find influential legislators who were sympathetic to small companies seeking to compete against the world's largest firm. The other important MCI political strategy was to persist in litigation. As the Series 11000 matter indicated, MCI would intervene in all possible F.C.C. proceedings against AT&T.

The F.C.C.'s MCI Decision and the Specialized Common Carriers (SCC) Investigation

On August 13, 1969, in a 4–3 decision, the F.C.C. granted MCI's Chicago–St. Louis application. The agency limited service to "transmissions between MCI's microwave sites making it incumbent upon each subscriber to supply his own communications link between MCI's sites and his place of business (loop service)."[17] The F.C.C. claimed that MCI's principal market would consist of subscribers willing to sacrifice quality for cost saving: "while no new technology is involved in MCI's proposal, it does present a concept of common carrier microwave offerings which differs from those of the established carriers."[18] Commissioner Nicholas Johnson interpreted the MCI decision in a more general way: "I am still looking, at this juncture, for ways to add a little salt and pepper of competition to the rather tasteless stew of regulatory protection that this Commission and Bell have cooked up."[19] The dissenting opinion of Chairman Rosel H. Hyde focused more on the principles involved than on the particular facts of the MCI Chicago–St. Louis application. Hyde pointed out that the public interest, not competition, was the F.C.C.'s standard, and that the Supreme Court explicitly directed the agency to avoid a standard of competition.[20] In this view, if a new innovation such as domestic satellites best serves the public interest through competition, it should be favored, but if competition is unnecessary, redundant, unproved, or inefficient, it should be avoided.

Predictably, MCI's success before the F.C.C. encouraged others to seek entrance into different forms of long-distance transmission, particularly in the most lucrative markets. By the mid-1970s, the applicants included, among others, seventeen other companies affiliated with MCI, several miscellaneous common carriers, and the Southern Pacific Communications Corporation, a subsidiary of Southern Pacific Company (primarily a railroad holding company), which owned a large private microwave system. AT&T, GTE Corporation, and other common carriers routinely opposed the applications, contending that they were better able to provide higher capacity and lower-cost facilities. Most importantly, they pointed to the underlying rationale of Section 214 of the Communications Act, which sought to prevent useless duplication of facilities with consequent higher charges. At the very least, they argued, the F.C.C. should have sought to determine whether the existing carriers or newcomers could more efficiently bring novel services to consumers.

By June 1970 it was apparent that the F.C.C.'s 1969 *Microwave Communications* decision had opened a can of worms and that general principles were necessary. On July 17, 1970, the F.C.C., accordingly, instituted Docket no. 18920—the Specialized Common Carrier (SCC) inquiry. The issues to be considered included (1) whether as a general policy SCCs should be permitted, (2) whether comparative hearings among the applicants are necessary, (3) technical problems, (4) service quality and reliability, and (5) the appropriate means of local distribution of the SCC service. The F.C.C.'s Common Carrier Bureau argued that competition directed toward the development of new communications services, markets, and technologies was in order. It urged that the new firms would expand the size of the communications market, not draw customers from the established carriers.

MCI conceded that its market was not the public switched network, claiming that there is "a distinct difference between a public telephone service which is a natural monopoly and a customized communications service offered on a private point-to-point basis." This distinction was critical in the F.C.C.'s approval of MCI's offering. In other words, if MCI had advanced a proposal to construct and operate a rival long-distance network (which it conceded to be a natural monopoly), the proposal would have been flatly rejected by the F.C.C. Instead, it delineated a market that was private "point-to-point." MCI's conception of point-to-point communications was taken from the way in which railroads employed private communications along their lines. A railroad could only communicate with certain points along its designated path and only the railroad was involved in using those facilities, which were not in the public switched network. And just as the private point-to-point service would be largely excluded from the public switched network, so also would the public switched network be excluded from the private point-to-point service.[21] However, there were exceptions in which a private point-to-point service could interconnect into the public switched network. As the F.C.C. undertook the SCC decision, the railroad private-line services provided the model for exceptions. Private lines, with AT&T's permission, could interconnect into the public switched network for designated reasons, such as emergencies involving safety.

In late May 1971 the F.C.C. issued its "First Report and Order" in the SCC inquiry. The commission, without dissent, opted for free entry in the services that the SCCs would provide. The lengthy decision accepted the Common Carrier Bureau's analysis and added much to it. Those who had expected a strict party vote (which had occurred in the MCI matter) were surprised at the unanimity in favor of competition. But the Nixon administration had made its predisposition toward open competition known in the prior year in its comments on domestic satellites. In brief, the regulated network manager system was left with few defenders within the community of those who influenced communications policy. As is made evident in the decision, the F.C.C. became favorably disposed to SCC licensing because it believed AT&T and the other common carriers would not be able to handle the enormously expanding market in data communications. In view of this conclusion, which stemmed primarily from the F.C.C.'s computer inquiry, the F.C.C. had no difficulty in its decision to allow new carriers to operate in that market. Because the voice market—Bell's dominant source of income—was also expected to grow at a rapid rate, the new entrants in the data-communications market would not engage in cream-skimming. One cannot emphasize enough how important it was to the SCC decision that the SCCs were viewed as market expanders and not principally as competitors of AT&T's long-distance, local-loop, or other services. The necessary tenor of the entire decision was that if the SCCs competed with AT&T in the Bell system's major markets, they would not be needed.[22] At this stage, then, the older public philosophy embracing the regulated network manager system had not been overturned, but it was clearly under stress.

The Dispute Intensifies

One of the principal themes that characterizes F.C.C. decisions from this period forward is that the agency, instead of clarifying issues and providing lucid rules, did the opposite. A straightforward public philosophy had been supplanted, not by another such philosophy, but by confusion. The principal evidence in support of this conclusion is the large number of hotly contested judicial cases and administrative proceedings that followed the agency's SCC decision. Yet at the time the SCC decision was handed down, neither the F.C.C. nor AT&T thought that any great variation from the old public utility principle had occurred.

In summary, the F.C.C.'s conception of competition in the SCC decision was narrow. The SCCs were not expected to compete directly against AT&T in the principal markets in which AT&T was engaged; rather, they were expected to enlarge the market by developing submarkets that AT&T had either not or insufficiently exploited. The SCC decision further emphasized that these markets were principally in the data field. Thus, at the time of the decision, a reasonable observer could assume several rules: that (1) the SCCs could not compete with AT&T in a public switched network; (2) the SCCs could not compete against AT&T in private-line or other services in which AT&T had an established position at the time of the SCC decision; (3) the SCCs could compete in private point-to-point or private-network service if AT&T either did not occupy the submarket or did so only marginally; and (4) AT&T could compete with the SCCs (which, in turn, could compete with each other) within the new submarkets. Based on this reasonable understanding of the SCC decision, AT&T was not displeased and saw no need to appeal, stressing that it might depart from rate averaging and instead price directly competitive services.

The difficulty with this understanding from MCI's perspective was that the submarkets carved out were small at the time. Accordingly, MCI soon sought to expand into AT&T's older, more traditional markets. And once the F.C.C. had made its substantial commitment to the SCCs, it was predictable that the agency would enlarge the decision far beyond its close bounds, rather than allow SCCs to fail. Contrary to the myth that large, successful companies dominate regulatory agencies, the MCI episodes that we will detail show that agencies will more likely use their powers to support weak firms in order to justify the "wisdom" of risky decisions. The large, powerful firms, like AT&T, can take care of themselves. Accordingly, the agency can impose costs on them—within reasonable limits—to benefit the newer or weaker firms. The next set of issues concerning services whose acronyms are FX and CCSA illustrate this. The context in which the dispute should be considered is the increasing value of special services that began in the early 1960s. For example, WATS (wide area telephone service) was born in 1961. AT&T's WATS revenues grew from $18 million in 1961 to more than $1 billion in 1976. The same exponential growth might occur in the cases of other special services.

Foreign exchange (FX) allows a customer to make or receive local telephone calls through a distant switching center. FX effectively provides a long extension cord in the form of a dedicated line between the customer's location and a telephone company switching center at the distant location. As such, FX was especially popular among airlines and hotels because they could centralize their reservation systems. A person seeking to make a reservation calls a local rather than a long-distance number, which is routed to the foreign exchange. The FX customer receives two bills—one for the private line that connects the customer to the foreign exchange and another for the telephone service that the customer used through the foreign exchange. Although it had certain private-line features, FX service was also integrally tied to the public switched network. Conceivably, FX could be used as an internal private system, but its principal and customary use was to link calls originating in the public switched network to a dedicated line. Thus, under any reasonable construction, FX was neither a private-line nor a private-network service under the SCC decision.

The other service at issue between MCI and AT&T—common control switching arrangement (CCSA)—granted a customer with large communications needs (primarily voice grade) among many points access to the telephone company's central-office switch, which routed calls to the customer's dedicated lines. CCSA, which originated in 1963, was an established AT&T service by the time of the SCC decision and, therefore, could not then be considered a unique or innovative service that AT&T was failing to provide. The public switch was used for many economic and technological reasons stemming from the fact that large users' PBXs and other equipment could not handle the volume of message traffic desired. Accordingly, additional hardware programming in a sophisticated switch, such as the Number 5 Crossbar, allowed a portion of the switch to be dedicated to a single customer. For instance, the large-user customer (such as the United States government) would dial an access code (usually "8") followed by a telephone number; the common control equipment in the Number 5 Crossbar switch would then translate this information into a route and destination, advance the call to an alternate route, forward the call to other switches, and so forth. A notable feature offered with CCSA was automatic off-net dialing, which enabled the customer to place a call to a telephone not on the CCSA network. Government systems established under CCSA during the early 1960s included the Federal Telephone System (FTS) for civilian use and the Switched Circuit Automatic Network (SCAN) for use by the U.S. Army. By 1971, more than twenty-five CCSA networks had been established for commercial customers. Thus, at the time of the SCC decision, CCSA was an AT&T commercially viable service offering. Further, it was much more than the novel private-line service contemplated by the SCC decision.

MCI's success in enlarging its service offerings to FX and CCSA—and beyond—stemmed in large part from its political stratagems, certainly not from any technological prowess. MCI employed negotiations with AT&T to establish a record of AT&T recalcitrance that it could use before the courts, Congress, and the F.C.C. Notably, former F.C.C. commissioner Kenneth Cox, who had sided with MCI in its authorization proceeding before the F.C.C., joined the company on September 30, 1970 (only one day after leaving the F.C.C.). MCI already had excellent legal representation before Cox joined the company,[23] but Cox would be expected to employ his political expertise. The company's political strategy was to put AT&T on the defensive and to expand MCI offerings into services already provided by AT&T. As noted at a July 13, 1971, AT&T-MCI meeting, MCI, in addition to an interconnection contract, "wanted to have the freedom to offer its customers every service available from either long lines or Western Union."[24] Clearly, this posture went far beyond the limits of the SCC decision. And if MCI failed in this strategy, it intended to take the issue to the F.C.C. for resolution, knowing full well the agency's commitment to making the SCC experiment successful. In view of this, AT&T sought to reduce the negotiating tensions between itself and MCI rather than face F.C.C. pressure. Thus, Illinois Bell agreed to provide more costly dial access to the network instead of manual interconnection, even though the Bell system could have resisted doing so in light of the SCC decision's ambiguity on the point.[25]

Notwithstanding their differences, MCI and AT&T reached an agreement in late September 1971, which was approved by the Illinois Commerce Commission. AT&T, however, made most of the concessions and MCI began its operations in January 1972. But controversy over rate issues erupted almost immediately. These issues paled, however, before the FX and CCSA disputes that are considered in the context of the general tariff changes called for in the *Carterfone* decision. Although the 1968 *Carterfone* decision, which dealt with terminal devices, did not discuss FX or

CCSA, it did require the Bell system to revise the interconnection provisions of its tariffs. AT&T thus drafted its new tariff revisions and, in October 1968, it filed further revisions together with an explanation of its new private-line interconnection arrangement: "Connection is made on a voice grade basis at a customer's service point."[26] The phrase "service point" (later defined as "customer premises") was sufficiently clear to be limited to "the point *on the customer's premises* where such channels or facilities are terminated in switching equipment used for communications with stations or customer provided terminal equipment *located on the premises*" (emphasis added).[27] That is, connections at premises other than the customer's were not contemplated by the tariff revision. Among the considerations that contributed to the AT&T Tariff Review Committee's hostility toward looser interconnection restrictions, quality and maintenance were the most influential. Bell argued that divided maintenance responsibility can lead to service deterioration and, hence, cost increases. The need to test all proposed interconnection arrangements would impose high information costs on AT&T and its subscribers.

Within the month, MCI petitioned the F.C.C. to reject AT&T's post-*Carterfone* tariff revisions on the ground that they were overly restrictive. The F.C.C. rejected MCI's arguments, specifically holding that AT&T could bar the use of customer-provided, network-control signaling units and that the *Carterfone* decision applied to interconnection, not substitution for AT&T facilities.[28] Among the categories covered by the tariff revisions and the F.C.C.'s rules was private-line service, which the agency defined as "a separate service *that does not use the switched telephone network*" (emphasis added).[29] Because MCI-provided FX or CCSA would use the switched network and would directly compete with AT&T in the provision of such services, one cannot conclude that MCI was entitled to provide these services at the time it demanded them. Nevertheless, the defeats that AT&T had sustained encouraged MCI to continue pressing its demands. Thus, following a 1971 F.C.C. decision in the SCC matter, MCI again demanded FX-type interconnection, which AT&T rejected. The novel twist that MCI conceived to overcome the F.C.C.'s objections was to lease space in MCI's premises to its customers who would then demand interconnection at their "business premises"—MCI's offices—instead of the customer's regular business facilities.

On April 18, 1972, Cone Mills Corporation, an important MCI customer, wrote a letter to Illinois Bell (sending a copy to MCI) demanding FX service. In essence, Cone Mills demanded a local telephone at its "offices" on the ninety-seventh floor of the John Hancock Building in Chicago, which happened also to be MCI's Chicago office. Further, Cone Mills's contact person was an MCI employee, and the telephone number it provided to Illinois Bell was assigned to MCI. The purpose of the demand was to enable MCI to connect an MCI interexchange channel to the Cone Mills local telephone line—that is, to provide an FX-type service. Illinois Bell refused the request on the ground that MCI was not entitled to FX service.

The stakes were high because FX and CCSA were larger than the conventional private-line market, and during this period MCI was under considerable financial pressure. MCI desperately sought to enlarge its market in 1972 and 1973 because its original private-line projections were inflated and its financial position was distressing. MCI needed FX and CCSA badly. For example, in June 1972, MCI contemplated a 165-city network at a cost of $80 million, yet a September 1972 internal memorandum estimated that a sharply curtailed 34- to 41-city network would cost $100 million.[30] On April 11, 1973, MCI's strategy of using government to meet its objectives was employed when Cone Mills complained to the F.C.C. about Illinois Bell's refusal (the complaint was prepared with MCI's "assistance"). During the same period, MCI began its series of complaints to the F.C.C. and the Common Carrier Bureau about AT&T's alleged high-handedness. Portraying itself as a victim of AT&T, MCI was able to gain the support of those regulators who had put so much effort into the SCC decision and the new policies favoring competition in novel services and equipment; MCI's failure would undermine their hard work. In a variation of the then popular theme "what is good for General Motors is good for the country," MCI attempted to show that what was good for MCI was also good for the F.C.C. and its new policies.

The Bell of Pennsylvania Case

During this period MCI launched another attack against AT&T using a second front—the courts. The event that triggered the first court contest between MCI and AT&T began on October 23, 1973, when MCI learned that Bell of Pennsylvania would not provide a loop to serve MCI customer Keystone Tubular in Butler, Pennsylvania. Bell of Pennsylvania denied the request on the ground that AT&T's obligation was to provide local interconnection only and that Butler was outside the Pittsburgh local distribution area—a concept AT&T employed to delineate the area in which it could provide interconnection to Western Union, MCI, and the other SCCs. Butler was approximately thirty-six miles from the MCI terminal and was located within an area served by an independent telephone company. The incident was only one of many in which MCI made demands for connections far outside the local distribution areas, including demands for areas considerably greater than one microwave hop as well as areas outside the state in which the principal city (such as Chicago) was located. Perhaps most importantly, while one could have questioned AT&T's definition of a local distribution area, MCI did not offer an alternative one but instead chose to forcefully demand and to involve the F.C.C. and others. Ambiguity was a way to challenge AT&T's FX and CCSA policy. Late in 1973 was clearly an opportune time for MCI to strike hard, as AT&T was on the defensive on many fronts. It was besieged with equipment-connection requests stemming from *Carterfone*; the F.C.C.'s restrictions on AT&T in satellite services; and a senatorial investigation led by Senator Philip A. Hart on alleged abuses of monopoly and oligopoly power in several industries, including telecommunications. In Hart's hostile investigation, former F.C.C. commissioner Kenneth Cox, then a top MCI official, was an important witness.[31]

MCI brought suit against AT&T in the fall of 1973, challenging Bell of Pennsylvania's Keystone Tubular action in particular and AT&T's interconnection policies under the SCC decision in general. During the same period, the F.C.C. instituted Docket no. 19866 to clarify the complaints concerning local distribution areas and other matters arising under the SCC decision. Meanwhile, AT&T had announced its proposed HI/LO tariff offering, which departed from the concept of rate averaging to compete with MCI and other SCCs in their markets and services. MCI's own study, conducted by the highly reputable Arthur D. Little Company, concluded that private microwave was able to undercut Bell only because AT&T scrupulously followed the principle of rate averaging. MCI's concept of competition sought to preclude AT&T's ability to respond as it used the government to defeat AT&T at most every turn. In this respect, it had a valuable ally in Bernard Strassburg, the chief of the Common Carrier Bureau, a principal architect of the F.C.C.'s limited competition policy. The F.C.C. conceded that its SCC policy was not meeting the expectations that services were to be novel and innovative. But, it claimed that experience was yet too limited for the agency to accede in AT&T's favor.

On the last day of December 1973, the federal district court for the Eastern District of Pennsylvania upheld MCI's position on the local distribution area issue. Moreover, the court required AT&T to provide FX and CCSA connections, to enlarge the local service areas, and to provide "such other interconnection facilities as are necessary to enable plaintiffs to furnish the interstate services they are authorized by the F.C.C. to perform.[32] MCI won in large part because it relied on an October 19, 1973, letter from Common Carrier Bureau chief Strassburg, which stated that MCI was entitled to everything it sought from the court. That the letter was advisory, from an F.C.C. staff person, and that the F.C.C. was in the process of deciding the very issues under consideration did not give pause to the district court. The judge did not come to terms with the rationale behind the basic SCC decision or of the December 1973 reconsideration, did not understand the concept of a private line or how it differed from FX and CCSA, and did not consider rate averaging and other matters in his decision. Instead, Judge Clarence Newcomer relied on such lesser matters as that because Bell included FX and CCSA in its private-line sales literature, they must be private-line offerings.

However, in April 1974, the Court of Appeals for the Third Circuit vacated the district court injunction. In keeping with established principles of administrative law, the court of appeals unanimously held that the district court should have deferred to the appropriate administrative agency in the complex technical issues of FX, CCSA, and local distribution facilities. Moreover, the F.C.C. was then considering the issues that Judge Newcomer had failed to consider. In keeping with its views on the proper role of the courts in such matters, the court of appeals stated: "An examination of these two Commission pronouncements reveals that the existence and scope of any such obligation on the part of AT&T is so unclear that deferral to the expertise of the F.C.C. is both desirable and appropriate."[33] Noting that none of the SCC decisions had mentioned FX, CCSA, or local distribution areas specifically or by implication, the court of appeals decided that it would be presumptuous for it to decide the issues in MCI's favor, in that such a decision would inappropriately substitute the court for the F.C.C. as the body responsible for deciding competition issues in telecommunications.

AT&T's victory was, however, short-lived. Spurred by Common Carrier Bureau chief Strassburg, the F.C.C. was strongly committed to preserving—indeed, encouraging—the SCCs. In its important 1974 *Bell System Tariff Offerings* decision, the agency, in a classic understatement, conceded that "its prior orders may not have been perfectly clear."[34] Reaffirming its belief in the SCCs' ability to serve the public interest, the commission declared that FX and CCSA were private-line services on the same ground that Judge Newcomer chose—because they were so described in AT&T's written materials. Neglected was the previously held idea that SCCs were to provide innovative and unique services, principally in the data field, as FX and CCSA clearly would not fit into the older concept. The F.C.C. thus became further committed to the survival of the SCCs, and its concept of competition had changed—the SCCs would be allowed to expand their service offerings in order to survive. For the same reason, AT&T was severely restrained in how it could compete. Thus, AT&T's executive policy committee authorized the filing of the HI/LO tariff in January 1973 in order to compete with the SCCs. In January 1976, after numerous proceedings and delays largely caused by AT&T's rivals, the commission ruled the tariff unlawful.

MCI's Renewed Attack

MCI was not to be satisfied with its FX and CCSA victories. Sensing that its claims were in the vanguard of a shift in public philosophy, MCI continued to press the attack. During this time, large firms were once again under attack. For example, the Federal Trade Commission in 1973 attacked the four largest breakfast cereal manufacturers in one case and the eight largest integrated oil companies in another on the novel view that these firms "shared" monopolies. Impetus for restructuring and deregulating American industry stemmed from the changing structure of the world economy and the fear that without drastic changes American firms would not be able to compete effectively. Although President Jimmy Carter's statement in signing a key rail deregulation statute was uttered in 1980, it captures the sentiment that was already ascendant in 1973. The president expected that the statute would be "a major boost for the revitalization of the American economy, a revitalization that I intend will restore America's competitive edge and make possible full employment, and, at the same time, stable prices."[35] Traditional regulatory principles were clearly on the defensive. Although regulation would continue to exist, the agencies would have to show what areas within their domains should continue to be regulated and why. To defend their domains against the deregulation onslaught, they would have to develop coherent theories showing why competitive behavior should not prevail in certain activities. Of course, the competition concept that now applied would mean protecting new competitors, not the fierce rivalry that believers in laissez-faire envision. MCI correctly appraised the shift in public philosophy.

On August 24, 1974, MCI's vice president, Bert C. Roberts, Jr., sent a confidential memorandum to William McGowan outlining the company's need to act on a new service called Execunet. The company's original plan—to rely on private-line offerings largely in the data field—had not met expectations. Consequently, the company devised Execunet, which, as we shall see, was tantamount to WATS and MTS (ordinary long-distance service). Roberts commented in his August 24 memorandum to McGowan that many at MCI doubted that Execunet was a private-line offering (although he did not), and that "each day that goes by will tend to put MCI into a negative cash flow position on the start up of the project."[36] Generally, MCI was in a cash-negative situation in the fall of 1973 and sought to use government policies to reverse the problem. MCI admitted that it could not compete with Bell's TELPAK offerings in the private-line market. Even earlier, MCI had drastically miscalculated the cost of constructing a private network. In June 1972, it estimated that $80 million would build a 165-city network, but Stanley Scheinman, MCI's chief financial officer, prepared an analysis in September 1972 that concluded $100 million would be required to build only a 41-city network. Scheinman further calculated that at the end of 1973, MCI would be in a deficit cash position of $15–$20 million. Further, a 1974 internal audit report prepared at the behest of MCI management concluded that the company was itself largely responsible for its difficulties. The report stated that the major cause of circuit installation delay was "poor coordination between and among salesmen, customers, one or both terminating branches in telco personnel. In many instances, this poor coordination has materialized as a general lack of direction and aggressiveness on the part of MCI to solve problems, or to obtain and communicate vital information in a timely manner."[37]

With an understanding of MCI's financial background, it is clear why it sought to expand its offerings far beyond private line. But to do so successfully, it would have to put AT&T even further on the defensive through a private antitrust suit. As early as January 9, 1973, MCI's top command decided to prepare a private antitrust suit against AT&T and the operating companies. At the same time, MCI officials agreed to prod the Antitrust Division into a major action against AT&T as well as to spur sympathetic F.C.C. staff into action against AT&T in the administrative arena. McGowan mentioned the possibility of a private antitrust suit in a March 2 meeting with AT&T's John de Butts. Then, on September 28, 1973 (and at other times), MCI officials met with Antitrust Division officials, including chief Donald Baker, in an attempt to convince the Justice Department to bring a major action against AT&T. Obviously, a multipronged attack would be more effective, of which the private antitrust suit would be the first step.

MCI filed its private antitrust suit against AT&T on March 6, 1974, in the federal district court in Chicago. The complaint contained four separate counts: monopolization, attempt to monopolize, conspiracy to monopolize under Section 2 of the Sherman Act, and conspiracy in restraint of trade under Section 1 of the Sherman Act. MCI alleged that AT&T had committed twenty-two different types of misconduct that could be grouped into several categories held by the courts as antitrust violations—predatory pricing, monopolistic refusal to deal through denial of interconnections, bad-faith negotiations, and unlawful tying. MCI requested a jury trial and stated that the full amount of damages sustained would be determined after discovery and proof during the trial. Under Section 4 of the Clayton Act, a successful plaintiff in an antitrust action is entitled to threefold the damages sustained and the cost of suit, including reasonable attorneys' fees. The case was assigned to Judge John Grady, who began pretrial proceedings and decided a series of preliminary issues, including a denial of AT&T's motion to dismiss the complaint, on October 6, 1978. The trial eventually began on February 5, 1980, and was submitted to the jury on June 11 after the taking of 11,514 pages of testimony and the submission of about one thousand documents into evidence. Two days after it began its deliberations, the jury rendered its special verdict in the amount of $600 million, which was tripled in accordance with Section 4 of the Clayton Act to $1.8 billion—the largest antitrust damage award in history.

MCI had grand plans to finance expansion from the proceeds of its antitrust award. Considering that MCI's earnings in the fiscal year prior to the verdict were approximately $13.3 million, a $1.8 billion award was quite substantial. Even Judge Grady was reported as saying that the total judgment "seems unseemly, maybe even obscene." Half the jurors did not know the damage award would be trebled. One juror said she knew about treble damages from having typed a report for a college student the year before.[38] Unfortunately for MCI, the Court of Appeals for the Seventh Circuit overturned the verdict. On January 12, 1983, the Seventh Circuit court rendered its 258-typed-page opinion and 40–page appendix, ordering a new trial on the issue of damages.[39] The second trial began in early 1985 with Judge Grady again presiding. The verdict finally handed down in May 1985 was in the sum of $37.8 million, which was tripled to $113.3 million. MCI had certainly replenished its coffers at AT&T's expense, although not to the extent that the first verdict would have. But even this MCI victory paled before its legal triumph in the Execunet case.

Execunet

Each MCI success in enlarging its offerings only whetted the company's appetite to expand further. A critical breakthrough was in the service MCI called Execunet. In this service, an Execunet customer gained access to an MCI intercity line by calling a particular MCI local telephone number in the originating city from any push-button telephone. When the connection was made and the customer was identified through an identification number, he or she obtained access to MCI intercity circuits. The customer then dialed any telephone in any city where MCI offered Execunet service. The call was transmitted over MCI's intercity circuits, which were interconnected through the local telephone company's switching facilities to the local exchange facilities in the distant city. The call then reached the telephone called. A push-button telephone was ordinarily used in the originating city because MCI's switching equipment responded to the signal tones generated by this equipment. However, a customer could use a dial telephone and generate the appropriate tones through a readily available "Touch-Tone" pad.

With Execunet, MCI abandoned any reasonable pretense to offering only private-line service. It was a service that more closely approximated ordinary long-distance (MTS) or WATS service. Neither MTS nor Execunet dedicated particular intercity circuits to specific customers; rather, both used whatever intercity circuits were available as well as local telephone company switching facilities and circuits. Second, like MTS, any telephone, not only one within a private subscriber's ambit, could access Execunet. Third, any telephone in a large number of distant cities could be reached. Fourth, the Execunet customer used common local exchange plants at both ends, and, finally, the Execunet customer, like ordinary long-distance customers, was billed for each call, based on time and distance, with no charge added at the distant city.[40] Once again MCI did not offer an innovative service as contemplated by the SCC decision, but rather used government processes to gradually encroach on AT&T's public service monopoly and, with it, the old public philosophy.

MCI began offering the Execunet service in January 1975. AT&T contacted the F.C.C. in May 1975 (with a copy to MCI), claiming that Execunet was long-distance message telephone service and that MCI was not authorized to offer such a service. AT&T's position was that Execunet threatened the entire structure of telephone service. AT&T's MTS service was offered at nationwide averaged rates and, therefore, was susceptible to carriers aiming primarily at low-cost, high-density routes that yield high profits. Execunet also threatened the subsidy contribution that long distance made to local service through the separations process. The Execunet service would remove substantial revenues from the separations process, which would result in increased local rates. After MCI responded to AT&T's letter, the F.C.C., on July 2, 1975, released an order rejecting the Execunet service on the ground that it was a switched public message service and MCI was authorized only to offer private-line service. Latent in the F.C.C.'s response was the anger of its staff and commissioners that MCI had deceived and betrayed them.[41]

After MCI appealed the F.C.C. order to the court of appeals, the matter was held in abeyance until MCI and other interested parties could file briefs and comments. On July 13, 1976, the F.C.C. released a decision, reaffirming that Execunet was an unlawful tariff and reminding MCI of the original rationale for its specialized service: "MCI asserted that there was distinct difference between a public telephone service which is a natural monopoly and a customized communications service offered on a private line basis."[42] The F.C.C. also reminded MCI that every filing the company had made before the agency and the courts was premised on this distinction.

MCI appealed the F.C.C. decision to the Court of Appeals for the District of Columbia Circuit, the court then at the cutting edge of judicial activism. The focus of the court's 1978 decision was on Section 214 of the Communications Act of 1934, entitled "Extension Lines," the only section that dealt with entry into the telephone business. Completely ignoring the legislative history of the act, which showed that Congress intended telephone service to be delivered by monopolies, Judge Skelly Wright ruled that the F.C.C. should have considered whether the Execunet service should be permitted regardless of the limits imposed by the SCC decision and the operating authority to MCI based on it. And in a remarkable leap of faith, the court concluded, without supporting evidence, that MCI intended to compete only "on the fringes of the message telephone market."[43] Again, the F.C.C., on remand, concluded that AT&T did not have to interconnect with Execunet and a similar Sprint service. And again the court of appeals reversed the F.C.C. decision, holding that AT&T must provide local interconnections for Execunet and similar services.[44]

To all intents and purposes competition in long distance had been established through the long road described in this chapter. But it was a strange form of competition in which the F.C.C. would favor the newer entrants at the expense of AT&T, to which the F.C.C. gave a new appellation—the dominant carrier.[45] Under that doctrine AT&T would be subjected to regulatory burdens and inflexibilities in rates, services, and facilities from which competitors would be exempt.[46] But MCI's protracted attack would lead to another devastating impact in telecommunications that we will examine in the next chapter—the dismantling of AT&T.

5

The Biggest Case in History

Ma Bell

American telecommunications from the invention of the telephone through the present day has been dominated by a single firm—AT&T and its predecessors—nicknamed Ma Bell. As we have seen, the company has been challenged by business rivals and government actions from its beginnings in 1876, but AT&T managed to come through all of its travails as the dominant player in telecommunications. Each of these struggles led to important adjustments, but remarkably the company's leadership adopted strategies that led to its continued primacy. We have examined many of the firm's past challenges, including the 1949 antitrust suit that initially sought to break up the company but resulted in a settlement, leaving intact the company's structure consisting of local operating companies, equipment supplier, long-distance operator, and research arm.

Its greatest challenge occurred in 1974 when the Justice Department brought another suit seeking the dismemberment of the Bell system. In this chapter we will examine that case, which AT&T and the Justice Department agreed to settle in 1982. In broad outline AT&T agreed to divest its twenty-two local operating companies and withdraw from the local-loop business. In exchange, the Justice Department agreed to let AT&T keep its manufacturing arm and retain Bell Labs, the research facility, although AT&T agreed to help the seven newly formed regional Bell operating companies (RBOCs) set up Bellcore, their own research facility. Most importantly, from AT&T's perspective, many of the restrictions on AT&T contained in the 1956 consent decree were lifted. Technically, in fact, the AT&T case was dismissed and the 1956 decree was amended to incorporate the terms to which the parties agreed. By 1984 the divestiture was completed and the stock shares distributed to AT&T's investors in a remarkably smooth manner. Shareholders were given a variety of choices that they could make in the new AT&T and the seven RBOCs. But if the optimists felt that the terms of the agreement would fundamentally resolve the public policy and business issues in telecommunications, they were sadly mistaken. Judge Harold F. Greene, who presided over the settlement agreement, became virtually a new telecommunications regulatory agency in competition with the F.C.C. and state regulators. Legal battles began almost immediately, calling for resolution by Judge Greene. At the same time AT&T began the continuing process of changing its internal structure and making acquisitions, the most important of which were the NCR Corporation, a major firm, purchased in 1991 for $7.48 billion, and McCaw Cellular Communications, the nation's largest cellular telephone company, in 1994 for $11.5 billion. But then, irony of ironies, AT&T in 1995 announced that it would voluntarily split itself into three companies. Thus, the *United States v. AT&T* case did not permanently resolve most of the issues in American telecommunications. Nevertheless, it was one of the most important events in telecommunications history, and its ramifications are still with us. In this chapter we will look at the case in detail.

Before examining the AT&T case, it is important to consider again Coase's theory of the firm that was discussed in Chapter 1, since AT&T's structure was a central concern in the case. As that distinguished economist showed, companies frequently experiment to determine whether some things should be made or done internally or whether, at the margin, the product or service should be acquired on the open market.[1] Different firms in the same industry often have different answers because assessments and costs can vary from company to company. But in a world of incomplete information, outcomes do not necessarily accord with intentions and expectations. Further, production costs and technologies change over time. Consequently, Coase's theory of the firm should not be conceived in a static manner as if once a decision is made to produce something internally, the decision is unchangeable. To the contrary, firms—at least well-run ones—frequently reexamine the internal production versus purchase in the open market issue with respect to many activities. Thus, it is entirely consistent for AT&T management to have concluded that a vertically integrated structure made sound economic sense in 1974, but that it no longer did in 1995.[2] But it is one thing for firms to experiment with structures in the hope of becoming more efficient and profitable; it is quite another for government bureaucrats and courts, devoid of the company's accumulated business experience, to restructure firms by complaint and decision. Indeed, as the history of socialist economies illustrates, industrial structures devised by government bureaucrats are generally wrongheaded, if not disastrous.

The Beginnings of the AT&T Case

In the spring of 1968, Antitrust Division chief Donald Turner expressed his dissatisfaction with the settlement of the 1956 *Western Electric* suit. His comments caused such great activity in AT&T stock that trading had to be stopped temporarily.[3] Not only were many Antitrust Division staff members and others (notably some legislators) dissatisfied with what they conceived to be a "sellout" in 1956, but the Antitrust Division had also become active in intervening in F.C.C. proceedings, including *Carterfone*. Not surprisingly, the Antitrust Division's intervention was always on the side of more competition, for its task was to protect "competition" through the antitrust laws. But "competition," as the word has been used in antitrust circles, is inherently ambiguous. One meaning concerns the number of competitors while the other applies to behavior—that is, rivalry in price, quality, and so on. The Antitrust Division chose whatever concept would most effectively help it to bring a case. In the Antitrust Division's opinion, regulated monopoly undertaken by a large company could never perform well.[4] To the believers in these views, the fact of good—indeed, excellent—performance, as we saw in Chapter 4, was less important than the sentiment best expressed by economist Almarin Phillips: "There is an aversion to large businesses whether they are efficient or not. Part of AT&T's problem is that they are big and they do things efficiently and well. . . . Every time AT&T does something well, there are new antitrust regulations and suits. To the extent AT&T does well, it faces this dilemma."[5] Again, as Suzanne Weaver concluded in her excellent study of the Antitrust Division, "the presence of a large firm in an investigation will prompt not simply a search for the anti-competitive efforts but a search that tends to construe even probably harmless things in an anti-competitive light. . . . [T]he presence of bigness in a case at hand will convince many lawyers that they will find 'something bad' about the situation if only they look long and hard enough."[6]

However, many factors determine whether the Justice Department will bring a novel and difficult case such as AT&T's. Complex cases consume substantial resources and, of course, a department loss in a big case can be embarrassing. For this reason, it is more likely that an attorney general will agree to bringing a big case when additional factors are present. In *United States v. AT&T*, although there was dissatisfaction with the 1956 *Western Electric* consent judgment and the Antitrust Division had consistently taken positions in conflict with AT&T's before the F.C.C., these factors were probably not enough to push the case. Certainly, Senator Phillip A. Hart's

Industrial Reorganization Act proposals and his specific attacks on AT&T provided valuable support.[7] Almost every potential and actual SCC and CPE firm appeared before Hart's subcommittee complaining about AT&T in 1973 and 1974. But while executive-branch administrators do not ignore legislative pressures, they will not move simply because a certain legislator may want them to do so. Often there are legislators who are as vehemently opposed to an action as those who are in favor of it.

Two major factors greatly influenced the Justice Department's decision to bring the case. The first of these stemmed from the department's ability to capitalize on the new public philosophy that was emerging during the Gerald Ford presidency. The starting point in understanding the change taking place is that the consumer price index (CPI) rose from an annual rate of 1.8 percent between 1950 and 1965 to 4.4 percent from 1965 to 1973, and then it skyrocketed to an annual rate of 9.4 percent from 1973 to the first half of 1980. Not only was inflation conceived as a major problem, but Americans were beginning to appreciate for the first time that they lived in a competitive world economy. The connections between inflation, competitiveness, and deregulation surfaced as a major topic during meetings that led up to President Ford's "economic summit" in late September 1974. The economists invited to those meetings "agreed that government regulation was a major cause of the high and rising cost of living, and that reforming it was one of the few useful things that could be done to control inflation. The consensus on this point was striking, being shared by economists of every political stripe—a fact not lost on President Ford."[8]

The cost of infrastructural services—particularly transportation, communications, credit provision, and energy—is incorporated in the prices paid by consumers and every industrial and service sector of the economy. In addition, several of these infrastructural services have experienced other serious economic performance problems, including supply problems (especially in energy); the general deterioration of certain of these industries (most notably rail transportation), and certain wasteful practices under regulation that promoted grossly inefficient resource use (such as rules that prevented regulated truckers from carrying return or full loads). The economists' answer was deregulation, and telecommunications—even though its economic performance had been the diametric opposite of railroads and other badly performing public services—was linked by association.

But, in addition, pressures in the judicial area virtually forced the Justice Department to pursue action. That is, the numerous private antitrust suits brought against AT&T and pressures exerted by AT&T's rivals, most importantly by MCI, made it appear as if inaction on the Justice Department's part would seem like avoidance of its duty. For example, in ITT Corporation's antitrust suit against GTE's acquisition of the Hawaiian Telephone Company, other operating companies, and equipment manufacturers, the federal district court criticized the Justice Department for the 1956 *Western Electric* settlement and subsequent Antitrust Division inaction in the telecommunications field.[9] That this 1972 decision was largely reversed in 1975 did not diminish the court's ability to prod the Justice Department in 1973 and 1974.[10]

President Ford had ample opportunity to make his views known; that he did not reject the suit implied his approval. Moreover, Antitrust Division staffers asserted that the president was kept informed of the investigation.[11] Thus, the AT&T antitrust suit was in accord with the administration's program and received Ford's "full approval."[12]

Although the Antitrust Division was backed by the Ford administration, it also needed support for its view that the F.C.C. and state regulators were incapable of resolving telecommunications issues adequately. To the Antitrust Division, the burgeoning number of private antitrust suits brought against AT&T was evidence of the F.C.C.'s inadequacy, in that AT&T's rivals were unable to obtain relief through the agency or the PUCs and had to resort instead to private antitrust action. The division argued further that both small and large firms had brought such cases, and that many private controversies had become public ones. The Antitrust Division used these facts together with its view of AT&T's use of the regulatory process to contest such cases as SCC or *Carterfone* to justify its conclusion, as stated in *Business Week*, that "the regulatory process was no longer able to contain AT&T's power."[13] Also, the lengthy records of the earlier regulatory proceedings and private antitrust cases were expected to save the Justice Department considerable time, effort, and money in preparing its case. The advice and materials provided by AT&T's competitors led Antitrust Division counsel Philip Verveer to proclaim, "We have not wanted for competitors who felt aggrieved and who have educated us in the business."[14]

The firm that provided the most important lessons for the Antitrust Division was MCI, which had brought its carefully prepared antitrust suit against AT&T in March 1974. MCI began its meetings with Antitrust Division officials as early as 1973. While its influence was certainly important in the Justice Department action, much more was involved. The information that MCI would provide and its collaboration in other ways would be of great value, and would save the Justice Department considerable resources in compiling data purporting to show that AT&T had violated the Sherman Act. Further, MCI's collaboration demonstrated that the Justice Department would have major support in the case—a clear incentive to take action. William McGowan was not exaggerating when he commented, after his

1980 Chicago federal district court verdict against AT&T, that "fully half of the Justice case against AT&T is our case."[15]

The Complaint

The complaint in *United States v. AT&T* was filed on November 20, 1974, in the District of Columbia federal district court, and the trial began on January 15, 1981. After several postponements, the Justice Department concluded the presentation of its case on July 2, 1981; the defendants began their case on August 3, 1981, and terminated it, unfinished, on December 18. The settlement agreement into which the Antitrust Division and AT&T entered in January 1982 terminated the trial portion of the case. However, AT&T had been scheduled to resume its case after the New Year's Day holiday and to complete its presentation on or about January 20, 1982. The Justice Department was then scheduled to present its rebuttal case, and the trial was scheduled to end by February 10, 1982.

Given the size of the record, it is likely that if the settlement had not intervened, Judge Greene would not have prepared a decision until late in 1982 or early 1983. An appeal to the court of appeals by one or both sides would have been inevitable as would an attempt to have the Supreme Court consider some of the questions the case raised. Thus, the settlement, modified and approved by Judge Greene on August 11, 1982, occurred almost eight years after the complaint was filed; without a settlement, the case could have taken as many as eleven or twelve to resolve. We should also consider that until the enactment of the Telecommunications Act of 1996, which superseded the settlement, Judge Greene was still being asked to consider problems under his August 11, 1982, order, known as the Modification of Final Judgment in *United States v. Western Electric*.

The complaint was only fourteen pages long—much shorter than the 1949 *United States v. Western Electric* complaint. Yet it spawned a volume of paper of legendary proportions. The pretrial phase had included 296 days of depositions and 45,000 pages of material. The trial testimony was recorded on 25,047 transcript pages. The plaintiff called 94 witnesses; the defendants listed 244 witnesses and 55 written testimonies. The Antitrust Division marked 8,103 exhibits totaling about 183,000 pages, but only 2,071 exhibits (totaling about 46,000 pages) were put in evidence. However, AT&T marked 15,477 exhibits of approximately 618,000 pages, of which only 2,521 totaling approximately 98,000 pages were received as evidence when the trial was suspended. In addition, of course, there were numerous motions and other procedural matters as well as court decisions based on the disputes between the parties. Finally, there were 73 stipulation packages, which constituted the basic organizing principle of the case (these are discussed later in more detail).

How did such a relatively small complaint generate such a torrent of paperwork? In general, monopolization cases under Section 2 of the Sherman Act are usually big cases because the stakes are high (a company may, after all, be restructured and divest assets if it loses such a case). Also, the high stakes tend to make monopoly cases intensely contested. In addition, they entail the presentation of numerous facts showing that the defendant has monopoly power or intends to acquire and maintain it. If a company is charged with monopolizing, the courts will conduct an inquiry into the peculiarities and nature of the industry, the defendants' market position within it, and the specific acts undertaken to acquire or maintain monopoly power. This can involve a written history of the industry and of the defendants' places within it.

The Antitrust Division named AT&T, Western Electric, and Bell Labs as defendants, charging them with three offenses: monopolization, attempt to monopolize, and conspiracy to monopolize. The other conspirators not made defendants included the local operating companies in which AT&T held shares, such as New Jersey Bell and Pacific Telephone and Telegraph. While there are different elements required than in the monopolizing charge, the attempt and conspiracy charges essentially fell within the claim that AT&T engaged in monopolization under Section 2. Further, the government's complaint was framed in terms of two elements required to prove monopolization. First, the defendants had to possess monopoly power in the relevant market. "Monopoly power" was defined as the power to control prices or to exclude competition. While this test has no readily apparent meaning and has been treated in a number of ways, the fundamental question is whether "a firm has a substantial degree of power to exclude competitors by reducing price and still be profitable."[16] The relevant product or service market is based on the notion of reasonable interchangeability. Do products serve the same use so that small reductions in price in one product result in large numbers of buyers turning to it from other products? If this occurs, both products are part of the same product market—they exhibit high cross elasticity of demand.

But the possession of such monopoly power alone is not sufficient to constitute a Sherman Act monopolization offense. One may, for example, attain monopoly power as a result of producing a product that is better than one's competitor's. Or, one's service, distribution, design, and so on may be so superior that all customers turn to it. Attaining a monopoly position in such ways is lawful; indeed, that is what competition is about. And if one attains market dominance as a result of such superior performance, the process of competition has worked well. Consequently, the second element in the offense of monopolization is that the charged firm's conduct goes beyond normal and honest business conduct. In the *AT&T* case, the Justice Department considered its burden of proof in the following terms: "Willful acquisition or maintenance of monopoly power does not require a showing of specific intent. . . . Where the offense alleged is monopolization, the requisite showing is one of a general or deliberate purpose or intent to exercise monopoly power. . . . It is sufficient to show that a monopoly results as the necessary consequence of a defendant's conduct or business arrangements."[17] In other words, the Justice Department sought to ease its burden considerably by abnegating the second element of a monopolization charge. However, the Justice Department still had to show as many situations of purportedly predatory conduct as it could locate.

Only two pages in the complaint actually sketched the actions about which the Antitrust Division complained, yet they did not tell what the government intended to prove. The charges included that (1) Western Electric supplied the telecommunications equipment needs of the Bell system, thereby eliminating competition from other manufacturers and suppliers; (2) AT&T obstructed the interconnection of SCCs and other carriers; and (3) AT&T obstructed the interconnection of customer-provided CPE into the Bell system. Thus, the Justice Department's case was based on only three factors: the Bell system's vertical integration and procurement practices, MCI's rate and interconnection complaints against AT&T, and CPE interconnection cases. Clearly, the second and third factors were viewed as examples of predatory conduct. Based solely on these alleged actions—and without mention of the F.C.C.'s or the PUCs' involvement in the events described in the complaint—the Justice Department called for AT&T's dismemberment. It hoped the court would require AT&T to divest all Western Electric stock and that Western, in turn, would be required to divest "assets sufficient to insure competition in the manufacture and sale of telecommunications equipment."[18] Additionally, the Justice Department called for AT&T to divest some or all of the Bell operating companies, and requested the court to impose unspecified, nonstructural relief. In short, the Justice Department wanted AT&T to serve as little more than a long-distance company with some connection to Bell Labs.

The Answer

That AT&T would vehemently denounce the antitrust suit, and that MCI and the other firms that had brought private actions against AT&T would be delighted with it, are not surprising. The recorded responses of the investment community were largely negative. According to an AT&T survey, newspaper editorials ran three to one against the suit. A *Wall Street Journal* editorial summarized this generally negative stream of sentiment against the suit:

> While the Justice Department can't promise any consumer benefits that might result from its suit to break up AT&T, it is sure of one thing. This is the largest antitrust action ever filed.
>
> So much for the mentality of modern day trustbusters. As long as they can tackle the biggest of all "big businesses" what is the difference whether the massive expenditure of federal money and effort is likely to cut anyone's phone bills? What the Justice Department suit attacks is not monopoly but vertical integration.
>
> A study [by] Touche, Ross & Co., the accounting firm, completed for the Federal Communications Commission earlier this year . . . was something of a disappointment to federal regulators and trustbusters.
>
> Its conclusion was that "the general effects of the interrelationship of Bell Systems companies are a reduction of cost and investment." . . . Out of all this we arrive at one question: Where is the problem that justifies risking possible damage to the efficiency of a vital part of the U.S. infrastructure. . . . If there is a problem that justifies all this we can't find it.[19]

AT&T sought, of course, to capitalize on the sentiment in its favor. After the suit was filed, CEO John de Butts announced that AT&T was not in violation of the law and that the action was undertaken in complete disregard of the interests of the general public. Fragmentation of responsibility, the principal goal of the suit, would lead to deterioration of telephone service. The regulated network manager system, de Butts pointed out, had withstood constant examination by state and federal regulatory agencies, courts, and legislative bodies almost from its inception. Notwithstanding criticism of certain specific activities, the system, on balance, had worked remarkably well. Virtually every household had telephone service, the level of telecommunications technology was the highest in the world, and costs had been kept down by productivity gains at twice the pace of the general economy. Finally, de Butts stated on several occasions that AT&T would not settle the suit.[20]

In contrast to the complaint, AT&T's formal answer was twenty-three pages long and replete with details. But, more importantly, instead of starting with recent times, as the complaint did, the AT&T answer briefly traced the history of the industry from the telephone's invention to the suit. The purpose of the history was to show why and how the regulated network manager system had evolved. In contrast to the Justice Department's portrayal of AT&T, the company showed that other models of government-business relationships in the telephone industry were tried in the past and found wanting. Accordingly, the regulated network manager system evolved, not all at once but gradually, in response to public service goals. AT&T then showed how it had been under constant scrutiny (much of this hostile) since well before the enactment of the 1934 Communications Act. The F.C.C. was invited by Congress to request new powers and enforcement tools if existing ones were found to be inadequate. Yet with minor exceptions, the agency concluded that it already had sufficient power to regulate AT&T and the other public service companies. But, AT&T questioned, was this because the F.C.C. was under AT&T's influence or because it had given up in response to the futility of adequately regulating the public service firms? The question was, of course, a vital one in that a major underpinning of the Justice Department case was the inadequacy of regulation and, therefore, the need to dissolve AT&T. Not only had AT&T's component telephone companies been adequately regulated, but Western Electric and Bell Labs as well. In view of the numerous contests that AT&T and its constituent companies lost by 1974 at the federal and state levels, there was almost a mythical quality to the notion of inadequate regulation. The proof of adequate regulation could be found in the high quality of telephone service, in AT&T's modest profit rates, and in the fact that the "interstate rates of the Bell System are substantially at the level of 20 years ago, and rates for local service have increased at only about one-third of the rate of increases of prices in the economy generally."[21] In short, then, AT&T claimed it had not behaved like a monopolist; that is, its monopoly position in long distance and many local markets came about not from predatory practices, but for the same reason that the tiny Tatum Telephone Company was the local monopolist in Tatum, Texas. The gradual evolution of the telephone industry was in the direction of single market providers. It noted, too, that the F.C.C. had demonstrated in many decisions that it, and not AT&T, had the power to exclude or license new competitors. The F.C.C. and the PUCs had the power to control rates through a variety of regulatory techniques. For these reasons, AT&T lacked monopoly power in the antitrust sense regardless of its size. Further, AT&T asserted that the court lacked jurisdiction over the matter because a comprehensive regulatory scheme inconsistent with antitrust primacy governed telecommunications. (While the F.C.C. had modified the old regulated network manager system in favor of what is termed here *contrived competition,* it was still a comprehensive system. No matter how ad hoc F.C.C. regulation had become, the numerous SCC, satellite, interconnection, long-distance, rate, technical, and other decisions showed that F.C.C. regulation was so comprehensive that there was no room for antitrust enforcement.) Finally, AT&T's answer argued that the matter had already been tried and settled by the parties. Since AT&T had fully complied with the terms of the 1956 consent decree, the Justice Department could not bring another suit on the same cause of action.

And the Case Drags On

The matter was initially assigned to Judge Joseph C. Waddy, who had never previously presided over an antitrust case. Almost immediately each side made massive document requests while, at the same time, resisting the other side's request as unreasonable. Judge Waddy at the outset was concerned with two interrelated issues. First, what *specifically* did the Justice Department claim that AT&T had done wrong? Second, did not the comprehensive F.C.C.–state PUC jurisdiction over telecommunications preclude Justice Department prosecution under the antitrust laws? Both sides anxiously awaited Judge Waddy's first decision to see if it could provide clues about his predisposition in the case. On November 24, 1976, he issued his first opinion on the threshold issues, concluding that AT&T was not immune from Sherman Act prosecution. Accordingly, he ordered the parties to proceed with pretrial procedures.[22] Notwithstanding this adverse ruling, it was nevertheless apparent from his statements that Judge Waddy was skeptical that the Justice Department could prove its case.

As the discovery process, rampant with disputes, progressed in 1978, Judge Waddy became terminally ill with cancer. The case was reassigned to Judge Harold F. Greene, who had been sworn in as a federal district court judge on June 22. Greene was uniformly regarded as a resolutely fair trial judge and an excellent judicial administrator.

Judge Greene had the immediate task of getting the proceedings moving. Almost four years had elapsed since the complaint was filed, yet little progress had been made. Greene wanted to avoid another *United States v. IBM* scenario, which began in January 1969 and was still far from completion. As a group studying big antitrust cases for the National Commission for the Review of Antitrust Laws and Procedures reported in January 1979 on the *IBM* case: "The number of non-substantive issues generated during discovery and trial is also prodigious. As of November 27, 1978, Judge Edelstein had issued 59 opinions, 127 memorandum endorsements, 21 pretrial orders, 13 amended pretrial orders and 63 stipulations and orders."[23] The advisory panel also discussed Judge Waddy's handling of the *United States v. AT&T* case, pointing out that virtually no discovery had taken place since the complaint was filed. While the report was filed after Judge Greene took charge, he undoubtedly knew of the existence of President Carter's National Commission for the Review of Antitrust Laws and Procedures, of which delay was a major topic of investigation. However, we cannot assume that delay is simply a defense tactic. The issues raised in procedural matters are often important ones, especially if they concern the government's potential for abuse—a subject about which Greene would be sensitive. Once a case is brought, the government lawyers involved are much like those in the private sector—they do not necessarily seek justice but rather to win and score heavily over their opponents. Judge Greene would have the difficult task of balancing fairness to the defendants with moving the case at a quicker pace.

One of Greene's first acts was to issue an order on July 6, 1978, directing the parties to file status memoranda on all issues preliminary to the trial. Then, on September 11, 1978, after reviewing prior proceedings, Judge Greene issued his first important decision in the case.[24] The decision was organized into four subjects. First there was the question of jurisdiction. The second was one of AT&T's principal defenses: that the United States government to a large extent compelled the conduct of which it now complained. But the Justice Department, in addition to disputing this contention, also argued that the government was not a monolith and that the Justice Department could not be prevented from complaining about conduct in which the F.C.C. and other agencies implicitly or explicitly concurred. The third was that the plaintiff sought access to documents produced in private antitrust suits brought against AT&T. And fourth, Judge Greene used the decision to plot the future course of action in the case. Once again the court rejected the argument that regulation was sufficiently pervasive to preempt completely the antitrust laws. In any event, there was no reason for this question to prevent discovery proceedings. If after discovery the court was wrong about jurisdiction with respect to some of the defendants' conduct, those issues would be referred to the F.C.C. Judge Greene, in deciding the second issue, first observed that one of AT&T's most important arguments was that its conduct largely resulted from government directives and policies. Moreover, AT&T claimed that its structure and practices benefited the United States government. Noting that AT&T's argument was plausible, that the United States as a plaintiff was the entire executive branch (except the independent regulatory agencies of which the F.C.C. was one), and that any relief would be national in impact and scope, Greene rejected the plaintiff's argument. Therefore, AT&T could subpoena documents from the entire executive branch, not just the Justice Department. While he could not order the production of documents from the F.C.C. because of its nominal independence from the executive branch, Greene promised to assist AT&T in securing documents from it—if the defendant would pare down its request.

The third major issue concerned documents produced by AT&T in private antitrust suits. At stake were approximately 2.5 million pages of AT&T

documents that were in the records of the *MCI* cases and others. Judge Greene, noting that it would be too time consuming for the Department of Justice to duplicate the document-selection process when it was already available, held for the government on the issue.

Judge Greene's most innovative effort concerned the fourth issue. His basic strategy in administering the *AT&T* case involved several considerations, the most important of which was that the case would be tried without a jury. By allowing nearly all evidence and testimony within a broad range of tolerance into the record, Greene avoided the pitfalls involved in deciding issues of inclusion and exclusion, many of which could lead to appeals. Greene would, after all, be able to evaluate the quality of evidence based on his legal skills and experience. At the same time, he assured AT&T that it would be able to obtain the evidence it needed for its defense. Although a record replete with the testimony and exhibits of both sides would help to guarantee fairness, it would also cause interminable delay.

Judge Greene's next task, then, was to outline procedures that would bring order and speed to this morass of documents without injuring his commitment to fairness. Although modified somewhat, the basic contours of Greene's original plan governed the administration of the case.

Thus, Pretrial Order No. 12 asked the parties to file four successive Statements of Contention and Proof (SCPs) over an eighteen-month period. The plaintiff's first SCP was to show (1) the government's legal and factual contentions, (2) a list of witnesses and the documentary evidence that would support each contention, and (3) the extent to which the evidence was in plaintiff's hands or where it could be found. The defendants' first SCP was to be organized in a manner similar to plaintiff's. After the filing of the first SCPs, a magistrate was to conduct a conference designed to simplify the issues, arrive at stipulations of uncontroverted facts, and reduce further unnecessary discovery. At the conclusion of the first pretrial conference, then, the parties would have a list of stipulations to which they both agreed and another of contentions about which they differed. It was hoped that the second SCPs would further narrow and simplify the issues and that the second pretrial conference would increase the number of stipulations and reduce the number of contentions. In this way, considerably less need for testimony and exhibits would exist when the trial began. However, Judge Greene allowed sufficient flexibility in the procedure to enlarge existing contentions or to add new ones in the second SCP. Therefore, the magistrate was instructed to be more stringent in applications for new contentions. The discovery process was scheduled to terminate on April 1, 1980.

Although Greene's pretrial process did not work exactly as planned, it marked a good beginning to what would lead to an orderly trial. The plaintiff's 530-page first SCP was filed on November 1, 1978, and outlined the nature of the telecommunications industry and its technology and participants. The document also described the structure of the Bell system and AT&T's role in it, and it stated the major themes of the Justice Department's case as well as the purported factual support. The themes included were (1) the alleged exclusionary acts that resulted from vertical integration, (2) the abuse of monopoly power to thwart competition—so-called predatory acts—and (3) the inability of state and federal regulation to control the acts of the defendants. The markets examined were broadly telecommunications transmission and equipment, and a discussion of the applicable law was followed by another of the relief necessary to remedy the violations of the law.

The defendants' first SCP, a 490-page document, was structured somewhat differently in keeping with its theory of the case. It began with a more detailed discussion of the technology of telecommunications, showing that the vertical and horizontal structures of the Bell system were due more to the technology of telecommunications than to any intent to monopolize the industry. The defendants also described the development of telephone regulation and the reasons for its increasing pervasiveness, including the widespread adoption of the natural-monopoly idea and the growth of federal regulation. Seeking to show that the regulated network manager system worked well, the historical exposition included, as well, material on the remarkable performance of the Bell system, such as the accomplishments of Bell Labs—topics that the Justice Department largely viewed as irrelevant. The lengthiest portion of the document consisted of rebuttals of the government's charges. Finally, AT&T argued its affirmative defenses and the proposed remedy, and an appendix described how it intended to prove its case. The second SCPs were briefer than anticipated, but the third SCPs were more comprehensive than the first set, largely because of the judge's insistence that the case should be organized into a set of episodes. By September 1980, the case had been organized into eighty-two separate episodes, many with subparts. The case had moved to a higher level. Both episode lists had much in common; for example, episodes one through seven as well as nine dealt with the technology of telecommunications as well as the history of government-industry relations through the *Carterfone* decision. Most of that material was a part of AT&T's defense that its structure and performance were to a large extent attributable to a combination of the nature of telecommunications technology and government regulation. The heart of the government's case was embodied in the episodes concerning specialized common carriers, most critically MCI, and various AT&T tariff offerings.

These were the most important and detailed episodes in the government's case. The government's most important witnesses included MCI's William McGowan, whose testimony covered approximately six hundred transcript pages, and other MCI officials who testified on FX, CCSA, Execunet, and other matters of controversy between MCI and AT&T. Its principal expert witness was Professor William H. Melody (a frequent expert for MCI), whose five-hundred-page testimony argued that the various AT&T tariffs were not compensatory. Through these testimonies and exhibits, the Justice Department hoped to show that the F.C.C., although well intentioned, was unable to control the monopolist AT&T.

It is crucial to appreciate the importance of these episodes to the government's case, for not only did MCI furnish the Justice Department with 1.5 million pages of materials from its first antitrust suit against AT&T, but it provided the work of its attorneys as well. In the words of the Court of Appeals, District of Columbia Circuit: "MCI furnished the Government the documents, depositions, and exhibits that MCI had discovered from AT&T. MCI also furnished certain documents pertaining to a 'database' consisting of computerized abstracts of documents, deposition transcripts and exhibits received from AT&T during discovery. MCI's counsel had prepared the database."[25] Considering the importance of the MCI episodes to the Justice Department, it is instructive to note the disposition of MCI's principal private antitrust suit against AT&T. In January 1983—approximately one year after the Justice Department and AT&T reached a settlement and four months after Judge Greene's basic decision on that settlement—the Seventh Circuit court of appeals reversed most of the trial court's findings in *MCI v. AT&T* and explicitly rejected Dr. Melody's testimony and the cost concepts he advanced. The Seventh Circuit found that each of AT&T's private-line tariffs was compensatory.[26] The court upheld the jury's finding on the FX and CCSA issues only by permitting the jury to interpret the F.C.C.'s complex SCC decision.

However, even though the SCC portion of the government's case was the most elaborate, the other parts of the case were important as well. The cumulative effect of the many episodes used to show AT&T's alleged abuse of its monopoly position was intended to prove regulators' failure in controlling AT&T's destructive conduct. Usually these episodes involved a representative of a company supposedly abused by AT&T, who purported to show that the company's product or service was remarkable and innovative and that AT&T's conduct harmed that company. AT&T had to justify its conduct in the highly complex world of telecommunications; for example, it had to show technical reasons for not purchasing certain equipment from independent manufacturers or for not interconnecting with particular

CPE. From Greene's decision on the motion to dismiss, it is clear that these episodes made a major impression on the court and that AT&T would endure a difficult burden in its defense. Nonetheless, the defendants' third statement and the Stipulation/Contention Package indicated that AT&T had a plausible and convincing justification for each such incident.[27] The government's presentation of evidence began on January 15, 1981, following an unsuccessful attempt to settle. At the conclusion of the plaintiff's case, AT&T filed a 553-page memorandum in support of its motion to dismiss the complaint on the ground that the Antitrust Division had failed to state a cause of action. Because the defendant takes no risks in making such a motion at the close of the plaintiff's case, it is not an uncommon action. Also, the defendant may obtain a better sense of the points the court considers most important as well as its general views on the case, and thus adjust its examination of witnesses accordingly. Generally such motions are rarely granted at the close of the plaintiff's case, and they are deferred for consideration at the conclusion of trials.

Judge Greene, however, took the opportunity in his forty-page decision to make a strong statement indicating that the court would support major portions of the government's case. Greene's general attitude may be surmised in this 1983 statement: "It is antithetical to our political and economic system for this key industry to be within the control of one company."[28]

AT&T had lost on nearly every point decided by Judge Greene in the motion to dismiss. Although AT&T sought to downplay the decision, it knew that the decision indicated a high probability of losing the case at the trial-court level. Indeed, AT&T responded by enlarging its witness list in an attempt to counterargue parts of the decision. But, at the same time, other important events occurred. Most notable was Judge Vincent Biunno's September 3, 1981, *Western Electric* decision, construing the 1956 judgment in AT&T's favor so that it could offer enhanced telecommunications services through a separate subsidiary in keeping with the F.C.C.'s proposals. This placed the prospect of a negotiated settlement in a new light, for AT&T's leadership realized that the old public philosophy was shattered and that the company could adjust to a new one.

Toward a Settlement

Any compromise settlement must, of course, involve perceived gains and losses on the part of both sides. From the Justice Department's perspective, many factors favored settlement. First, much of what it sought in the 1974 complaint had been accomplished or was in the process of being achieved in other proceedings. The Execunet decision and its aftereffects had opened up the long-distance market to at least a form of competition. F.C.C. proceedings were opening up the CPE market to easy entry. A divorce of AT&T from the operating companies would do the same for the switching and transmission equipment markets. Because so much had already been settled, the Justice Department had greater room for flexibility in arranging a settlement without invoking the ire of AT&T's rivals. The *AT&T* case was so unique that it would have little precedent value. Notwithstanding the Justice Department's victory in Judge Greene's denial of AT&T's motion to dismiss, there was much to lose from a lengthy prolongation of the matter, including appeals. At the conclusion of the trial, the record would have been so immense that much time necessarily would elapse before a final decision would be announced by Judge Greene. The inevitable appeal to the court of appeals would add years to the case as well, and it was far from certain that the Justice Department would win at the court of appeals level. An appeal to the Supreme Court would extend the time still further. The uncertain status of the telecommunications industry during these critical years could not help AT&T or its opponents plan effectively for the future. Nor could it help the Justice Department politically. Congress and members of the executive branch were already preparing a variety of remedies, and as different as these were, all could be implemented considerably more quickly than antitrust relief. Finally, even if the Justice Department won the case on its merits, it is far from certain that drastic relief involving divestiture would have been upheld. In summary, then, the Justice Department had many reasons to attempt to settle the dispute.

AT&T, too, had to consider the various trade-offs of litigation and settlement. In addition to the enormous resources consumed in litigation, prolonging the matter through the Supreme Court stage would limit the company's ability to engage in long-range planning. The company certainly did not want to put resources in a division that it may have had to divest. Again, such uncertainty enhanced risk and, therefore, probably made it more difficult and costly for the company to borrow funds, especially in the form of long-term bonds. Moreover, the ultimate outcome of AT&T's attempt to modify the 1956 consent decree was equally uncertain in that the Justice Department challenged AT&T on this interrelated matter as well. From AT&T's perspective, settlement considerations required the company to come to grips with the kind of structure that would be the least-worse alternative. AT&T also appreciated that Judge Greene would have to approve the terms of a settlement and that its many enemies in Congress and the private sector would closely scrutinize and exert influence on its terms. The AT&T top leadership had, indeed, been preparing for changes in light of the shift in public philosophy toward competition in regulated industries and the gradual demise of the public service philosophy.[29]

Based on its past record, AT&T could be reasonably confident of its ability to do well in the new competitive environment. Its 1978 *Annual Report* stated: "A key reason for this confidence lies in the unique resource of Bell Laboratories. For a high technology business such as ours to continue to innovate, it must be fueled by constant research that extends the boundaries of scientific knowledge and translates it into useful technology. . . . In short, Bell Laboratories assures the Bell System of being on the leading edge of new technology."[30] Thus, AT&T was far more reluctant to give up the research, development, and implementation of new technology—Bell Labs and Western Electric—than it was to give up long-distance or local-operating transmission. But if AT&T had to choose between keeping long distance or the local operating companies, its judgment was to keep the former because long distance had been far more susceptible to technological progressiveness and declining costs than had local service. Moreover, more that 90 percent of AT&T's construction budget was being absorbed by the local operating companies. Finally, some states, most importantly California, were adamantly resisting applications for rate increases. AT&T's strategic choice was, therefore, strongly in favor of retaining long distance at the expense of local service.

Prior to the enactment of the Antitrust Procedures and Penalties Act—the so-called Tunney Act—in 1974, only the parties to the suit had to agree for a consent decree to be entered. The Tunney Act arose in large part because of congressional suspicion about the 1956 *Western Electric* consent decree and the settlement terms of an antitrust suit against ITT during the Nixon administration. Under the procedures set up by the act, the Justice Department is required to submit for industry and public comment a copy of the proposed decree and a public impact statement that analyzes the decree and its probable impact. After public comments, the court is required to hold a hearing on the decree, making findings about whether the decree is in the public interest and what its probable effects will be. Since the court has the power to "take such other action in the public interest as the court may deem appropriate," the parties must consider what the court will do in reaching their final terms of agreement.

Although settlement was discussed almost from the outset of the case, the first serious attempt to settle occurred at the end of 1980 and the beginning of 1981. During the waning days of the Carter administration, both sides requested that the trial, then scheduled to begin on January 15, 1981, be postponed pending settlement negotiations. The parties stated that they had a framework for negotiations but that many complex and controversial features still needed to be resolved. Judge Greene, claiming not to understand why the parties waited so long to begin serious negotiations, turned down their request. Greene noted that the unresolved issues, which might derail the settlement, and the time required contributed most to his decision. In addition, incumbent assistant attorney general Sanford Litvack had not consulted with the incoming Reagan administration officials about the settlement plans. However, only one week later the parties reported that they had worked intensively on settlement and that a complete, detailed agreement had been prepared, in which there remained no complex or controversial issues to be resolved. Judge Greene described the agreement as "essentially complete," but noted that the new administration still had not been consulted about the terms.[31] After both sides planned to remedy this problem quickly, Judge Greene agreed to interrupt the trial proceedings until February 2, 1981, at which time the attorneys for both sides were to report back to the court. If at this time they were agreeable to the filing of a formal consent decree within thirty days, the court would delay the case further. However, if they could not agree to this by February 2, the trial would proceed.

When the settlement terms were revealed, they surprised many observers. First, AT&T would have been required to divest Pacific Telephone and Telegraph and its minority interests in Cincinnati Bell and Southern New England Telephone. AT&T would have given up difficult problems in the case of PT&T, and its minority shareholdings in two companies that, though parts of the Bell system, it did not control. By the divestiture of these local operating companies, the Justice Department would have arranged the creation of independent firms whose behavior on interconnection and other issues could readily be compared with the Bell local operating companies. If the Bell companies were found wanting in some respect, the F.C.C. could use the three former Bell-system companies operating independently as models of appropriate behavior. Further, the 1956 consent decree would have been vacated, allowing AT&T to enter noncommunications businesses. However, consistent with the F.C.C.'s decision in the *Computer II* case, a fully separated subsidiary would provide CPE and enhanced services. The Long Lines Department and the interstate long-distance network would have been placed under the control of a different, fully separate subsidiary. Finally, AT&T would have been required to spin off parts of Western Electric to create an equipment competitor. But for several reasons, importantly the very different settlement ideas of William Baxter, President Reagan's antitrust chief, the attempt failed.

The Settlement of 1982

Baxter's strong criticism of the proposed 1981 settlement would form the basis of the Justice Department's future negotiating position. Baxter held that AT&T should be divided into two piles of assets: the regulated side would be composed of those involved in local loops, and the competitive side would include equipment, enhanced services, data processing, and long distance. "We are well into the morn of the day when long lines should not be regulated at all. . . . [Long distance should be] put over on the competitive pile. The local loops would be on the other."[32] Others in the Reagan administration, most importantly the Defense Department, rejected any breakup of the Bell system because of its potentially adverse impact on defense procurement and for other reasons. In addition, Congress was actively considering telecommunications legislation that would reshape the industry. At the same time, the F.C.C. and the Justice Department were involved in judicial proceedings concerning proposed modifications of the 1956 *Western Electric* consent decree. The *AT&T* case, in a phrase, was becoming a political football over which the parties to the case were losing control. When AT&T's board of directors met promptly at 10:30 A.M. on December 16, 1981, Chief Executive Officer Charles Brown scrapped his prepared statement and instead described the Baxter divestiture plan that had been under discussion between Baxter and AT&T general counsel Howard Trienens. After Brown had been thoroughly questioned by the others present, the board authorized him to enter divestiture talks with the Justice Department. Baxter and his staff began preparing an agreement based on regulated and unregulated divisions of the company. Baxter did not care whether AT&T kept the local operating companies or the competitive parts of the business, as long as it did not keep both. AT&T received a first draft of the proposed consent decree on December 21. After Brown reviewed the original proposal, a modified proposed decree little different from the first one was prepared. At most, half a dozen Justice Department employees, AT&T's directors, and perhaps ten of its employees knew of the momentous events that were taking place.

As the agreement took shape, the lawyers turned their attention to the legal vehicle that was to embrace what they did. As we have seen, AT&T wanted to eliminate the restrictions in the 1956 consent decree. Both sides wanted to consolidate the New Jersey and District of Columbia cases before one judge—Judge Greene. Therefore, they concluded that the agreement should be a modification of the 1956 consent decree. Judge Biunno was asked to transfer the matter to Judge Greene's court but not to examine the substance of the agreement. Little known is that Judge Biunno did, in fact, approve the decree before transferring it to Judge Greene, who conducted his own review. Further, both sides argued that the Tunney Act did not apply to modifications of decrees but, expecting to lose on that issue, they followed the Tunney Act procedures.

At the heart of the settlement was the requirement that AT&T would spin off the Bell operating companies and submit a plan that would restructure the BOCs into viable entities. AT&T would no longer be in the local-exchange business (except for its minority ownership in Cincinnati Bell and Southern New England Telephone, which the settlement did not affect). Also, AT&T would retain control of Bell Labs and Western Electric and continue to operate its intercity long-distance network. The company would furnish all CPE, including that provided by the local Bell companies, but license and supply contracts then in effect between Western Electric and the local operating companies would be canceled. The new operating companies would, thus, be free to choose their own suppliers. Because the local operating companies would be suddenly divorced from Bell Labs—their principal resource for scientific and technological information and research—AT&T agreed to provide the new operating companies, on a priority basis, with research, development, and support services until September 1987. Finally, AT&T promised that it would not acquire the stock of any spun-off Bell operating company.

The settlement also specified the obligations of the new Bell operating companies. Foremost among these was to provide each long-distance carrier and information-service provider (that is, a company that transforms and communicates information) access into local loops equal in type, quality, and price to that provided to AT&T and its affiliates. For example, if a person dialed "1" to access AT&T's long-distance service, each new Bell operating company would have to make arrangements to treat the other long-distance carriers equally. The new operating companies would offer their customers a choice of which long-distance carrier they wanted that would be accessed by dialing "1." Similarly, each BOC was forbidden to discriminate in treatment between AT&T and other suppliers of various services, CPE, and switching and transmission equipment.

However, the most controversial aspects of the settlement followed from Baxter's rigorous distinction between regulated and unregulated businesses. The new operating companies (with a few exceptions relating to emergencies) were forbidden to manufacture or distribute CPE or other telecommunications products. For the same reason, they were excluded from the interexchange long-distance and information-service businesses. More generally, the BOCs were expected not to provide any other product or service, except local telephone service and local access, "that is not a natural monopoly service actually regulated by tariff."[33] Among the most important nonregulated services were the Yellow Pages.

Although the parties to the settlement formed a united front once they entered into the agreement, virtually every other interest criticized some aspect of it. These criticisms were quite varied; for example, some deplored the breakup while others felt that the breakup did not go far enough. The criticism continued in the formal comments authorized under the Tunney Act. More than six hundred individuals and organizations filed comments comprising approximately 8,750 pages.

Both the Justice Department and AT&T sought to complete the arrangements called for in the settlement as quickly as possible and to do so without undue shock to the component parts of the new system or subscribers. In February 1982, AT&T took the first step in reconstructing the twenty-two operating companies into more economically viable entities by reorganizing them into seven larger regional operation firms. In this way, smaller BOCs like Diamond State Telephone, which covered Delaware, would be better able to withstand the shock of divestiture. Each of the regional companies, which in fact constituted the firms eventually spun off, had local operations that were greater than GTE's. GTE was then the second largest integrated telephone company. The new regional Bell operating companies (RBOCs) would become:

New	Old
Pacific Telesis Group	Pacific Telephone & Telegraph
	Bell Telephone Co. of Nevada
Nynex Corp.	New York Telephone Co.
	New England Telephone & Telegraph Co.
BellSouth Corp.	Southern Bell Telephone Co.
	South Central Bell Telephone Co.
Ameritech Corp.	Illinois Bell Telephone Co.
	Indiana Bell Telephone Co.
	Michigan Bell Telephone Co.
	Ohio Bell Telephone Co.
	Wisconsin Telephone Co.
Southwestern Bell Corp.	Southwestern Bell Telephone Co.
US West, Inc.	Mountain States Telephone & Telegraph Co.
	Northwestern Bell Telephone Co.
	Pacific Northwest Bell Telephone Co.
Bell Atlantic Corp.	Diamond State Telephone Co.
	Bell Telephone Co. of Pennsylvania
	New Jersey Telephone Co.
	Chesapeake & Potomac Telephone Companies of
	Maryland, Virginia, West Virginia, and Washington, D.C.

On August 11, 1982, Judge Greene rendered his opinion and order agreeing to accept the Modification of Final Judgment subject to certain modifications that applied to both the new operating companies and AT&T.[34]

First, RBOCs would continue to provide the printed Yellow Pages. Second, they could lease or sell CPE to their customers but they could not manufacture them. In this way, Greene argued, they would not favor their manufacturing subsidiaries—thus solving the vertical integration problem. Third, the new RBOCs could enter other business markets if they were able to show that monopoly power would not be used to impede competition in the markets. Under this provision Judge Greene had been deluged by the operating companies with requests to enter new lines of business. Fourth, while the new RBOCs were prohibited from offering information and enhanced services, AT&T was precluded from engaging in electronic publishing over its own transmission facilities for seven years. Many of these changes were deviations from the rigorous division into competitive and regulated activities that Baxter had devised. Further, they reveal Greene's concern that without such opportunities and benefits, the RBOCs might not have become viable entities. Apparently concerned also about the possible adverse impact of the decree on the universal service goal, Greene did not object to a subsidy flow from the long-distance user to the local subscriber.

However, Greene would soon realize that he had not replaced the F.C.C. as a decision-making body and that the settlement would not resolve many of the controversies and problems within the industry. In December 1982, the F.C.C. adopted its long-debated access-charge rule (not to be confused with equal access), under which each local subscriber would be charged a flat fee to link into the toll network. The flat fee was intended to help local telephone companies avoid having to raise business subscriber rates. Traditionally, business rates had subsidized residential rates, but now the reduced costs of bypass technologies afforded more firms the opportunity to bypass local loops if they considered local rates unacceptable. The access-charge solution was expected to eliminate the incentive to bypass by shifting charges to residential subscribers.

Yet access charges would be only one of numerous controversies into which Judge Greene would be drawn as a result of his obligation to supervise the enforcement of the decree. Nevertheless, on August 24, 1982, when the Justice Department and AT&T signed a revised agreement incorporating the changes that Greene required, they undoubtedly believed that the agreement would solve more problems than it would create.

AT&T's plan for reorganization would become effective within the eighteen months following the entry of the approved Modification of Final Judgment. The new operating companies were to have sufficient facilities, personnel, systems, and rights to technical information to allow them to provide good performance—an obligation that AT&T fulfilled in exemplary fashion. In December 1982, AT&T filed its 471-page Plan of Reorganization. Under the plan, the former twenty-two BOCs were reorganized into the seven RBOCs. Approximately 75 percent of AT&T's assets were assigned to the RBOCs. Further, all Bell-system territory in the continental United States was divided into 161 geographical areas called Local Access and Transport Areas, or LATAs. The LATAs were generally centered around a city or other identifiable community of interest, and each one marked the boundaries within which operating-company subsidiaries of the RBOCs could provide telephone service. Thus, an operating company could provide local service and intra-LATA long distance, but inter-LATA long distance would be provided by AT&T and the other long-distance carriers, such as MCI (which argued that the LATAs were too large). For example, because one LATA in Ohio included Cleveland, Akron, and Lorain, a long-distance call from Cleveland to Akron would be handled by the Ohio Bell subsidiary of Ameritech, but a call from Cleveland to Columbus would be served by an interexchange carrier. Certain exceptions permitting RBOCs to cross LATA lines (such as the New York City–suburban New Jersey corridor) were allowed. The plan also required each new RBOC to provide all interexchange carriers equal access by September 1, 1986, as well as information access. Finally, for the seven RBOCs, AT&T set up a central services organization called Bellcore, which the RBOCs jointly owned. Bellcore's function was to provide the RBOCs and their subsidiaries with technical assistance, such as network planning, engineering, and software development. Patterned after Bell Labs, the new company would also provide consulting services and serve as a central contact point for coordinating the efforts of the RBOCs in meeting national security requirements.

On July 8, 1983, Judge Greene issued a decision largely accepting the plan of reorganization but requiring certain changes. First, he expanded the patent-licensing powers of the RBOCs. Second, AT&T would no longer be permitted to use the logo or name "Bell" (except in the case of Bell Telephone Laboratories). According to Greene, the continued use of "Bell" by AT&T would have caused such confusion that an Illinois Bell subscriber, for example, would have assumed that AT&T "is the natural or 'official' long distance company to be used in conjunction with the local services provided by the several Bell Operating Companies."[35] Symbolically, though, Greene's decision on this point was appropriate—it marked the end of a long period in telecommunications history (even if it didn't mark the end of controversy within the industry). In early August, AT&T, with some reluctance, and the Justice Department agreed to Greene's modifications of the reorganization plan. In November, AT&T sent to its shareholders a prospectus detailing the stock distribution plan (seven RBOC shares for every ten AT&T shares held). And at midnight on the last day of 1983, the

Bell system that had been gradually constructed for more than a century broke up.

We noted in Chapter 1 F.A. Hayek's observations on the extraordinary difficulties in predicting changes in the marketplace. No field illustrates his wisdom more than telecommunications. Contemporary giants like Intel Corporation and Microsoft Corporation were comparatively small firms in 1984, while Netscape Communications was not even conceived then. All became major players in telecommunications a little more than a decade after the breakup. While computers played a role in telecommunications long before 1984, few, if any, saw the extraordinary ways in which the technologies would soon converge. Words and phrases like "Internet," "World Wide Web," and "Gopher," which have become extremely important in telecommunications, were unknown in 1984. Even before the breakup, cellular radio was introduced in October 1983 by an Ameritech subsidiary, but the growth of wireless services in the next decade and beyond was barely perceived. The RBOCs would themselves become involved in numerous businesses throughout the world. In addition, by 1997 the seven RBOCs would become five, as Bell Atlantic merged with Nynex, and Southwestern Bell (now SBC Communications) acquired Pacific Telesis. Events overtook the decree, which was largely abrogated by the Telecommunications Act of 1996. The AT&T breakup was crucially important, nevertheless, in two respects: first, because it restructured the dominant player in telecommunications and, second, because it occurred on the eve of dramatic changes in telecommunications.

6

Internationalization and Competition

After the Fall

On February 9, 1996, President Bill Clinton signed the most important United States telecommunications statute enacted since the Communications Act of 1934. Congress had worked for more than five years to enact a statute that would accommodate the various interests involved in telecommunications and would take into account the new realities of 1996. Much had changed since the AT&T breakup in 1984; indeed, many of the important companies in modern telecommunications had either not been born or were not involved in 1984. Netscape and America Online, for example, were unknown in 1984, while Microsoft at that time was concerned only with software development, not telecommunications. In 1984 most of the telephone systems in Western Europe and Asia were publicly owned monopolies. So strongly entrenched was the public-monopoly idea in telecommunications that it was contained in West Germany's fundamental law. In 1984, however, British Telecommunications (known as BT) was transformed into a public company and listed on the various stock exchanges. Since that seminal event, public telephone systems throughout the world are gradually being privatized. At the same time competition is being introduced in many nations. These remarkable changes were as unthinkable as late as 1976, just as the fall of the Berlin Wall and the end of European communism were then. But the world had changed dramatically in many respects since then.

There is little question that one of the most important changes that has occurred, especially since the AT&T breakup, is the creation of a global telecommunications infrastructure as both response to and cause of the creation of a global economy. One week after President Clinton signed the new telecommunications law, Merrill Lynch and Salomon Brothers, two of the largest Wall Street brokerage houses, stated that they expected approximately 20 percent of their future investment banking revenues to come from global telecommunications.[1] The contrast with earlier periods is dramatic. In 1980, while a number of telephone stocks (principally American firms) were traded on the world's stock exchanges, AT&T was overwhelmingly the dominant factor. Between 1986 and 1995 the value of the telecommunications sector had quadrupled, with more and more firms in that industry listing on one of the major exchanges each year. Every major telecommunications firm has been investing heavily in an international presence, either separately or through an alliance with other firms. AT&T, for example, which derived little of its revenue from international sources before the 1984 breakup, expects to earn half of its revenue outside the United States before the year 2000.[2] If one looks at cross-border telecommunications acquisitions, the number and value of such transactions has been accelerating rapidly since the crucial year of 1984. For example, from 1985 to 1990 alone, the number of deals increased from five to sixty-seven, while their value jumped from $399 million to $16.5 billion.[3]

Three interrelated trends must be considered to appreciate the international importance of the U.S. telecommunications sector: foreign trade, foreign investment, and globalization. Modern telecommunications is a contributing cause of these trends. At the same time, the increasing internationalization of telecommunications is also an effect of the trends. Let us begin with the exports of goods and services (measured in constant 1987 dollars). In 1994 the value of exported goods and services constituted about 12 percent of gross domestic product (GDP)—more than 2.5 times the 1960 percentage. At the same time, imports constituted more than 14 percent of GDP in 1994, more than three times the 1960 figure. If we look at just the goods-producing sectors of the U.S. economy, the changes that have occurred are even more dramatic. In 1994 exports of U.S. goods were 24 percent of the domestic output of goods. The comparable figures for 1960 and 1980 were 8 percent and 16 percent. Imported goods illustrated comparable trends. In 1960 approximately 9 percent of the goods consumed in the United States were imported. By 1994 that figure had grown to about 28 percent. Thus, the United States has become more dependent on exports and imports than at any time in the era following World War II.[4] And the upward import and export trends give every evidence of continuing as the successfully enacted North American Free Trade Agreement (NAFTA) and the signing of the Uruguay Round world trade agreements attest. At the most obvious level, the increased volume of international trade transactions inexorably leads to increased demand for telecommunications services. All other things being equal, business customers engaged in telecommunications activities in many countries would clearly prefer to purchase services from a single provider rather than from many because transaction costs will be lower. The fact that all other things are often not equal provides an incentive, in turn, for telecommunications providers to place themselves in the position of being a one-stop provider.

Trends in investment have followed the same path as foreign trade. The market value of direct U.S. investments abroad (in current dollars) escalated from $379.1 billion in 1985 to $993.2 billion in 1993. In that same short period, foreign direct investment in the United States jumped in market value from $220 billion to $745.6 billion. These figures do not include, we should note, indirect investment. We may reasonably conclude that the telecommunications needs of foreign firms with American investment and American firms investing abroad will be even greater than in the export and import situations. The reason is the daily need that home offices have to constantly stay in touch with branch plants and offices in other nations. In contrast, sales and negotiations are apt to be more intermittent. In addition, international firms will often demand secure private networks. For example, in the 1960s IBM began building an internal global network; by 1988 it extended to 145 countries and could serve to link employees throughout the company's far-flung empire. By 1987 IBM was moving three trillion characters of internal information annually.[5]

While increased cross-border trade and investment together account for much of the expanded scope of telecommunications, there is a subtler concept at work, the impact of which will be even more dramatic. This is the concept of the global economy, which, while incorporating increased levels of trade and investment, includes far more. The idea of the global economy has both a consumer side and a producer side. The speed with which information can electronically move around the world is the most important facet of the global economy. Obviously, in every country there is much nationalism that resists cooperation, openness, and interdependence. Nevertheless, consumers have voted with their pocketbooks for a global economy. Consumers in the developed regions of the world gradually achieved what management expert Kenichi Ohmae has termed the "Californiaization of need," and telecommunications has played a major role in this process. The products of McDonald's, Adidas, and Coca-Cola, among many other firms, are sold almost everywhere. "Whatever their nationality, consumers . . . increasingly receive the same information, seek the same kinds of life styles, and desire the same kinds of products. They all want the best products available, at the lowest prices possible. Everyone, in a sense, wants to live—and shop—in California."[6] At the cash register, very few of us care whether the Sanyo boom box we are buying was assembled by a Japanese company in a Thai factory and contains components made in many countries.

Consumer wants are not, however, permanent. Indeed, new trends and fads replace older ones more rapidly than ever before in some industries and services, such as apparel. Trends discerned in one market can readily be imitated in another one. At the same time, there are still national or regional trends that are not imitated elsewhere—which may provide an opportunity for introduction in another market. Regardless of how consumers may respond and the differences between various groups or nationalities, making sound marketing decisions for the future requires, in the first place, the collection of a considerable amount of information and, in the second place, the dissemination of that information throughout a global network. A product variation that is successful in Indonesia may, for example, be unpromising in the United States. Nevertheless, it is better that American firms receive such information than remain in blissful ignorance of it. We spoke in Chapter 1 about the importance of feedback, accuracy, and dialectic, and the power of modern telecommunications to solve the problems raised by these conceptions. Nowhere is the capability of resolving such issues greater than in the global arena. When one factors in the capabilities to store, manipulate, and retransmit marketing and other information that was unavailable only a few years ago, one can readily appreciate the extraordinary importance that modern telecommunications provides to companies assessing and seeking to fulfill consumer demand.

When one moves from the demand side of the ledger to the supply side, the enhanced benefits of modern telecommunications come even more to the fore. These advantages can be divided into two categories: those that reduce costs within a firm, and those that reduce costs between the subject firm and those with which it undertakes or may undertake transactions. Although Wal-Mart is largely a domestic company, it concretely typifies what may be done globally. Wal-Mart, a leader in the application of modern information technology, has created a massive communications system that transmits data from the cash registers of more than two thousand stores into an enormous database containing its vendors' weekly point-of-sale data. Collecting and analyzing such data, Wal-Mart can rapidly determine how well particular product lines are selling and adopt new strategies very quickly. Out-of-stock information can focus on the responses of suppliers and encourage them to boost or lower production and adjust inventory carrying costs. Wal-Mart's quick response time, thanks to modern telecommunications, has provided the company with an enormous advantage over less information-intensive competitors.[7]

This case only begins to illustrate the many ways in which modern telecommunications shapes Wal-Mart's business activities and strategies. And, it is difficult to consider the thousands of ways in which most other large enterprises are being transformed by the same forces. The Wal-Mart case illustrates the enlargement of the network idea in which information can flow from point to point at the speed of light and is processed and analyzed more quickly than ever before. It requires no leap of the imagination to appreciate that information can flow across oceans in the same blink of an eyelash that it can flow from Key West, Florida, to Bellingham, Washington. "New network services will make it possible for companies to be effectively managed and to compete anywhere, anytime. A top executive can hold a meeting with senior executives who remain in Tokyo, London, New York, and Des Moines in virtual reality. . . . Already it is possible to schedule, monitor, and coordinate the production of multiple factories in a number of countries from a single location."[8]

Based on a large number of case studies, Michael Porter and Victor E. Millar, two of the leading scholars of business strategy, have provided a set of generalizations about the dramatic changes that are being wrought by the telecommunications revolution, especially in the international area.[9] They have concluded that information technology allows firms to collect and process more information up and down the value chain than ever before. Markets are thereby enlarged and competitiveness is intensified because of the more systematic and comprehensive ways in which pricing and other business information can be obtained and evaluated. Similarly, production can be made more efficient than ever before because of the information revolution. For example, fishermen now employ weather satellite data on ocean temperatures to more accurately identify promising fishing areas. Again, engineering and supply data about components in a finished product can be more readily evaluated (and sometimes corrected) through advanced telecommunications than ever before, thereby greatly lessening the "snafu" problems that have so often plagued producers.

Porter and Millar conclude that the most important implication of the information revolution is its contribution to the globalization of the world economy. By dramatically reducing information and transaction costs, globalization allows firms to efficiently coordinate activities around the globe. This does not necessarily mean that large companies extend their own operations around the globe, for the very same kinds of telecommunications networks also explain the expansion of outsourcing, in which manufacturers link closely with independent suppliers with whom they are in constant contact and over whom they can exercise vigilant quality controls.[10]

We can concisely sum up this section by noting Vice President Albert Gore's observation that "time zones, not cost, will be the biggest barrier to keeping in touch."[11] And, as the cost of telecommunications drops, the power of telecommunications increases. Globalization can only be stopped by foolish government nationalism.

Response of Telecommunications Companies

The globalization of the world economy and the central role that modern telecommunications plays in it is, of course, no surprise to either the telecommunications industry or government leaders. The telecommunications industry has an obvious incentive to meet the enormous consumer and producer demand latent in globalization. As we will see, they have done so through a variety of strategies, such as joint ventures and alliances with foreign firms, that are intended to create a single information supplier that can serve a customer throughout the world. The strategy, in short, is to serve as a one-step supplier of telecommunications services so that firms do not have to enter into separate agreements in different countries or regions. At the same time, the service provider can offer both a seamless telecommunications system with uniform standards throughout the customer's marketing areas and a wide range of services including basic and advanced telecommunications services. One-stop telecommunications services from a single provider can, thus, lower transaction costs materially below what they would be if a customer had to arrange separate contracts with telecommunications firms in each nation or region. From the perspective of the telecommunications industry, the stakes in the global market are huge. In the first half of the 1990s corporate voice, data, and teleconferencing traffic volume between countries in messages per minute was increasing at an annual rate of 15 to 20 percent—about double the U.S. corporate domestic rate. Estimates of the total world communications market by the year 2000 range as high as $750 billion.[12]

While the enormous capital requirements to satisfy this demand alone indicate a principal reason for international alliances and *might* imply that only large firms can be significant players in international telecommunications, small companies, indeed, play roles in satisfying niche markets. Consider for example Verifone, Inc., which gathers and transmits election data in Mexico. In the United States and other nations, Verifone makes and sells terminals that verify credit card and check transactions. Or consider Synoptics Communications, a leading provider in many countries of intelligent hubs that allow computers to talk to each other. Or consider IDB Communications Group, Inc., which specializes in transmitting sporting events in the United States, Europe, and Asia. One could go on and on, but the point is eminently clear. The enormous international telecommunications market has spurred the creation of numerous specialty firms, some of which will become major players, some of which will fail, and some of which will remain niche players. In addition, the burgeoning telecommunications market has stimulated established firms in other fields to supply services and equipment. Thus, for example, by 1997 in Germany, savings banks, railways, utilities, industrial companies, and insurance companies were pushing hard to establish networks for specialized services.[13]

The evidence presently indicates that international telecommunications is becoming increasingly competitive and, at the same time, increasingly heterogeneous, with a large number of services available in addition to POTS—plain old telephone service. Increasingly crucial to a modern business system are such newer services as electronic data exchange (including processing) for orders, offers, invoices, confirmations, delivery, restocking; videoconferencing; videotex (interactive screen-assisted data communications services); on-line database services; electronic mail; high-speed facsimile and other visual information; and electronic banking services.

At the same time other new technologies allow the existing wireline network to be bypassed, including cellular telephone, cable television, satellite, personal communications services, new fiber-optic lines along railway or utility lines, and so on. This consideration has extremely important consequences for intensifying global telecommunications competition.

Consider the history of Sprint Corporation, the United States's third largest long-distance company, to see the implications for global competition. Sprint's long-distance business was born in January 1970 when the Southern Pacific Company, the holding company controlling important railroad properties, established it to provide private-line communications services to businesses, government agencies, and educational institutions. Southern Pacific Communications Corporation (SPCC) was the outgrowth of Southern Pacific's large internal communication system along the company's rights-of-way, which in 1969 covered almost 8,000 track miles.[14] In 1983 GTE, then the United States's second largest telephone company, purchased SPCC, becoming a long-distance provider. GTE Sprint, the reorganized firm, was gradually purchased by United Telecommunications, a large operator of local telephone systems, and in 1990 officially adopted Sprint as its name. Sprint expanded internationally and into a variety of other services. For example, in 1993 Sprint instituted KINKO'S, a public videoconferencing network and in 1994 began long-distance service in the United Kingdom.

The morals of the Sprint story are two. First, rights-of-way are an enormously valuable resource in entering the telecommunications business. Rights-of-way that can be deployed to transmit electricity, gas, or railroad traffic may also be used to transmit telecommunications traffic. Second, experience in private telecommunications systems can suggest entering into the public network business, and then into advanced services. The United States led the way in permitting new entry into long distance and other telecommunications services, but other nations have been following a similar path. For example, in May 1994 RWE, the German utility, and the Deutsche Bank won a contract to operate a data-transmission network in Germany to compete against Deutsche Telekom, then a government-owned carrier. Similarly, only one day before that announcement, two large German industrial corporations, BellSouth, the American regional Bell operating company, and Vodafone, a British group, began operating E-PLUS, a mobile telephone network.[15] The inevitable next steps are internationalization and adding more services to the original ones deployed by the entrant, for the same distribution pipes—whether wireless, optical fiber, satellite, or some combination—can frequently accommodate any kind of transmittable information. In other words, information is the relevant product market, not voice, video, and so on. Thus, older firms, start-up enterprises, and companies entering telecommunications from other industries all may portend intense and widespread telecommunications competition in the global economy and its major markets.

Two potential roadblocks lie in the way of this vision: capital requirements and governmental policy, including not only the traditional entry and regulatory barriers, but also the more difficult ones involving establishing international standards. Let us first look at the capital issues. According to one widely respected 1995 engineering economics study: "There's a worldwide capital crisis right now, and there isn't enough money in the world's capital markets to build the flashy new networks we keep hearing so much about. . . . The harsh reality is that there simply is not enough money in the world to meet all the demands of the telecommunications industry, let alone those of anyone else."[16] For this reason Nippon Telephone and Telegraph (NTT), the world's largest company, had to delay its plan to upgrade its local access network beyond 2015, the initial target year. One method of increasing cash as well as attracting financial backing is to sharply cut costs, especially labor costs. Many important telecommunications carriers, especially current and formerly publicly owned ones, are under intense cost-cutting pressures in order to effectively compete in the global arena. For example, Deutsche Telekom in 1995 had twice as many employees per customer as the average American telephone carrier and four times as many as a typical American cable company. According to the foregoing study, Deutsche Telekom would have to discharge many employees in order to compete effectively against American carriers.

Two other consequences follow from the capital-shortage problem. First, there is an incentive to reduce embedded costs. Thus, major global projects will be largely wireless. Second, since any single firm would be hard pressed to meet very ambitious global plans, there is a very strong incentive to form cross-border alliances and joint ventures. There are a number of incentives that have led to the spate of cross-border alliances, but certainly increasing capital as well as reducing risk in a large-scale capital commitment are among them. Iridium World Communications, one of the most ambitious projects ever conceived in telecommunications, illustrates these consequences. In June 1990, Motorola announced the Iridium project, the purpose of which was to allow small portable telephones to communicate with other telephones from any location in the world to any other place. The twenty-five-ounce handset could conveniently fit in an overcoat pocket. The system was originally intended to deploy seventy-seven low-earth-orbit satellites. While Motorola was confident of the technology, it viewed financing as the major obstacle in implementing the plan, anticipating that the cost of putting the service into operation within six years would be $2.3 billion. Accordingly, it sought partners in the operation. By January 1993 Motorola announced that it had received only tentative commitments from potential investors, but no binding commitments. The number of satellites had been scaled back to sixty-six. Notwithstanding these difficulties, Motorola was able to announce in September 1994 that it had obtained $733.5 million in new equity capital in Japan to supplement the $840 million it had raised in 1993. Motorola, however, had to put in more of its own money than it had originally planned. But its partners included DDI (Japan's second largest telephone company), a Brazilian construction company, VEBA (the German utility), Sony, Mitsubishi, Sprint, and other investors throughout the world.[17]

Motorola's difficulties, however, were far from over. In September 1995 it had to cancel plans to sell $300 million in junk bonds because of lack of investor interest. In part, investor resistance stemmed from the fact that by late 1995 Iridium faced other large consortia, most importantly Globalstar, seeking to be the first to deploy a global satellite phone network. Financial experts doubted whether all could raise sufficient capital, notwithstanding that the participants included some of the world's largest corporations, such as Microsoft. Nevertheless, a market that could be worth $15 billion and have thirty-five million customers in developing countries alone in the first decade of the twenty-first century was a powerful magnet. In mid-1996, however, Iridium continued to face financial difficulties, selecting two of the world's largest banks to arrange short-term and permanent financing amounting to approximately $3.15 billion. In spring 1977 an initial public offering of stock was announced. Network launch was scheduled for late

1998.[18] The Iridium project is one of the most ambitious ever conceived. Nonetheless, it typifies two of the strongest themes in global telecommunications stemming from capital issues: the search for partners and the search for ways of lowering embedded costs.

The Government Response

We have seen in this chapter the growth of international connections and telecommunication's role in globalization. We have observed the increasing importance of information technology in the future prospects of large and small firms and the economies of nations and regions. Business, culture, education, entertainment, and virtually every other facet of life are nourished by modern telecommunications. In the last section we looked briefly at telecommunications firms' responses and intentions to the new opportunities. In this section we will look at government responses to the new situation. François Bar, a leading expert in the area, succinctly summarized a widely held view on government's roles in the process: "If technology diffusion is to be the overarching policy goal, governments have an important role to play in facilitating access to the technology, in preparing the grounds for its diffusion, in stimulating its implementation."[19] Governments can play a variety of roles, including removing regulatory and other impediments to telecommunications development, encouraging competition and diversity, providing and assisting the provision of rights-of-way, encouraging the adoption of uniform standards, and facilitating the interconnection of the various subnetworks into larger ones. On the other hand, it is possible for government bureaucrats to go too far and start dictating business policy and technological choices. National governments throughout the world as well as regional authorities and international organizations are groping their ways to the adoption of appropriate policies.

The inexorable direction that most governments in the world have taken is toward privatization of government monopolies and the introduction of competition in the provision of services and equipment. Several case studies in this section will illustrate these processes. Privatization ends the dependence of telecommunications firms on governments, which in almost all cases are hard pressed to solve budget deficit problems. Indeed, the sales of those huge properties to investors help to reduce deficits. At the same time, privatized firms have easier access to capital markets and more flexibility in attracting additional capital through joint ventures, the sale of stock, borrowing on more flexible terms, and so on. The introduction of competition (often called liberalization) permits the introduction of still more capital in telecommunications. At the same time, the force of competition provides strong incentives for efficient operation and the introduction of novel and diverse technologies. United States firms, the clear leaders in technology and efficiency, have of course taken advantage of the new situation to invest heavily throughout the world. And this, in turn, further assists the process of globalization. Thus, we might say that government's most important new role is getting out of the way!

Prior to 1982 the world's information infrastructure and government's role in it is simply described. The United States, as we have seen, was dominated by AT&T, the vertically integrated network manager that controlled the local loop, long distance, switching and transmission gear, and customer premises equipment. Legal controversies that ultimately upset the system had erupted in long-distance and customer premises equipment. As we will see in Chapter 8, the computer-communications interface provided a particularly vexing set of issues. Associated with AT&T were a large number of local-loop carriers ranging in size from GTE, a giant in its own right with major operations in such rapidly expanding areas as southern California and the west coast of Florida, to very small carriers such as the Ragland Telephone Company of Ragland, Alabama, and the Valley Telephone Company of Baggs, Wyoming. Texas alone had more than sixty such companies not affiliated with AT&T, GTE, or any other large holding company.[20] Regulating this cooperating structure were the F.C.C. and the various state regulatory commissions.

The systems that prevailed in most of the rest of the world in 1982 were quite different, but similarly straightforward. Canada was a hybrid system consisting of privately owned carriers in the most populous parts of the country and government ownership in the prairie provinces. A national administrative commission regulated the private monopolies. But the model that prevailed in most of the rest of the world was different again. A government monopoly typically owned and operated the post office and telephone and telegraph systems (hence the acronym PTT). Typifying the extent to which the system was deeply ingrained and universally accepted, the West German constitution (Grundgesetz) of 1949 proclaimed that the new federal government would be regulator, operator, and provider of the telecommunications infrastructure. Thus, a constitutional amendment was required to change the structure.[21] In each case the telephone monopoly's equipment was supplied by one or a few privately owned companies. In the case of the larger nations, such as West Germany or France, the equipment suppliers were frequently national firms. For example, Siemens and AEG were the largest equipment suppliers in Germany, while Thomson-CSF (nationalized by the Socialist government in 1981) was the dominant such firm in France.[22] While, of course, less developed countries did not have telecommunications equipment manufacturing industries, the pattern remained the same: a publicly owned operating monopoly and a few favored suppliers.

Another way of appreciating how deeply ingrained this system was is to consider it historically. Germany provides a good example. The German public monopoly system can be traced back to 1505 when the Hapsburg emperor Maximilian granted exclusive mail-carrying privileges to the Italian Taxis family in exchange for a large share of the profits. The system's profitability was greater than expected and led to a corollary policy that stemmed from the monopoly grant—vigorous protection from others who sought to operate rival systems. In 1614 Prussia made the next important policy development by establishing a state-run monopoly. Those persons who instituted the Prussian system made no bones about their fundamental intention of using the system to generate revenues for the state's activities. When the telegraph came into use in the nineteenth century, it was integrated into the overall publicly owned communications system, a decision reinforced by the new device's military importance. When the telephone was invented in 1876, it, too, was incorporated in the public communications systems. In 1892 the Telegraph Act was amended, guaranteeing that the Telegraph Administration would exclusively provide telephone service. As we noted, these systems became known as PTTs in view of their three major activities.[23] Before examining the pressures and incentives for the changes to privatization and competition in Germany and elsewhere, it should be observed that residential consumer dissatisfaction was clearly not a factor. In fact, the trade unions, social-democratic parties, and consumer organizations resisted the transformation. Further, we should not underestimate the sheer force of inertia and tradition that would make it difficult to radically reform centuries-old institutional arrangements.

Again, Germany is the most instructive case to illustrate the forces arrayed against the dramatic transformation. As late as 1985 the *Economist* reported, "The Bundespost has no plans, secret or not, to deregulate anything. Its near absolute control over German telecommunications is secured by constitutional protection, by its position as West Germany's biggest employer (with 500,000 employees, about 200,000 of them in telecoms) and government cash cow ... and by its administrative independence."[24] Supervision was extremely light and telecommunications revenues were deployed to subsidize, in part, the postal operation's enormous losses. While it was true that telephone rental charges were twice those of Britain's, Gerd Tanzer, Bundespost's telecommunications chief, nonetheless confidently asserted that there was a social consensus in favor of retaining the publicly owned monopoly system. And yet later it was transformed.

Although each nation has its distinctive history, Japan—with the world's second largest economy and telecommunications system—provides a good illustration of the forces leading to change as well as those whose objections had to be overcome. The Japanese telecommunications system can be traced back to 1869, when the Ministry of Technology established telegraph service between Tokyo and Yokohama.[25] The progress that had been achieved until World War II was reversed by the devastation visited on Japan in that conflict; Osaka, for example, had only 51 percent of the telephones installed in March 1951 that it had in 1940. The postwar government's response was the Telecommunications Law of 1953 and the Nippon Telegraph and Telephone Law of 1952. The effect of these laws was to create a government corporation with a monopoly over domestic telecommunications. The new corporation (NTT), although government owned, was modeled on AT&T. Early on, NTT established major research facilities patterned on Bell Labs, which laid much of the groundwork for Japan's widespread transistor technology as well as making important advances in memory chips, electronic switching, and data processing.[26] Like AT&T, NTT could argue that tampering with its structure might destroy an invaluable research resource. Additionally, the new public-monopoly corporation was assumed to be more efficient than competitive or smaller-scale enterprises, and its monopoly status would prevent wasteful duplicative capital investment that could be deployed more effectively elsewhere. The Diet desired the creation of a nationwide system that would reach the remotest parts of the nation at uniformly low local rates. A government monopoly was conceived as the best mechanism to attain these results.

On April 1, 1985, Japan began the process of transforming its telecommunications system. NTT began transforming itself into a private company and liberalization, previously restricted to peripheral markets, began. United States trade pressures intended to open the equipment market played a role. But it must be remembered that Japan, an export-led economy, was in the forefront of establishing the global economy. Thus, Japan's fear of United States trade retaliation was a recognition of the new global economy as was the American pressure on Japan. But more important was the role of the Ministry of International Trade and Industry (MITI), the powerful government agency that plays a caretaker role for Japan's export industries. MITI's planners strongly urged further deregulation of data communications so that private carriers could offer innovative new services to Japanese firms that would assure their competitiveness in the global economy. MITI officials held that the NTT monopoly was delaying the necessary integration of computers and telecommunications without which Japanese firms, especially in the leading electronics sector, would fall behind in foreign markets. NTT, it was also noted, was becoming grossly inefficient, generating far less revenue per employee than the Bell operating companies. Additionally, since NTT purchased more than one-half of its equipment from only four domestic firms, both potential foreign and domestic suppliers joined in the push for NTT privatization and liberalization. Further, large and small Japanese firms, including electronics manufacturers, computer firms, trading companies, and transport companies sought the opportunity to compete in the potentially lucrative telecommunications network market. Even some NTT executives saw the benefits of competition to their company, especially in the provision of newer, more lucrative services.[27]

The change in Japan did not, of course, instantly create a competitive market. Much resistance remained (and remains). Opponents can still place roadblocks in the path. The important message, however, is that the general direction of telecommunications policy did an about-face, just as it had in the United States and the United Kingdom. The basic theme of the increasing importance of modern telecommunications to the competitiveness of local business interests in the global marketplace was, once again, a central one. Without the full complement of telecommunications services that a competitive environment could provide, national competitiveness in virtually every industrial and service sector would be severely handicapped. Accordingly, governmental actors got behind the movement to privatize and liberalize. Precisely the same considerations applied in the nations of Western Europe, although (with the exception of the United Kingdom) their wake-up call came much later than in the United States and Japan.

The principal agency of change in Western Europe has been the institutions of the European Union, which bind together economic and social policies of France, Germany, Italy, the United Kingdom, and smaller Western European nations. The documents produced under the auspices of the European Union's associated institutions are particularly explicit in asserting the themes mentioned in this section. A 1993 European Commission white paper (published in 1994), prepared at the request of the European Council to design a medium-term strategy for growth, competitiveness, and employment, gloomily acknowledged that in the prior twenty years Europe's rate of growth sharply declined, unemployment steadily rose from cycle to cycle, the investment rate had decreased, and, most importantly, the EU's competitive position in relation to North America and Japan had worsened in regard to research and development, innovation, and the introduction of new products.[28] At the heart of the white paper's conclusions was the observation that the information revolution that the world is undergoing is as radical a transformation as the industrial revolution. Acknowledging that the United States has taken a strong lead in the transformation, the white paper concluded, "This issue is a crucial aspect in the survival or decline of Europe. . . . It can provide an answer to the new needs of European societies: communications networks within companies; widespread teleworking; widespread access to scientific and leisure databases; development of preventative health care and home medicine for the elderly."[29]

The European Council at its December 1993 meeting fully endorsed the white paper, commissioning a report on the information society to be prepared by a group of prominent persons. The report, popularly called the Bangemann Report after Martin Bangemann, its chairperson, provided concrete recommendations for action. Its most important recommendation was that the EU should place primary faith in market mechanisms to carry the member states into the information age. Accordingly, it strenuously urged the EU and its member states to strike down the monopoly or deeply entrenched positions of the PTTs and their respective cozy relationships with favored national equipment suppliers. Finally, the Bangemann Report called for the adoption of common member nation technical standards and government regulations. Notably missing from the report was an explicit call for privatization of the country networks, but the implication was unmistakable in view of the other proposals.[30]

The Bangemann Report was submitted to the European Council for its meeting in Corfu in June 1994. The Council essentially endorsed the report's conclusion, emphasizing that primary responsibility for modernization and expansion of the networks lies with the private sector. The roles of the EU and the member states were conceived as providing encouragement and a stable, predictable regulatory framework. Referred back to the Commission pursuant to European Union law, the Commission released its crucial Communication to the Council and the European Parliament on July 19, 1994. Once again, the general conclusions contained in the prior documents were endorsed.[31] Indeed, the Commission called for accelerating the rate of ongoing liberalization. The document noted that the Commission had already taken an active role in liberalizing telecommunications competition under articles 85, 86, and 90 of the 1957 Treaty Establishing the European Communities (popularly called the Treaty of Rome) and amendments. Finally, the document generally reached the same conclusions as the previously cited documents had, noting that "The information society promises to create new jobs, enhanced social solidarity . . . and cultural diversity," but warning that "Its advent is likely to generate some fears, which should not be underestimated."[32]

The next step in the European process was the production of a green paper on telecommunications infrastructure, which the Commission's July 19, 1994, report requested. (A green paper is a formal Commission document with recommendations submitted to the Council and the European Parliament.) In the strongest statement made to that time, the Commission, in remarks worth quoting extensively, warned:

> Everyone is busy preparing for and adapting to the challenges of the new information age. It also includes the USA, Canada and Japan—Europe's principal economic competitors. The nature of that economic competition itself is also changing. To compete effectively today, one must have the means to access, to process, manipulate, stock and produce information quickly and effectively. One must also have good access to markets and to customers all around the globe. It is therefore vital that Europe places itself at the forefront of this inevitable drive towards a global information society.
>
> Telecommunications infrastructures will form the fundamental platform upon which Europe's society and economy will depend in the decades to come.[33]

And what is true of Europe is true of the rest of the world. The inevitable outcome is to strengthen globalization, in which transnational organizations will play an increasingly important role.

International Telecommunications Organizations

Soon after Samuel Morse successfully sent the first telegraph message between Washington, D.C., and Baltimore in 1844, the device was adopted in other nations. Because the telegraph was frequently used for military and political purposes, each user nation employed a different system and a distinctive code intended to safeguard the security of its messages. Accordingly, messages had to be transcribed, translated, and passed over to national authorities at borders. As the commercial use of the telegraph expanded, it was obvious that this system was unsatisfactory and wasteful. On May 17, 1865, the first breakthrough to international standards occurred when the International Telegraph Convention was signed by twenty countries and the International Telegraph Union was created to deal with subsequent issues and later technologies. Thus, in 1885 the International Telegraph Union began the task of drafting legislation concerning the telephone. In 1906 the first International Radiotelegraph Convention was signed. The original regulations have been revised and amended many times.[34]

As the power of telecommunications to easily travel the globe became a reality with the advent of commercial radio in the 1920s, the establishment of standards became a more technical one, requiring the creation of a separate international organization to deal with these increasingly complex issues. Accordingly, in 1927 the International Radio Consultative Committee (CCIR) was created. Together with parallel telegraph and telephone standards committees, the CCIR became responsible for coordinating technical studies, for testing and measurement, and for drawing up international standards. In 1927, the first fruits of CCIR's efforts were borne when frequency bands were allocated to the various radio services in use, such as maritime, broadcasting, and amateur. The rationale of CCIR's allocations scheme was to assign frequencies based on the technical characteristics of each service. Nevertheless, standard setting, although couched in the highly technical language of electrical engineering, sometimes conceals bitter political or intercorporate disputes.

Before continuing with the discussion of the development of international telecommunications institutions, one of the most important tasks of which is the development of standards, it will be useful to digress and look more closely at the conception of standards. Paul A. David has devised what many scholars view as the best classification system for telecommunications. He proposes three categories of standards, each of which raises different sets of issues: reference, minimum attribute, and compatibility.[35] *Reference standards* are those dealing with weights and measures. If one thinks that issues concerning reference standards are only technical, consider, for a moment, the political and economic ramifications if Congress proposed that the United States should adopt the metric system. David's second category is *minimum attribute standards,* by which he means minimum requirements before a product or service can be deemed acceptable, such as minimum tensile strength of a wire. *Compatibility standards* are those that allow a part to function within a system. For example, modems must be compatible with both the telephone networks and the computers that send and receive data. There are, of course, a variety of such standards that must be compatible with other parts of a network. Again, it is sometimes important for a new device to be compatible with older products. For example, color television signals, when introduced, had to be compatible with black and white television sets. In each situation the stakes can be high, and as telecommunications has become increasingly international, disputes are resolved at international levels.

With the paramount issue of standards in mind, we can proceed with the discussion of international telecommunications institutions, picking up with the important 1932 Madrid Conference, at which the various conventions were consolidated and the decision made to establish the International Telecommunications Union (ITU), effective January 1, 1934. The ITU assumed international jurisdiction over all forms of communication, recognizing their increasing interconnectability. The 1930s were a time of world disintegration, however, so the ITU did little until after the conclusion of World War II. In 1947 the ITU became a specialized agency of the United Nations. Among its initial measures was the establishment of the International Frequency Registration Board (IFRB), the task of which was to allocate the increasingly complex frequency spectrum among the various services. In 1956 advances in telecommunications spectrum use led to the establishment of the International Telephone and Telegraph Consultative Committee (CCITT) to deal with standards issues. The CCIR continued in existence, and its efforts were expected to be coordinated with CCITT.

The next year saw a dramatic event that set in motion a series of developments, eventually leading to the creation of the International Telecommunications Satellite Organization (Intelsat), the next important international organization. In that year the Soviet Union launched Sputnik I, the first artificial satellite. While the Soviet Union led the way into space, the United States soon overtook it in commercial applications. AT&T's Telestar satellite was launched in July 1962, and in April 1965 Early Bird, the first communications satellite in geosynchronous orbit (appearing relatively motionless from the earth) was launched. Based on the theories of British physicist Arthur Clarke, the central discovery was that three satellites, placed in a geosynchronous orbit 120 degrees apart, could deliver communications to the entire world.[36] While some satellites must orbit over the poles to provide communications to higher latitudes, the geostationary satellites do not move relative to the earth, thereby permitting antennae on the ground to remain stationary.

Responding to the momentous potential of communications satellites, Intelsat was created in 1964, largely through United States initiative. The preliminary step was the United States' creation of Communications Satellite Corporation (Comsat), pursuant to the Communications Satellite Act of 1962. After a bitter legislative battle over the issue of public or private ownership, Congress and President John Kennedy devised a compromise. Comsat was established as a corporation half-owned by carriers such as AT&T and half-owned by shareholders. Subsequently, the private carriers sold their shares and relinquished their right to select three of the corporation's nine directors. Three other directors were selected by the government and three by the shareholders. Comsat's initial mission was to help organize Intelsat, which occurred in August 1964 when eleven developed nations signed an interim agreement. Intelsat's membership was subsequently greatly expanded to about 130 members, and the United States's influence was diminished. Intelsat membership is open to any ITU member, but costs and revenues are based on each nation's investment, which in turn is based on percentage of use during the preceding six months. The organization began operating in 1965 when the United States launched Early Bird, the first commercial communications satellite, the development costs of which were borne by Comsat. In 1969, as Intelsat added satellites, it had established global coverage for international telecommunications.[37]

While Intelsat's major market was intended to be and still is overseas telephone calls, it has enlarged its market to offer other services to its members as well as other countries. These include the transmission of live international broadcasts; transcontinental airline booking; secure international banking transactions; international simultaneous remote printing of newspapers, such as the *Financial Times*; digital services that can offer integrated voice, data, telex, fax, and videoconferencing; and back-up service in cases of other service outages. Typically, a carrier, such as AT&T, orders Intelsat services through Comsat, while in other nations a carrier was required to go through the national PTT. Thus, at its formation and for years afterward, Intelsat was a monopolist in the provision of international telecommunications transmitted through satellite. Such an arrangement was, of course, to be expected in an organization set up when national telecommunications was either provided by a state-owned or private monopoly.

A combination of technology and the movement toward privatization and liberalization began to undermine Intelsat's monopoly status. The basic Intelsat agreement contained a provision that opened the door to international satellite service outside the Intelsat framework. In 1983 two American companies, Orion Satellite Corporation and International Satellite, Inc., applied to the F.C.C. requesting the opportunity to launch and operate independent commercial satellite systems linking North America and Europe. The issue of competition was now clearly on the agenda since the two firms intended to attract customers that had been doing such business with Intelsat. Because of the Intelsat agreement's implications, the Departments of State and Commerce requested the F.C.C. to delay proceedings pending the results of an interagency review. Nevertheless, the lucrative potential of international satellite communications attracted still other applicants seeking F.C.C. authorization to provide similar services. Comsat uniformly opposed the F.C.C. granting such authority on the ground that it would violate the Communications Satellite Act of 1962 and the Intelsat agreements. Intelsat took the unusual step of intervening in a domestic United States proceeding, essentially arguing that granting any such application would be inconsistent with Article XIV of the Intelsat agreements by substantially impairing the economic viability of the organization.[38]

But as we have seen in other contexts, 1984 was not a propitious year in the United States for restricting competition. The tides were clearly turning. Accordingly, President Ronald Reagan signed in November 1984 a Presidential Determination that alternative satellite systems are "required in the national interest" within the meaning of the Communications Satellite Act. At the same time the Departments of State and Commerce informed the F.C.C. of the criteria by which satellite competition could be furthered without impairing the United States's obligations to Intelsat. Essentially, new competitors would be required to provide long-lease service and could not connect into the public switched message network. Further, foreign authorities would consult with the United States to assure technical compatibility and avoid economic harm. The scenario that would inevitably follow was similar to the one by which MCI originally sought a niche market and gradually became a full-scale competitor of AT&T. And just as AT&T resisted what it perceived to be continuing encroachment, Comsat played much the same role in connection with international satellite communications. Thus, Comsat fought Pan Am Sat's application on the ground that its proposed international service in North, Central, and South America, the Caribbean, and Spain would cause substantial economic harm.[39]

The second prong of the attack on Intelsat's monopoly is fiber optics, over which it enjoys no jurisdiction. Fiber optics began to compete with satellites, converging into one market. Consider the advances in optical fiber technology and their implications for the future. TAT-1, the first transatlantic telephone cable, was built in 1956 and had a thirty-six-circuit capacity. (Previously high-frequency radio had been used for transatlantic voice communication.) The Early Bird satellite decisively outclassed telephone cable with its 480 telephone channels, compared with the 256 then carried by telephone cable. Additionally, satellites covered a much greater area. Thus, until the advent of fiber optics it appeared satellites would dominate international communications. In December 1988 TAT-8, the first fiber-optic transoceanic cable, became operational. Owned by thirty firms, including AT&T, MCI, British Telecom, and France Télécom, the optical cable had a capacity of 37,800 voice channels. TAT-8 was only the first of many such optical cables laid on the floors of the Atlantic and Pacific Oceans. Signaling the new competitive challenge to Intelsat, AT&T immediately reduced its transatlantic rates when TAT-8 opened. Not only did bandwidth costs drop, but line errors decreased and fiber optics overcame the time-delay problem of satellites.[40] The advance of fiber optics from the opening of TAT-8 was rapid; for example, by late 1995 optical links carried 65 percent of the United Kingdom's international connections. TAT-13 became operational in fall 1996. TAT-12 and TAT-13, owned by forty-eight carriers (linking the United States and Europe), have the capacity to carry more than one million telephone conversations at the same time.[41]

By 1991 it was clear that technology had forced the advent of competition. On November 27, 1991, the State Department and the Commerce Department's National Telecommunications and Information Administration fully endorsed eliminating interconnection restrictions for Intelsat's satellite competitors by 1997. The F.C.C. endorsed the interconnection principle in 1992, pointing out that the delay until 1997 would allow Intelsat a reasonable amount of time to adjust to the new competition. By late 1994, Intelsat's officials saw the clear handwriting on the wall. Irving Goldstein, its director general, proclaimed, "The spread of deregulation, the corporatization and privatization of national telecommunications providers, the growth of competitive industries, and the proliferation of new satellite companies have created greater choice in the marketplace, and, therefore, greater competition for market share. In light of these dynamic changes, Intelsat is transforming itself in order to remain competitive."[42] And looming as still another threat is the Internet (which we will look at in Chapter 8).[43]

Completing the Circuit: Alliances

The convergence of the political trends toward liberalization and privatization in communications, albeit at different rates throughout the world, globalization of the world economy (thanks significantly to telecommunications), new competitors, and new technologies have reshaped the global market for telecommunications. Industrial and service companies that conduct transactions throughout the world have an obvious incentive to reduce their communications costs, assure a high standard of service, and obtain a wide variety of information services. The preferred solution for large companies is one-stop shopping, in which a company enters into a single contract for all or most of its telecommunications needs. Consider the experience of Grand Metropolitan, a major British consumer-goods manufacturer: "Instead of haggling one-by-one with hundreds of the world's local telephone companies, Grand Met is turning its entire global voice and data network over to Concert, a joint venture of BT and MCI."[44] In general, companies that do business in many locations—an increasingly widespread phenomenon—have provided the impetus for the establishment of global communications networks. And, of course, it follows that these large consumers of telecommunications services desire intense competition between multiple providers.

The result of global companies' demand has been telephone company creation of a complex web of cross-border agreements, mergers, external growth, and so-called strategic alliances. Some of these arrangements have failed, while others have succeeded. Some arrangements have increased the number of their participants, while others have maintained the same number of participants as they had at the times of their creation. The most important global arrangements are those led by the two major American long-distance carriers, AT&T and Sprint, and by British Telecom PLC, which acquired MCI in 1996 and 1997. But before looking at these alliances, we will look more closely at what "strategic alliance" conventionally means and the important objectives, in addition to satisfying customer needs, that these arrangements serve. As we explore these issues, it is important to bear in mind that there may be several reasons two or more firms enter into such an arrangement. For example, two or more firms may collaborate not only because this provides a better opportunity to secure the business of a large customer, but also because technology sharing may benefit both telecommunications providers.

A strategic alliance "links specific facets of the businesses of two or more firms. At its core, this link is a trading partnership that enhances the effectiveness of the competitive strategies of the participating firms by providing for the mutually beneficial trade of technologies, skills or products based on them."[45] Thus, strategic alliances are neither mergers of two or more firms nor overseas subsidiaries. Nor are they agreements between firms that are country specific; their ambition is to circle the globe or large portions of it. Obviously, strategic alliances between potential rivals are made with the expectation (not always fulfilled) that the marginal benefit from cooperation will outweigh the marginal cost from conflict that inevitably arises when two or more different corporate cultures are blended. Based on a wealth of experience, the chief executive of Corning Glass offered four criteria for the success of a strategic alliance: compatible strategy and culture, comparable contribution, comparable strengths, and no conflict of interest. He emphasized that, in addition to these threshold factors, luck and determination were also required.[46]

In the telecommunications area strategic alliances as well as cross-border alliances can occur for a variety of reasons in addition to meeting the enlarged needs of customers. First, they can be driven by a disparity in the factors of production. For example, in telecommunications equipment manufacture, one partner may have large amounts of surplus cash while the other may be strapped for cash but have access to low-cost, efficient labor. Second, the huge sunken costs of capital equipment may create vast economies of scale so that the linkup can greatly enlarge the customer base over which costs may be amortized. Third, two or more firms may lower their individual research and development costs by collaborating. Fourth, the two or more firms may have complementary technologies or skills. For example, one firm may have great strengths in marketing while the other may have great technological prowess. Fifth, there may be regulatory or legal barriers that restrict one firm from operating effectively or at all in another country or region. An alliance is the answer. For example, Canada's Telecom Act requires that facilities-based carriers must have 80 percent Canadian directors and Canadians must own 80 percent of the voting shares. Sixth, even without formal barriers to entry, one firm may find it difficult to operate in another country or region because of the cozy business relationships between national companies that have been established over many years. For example, as early as 1983 AT&T entered into separate alliances with Olivetti and Philips (the Dutch electronics company), two giant European firms, to market telecommunications equipment in Europe. Both alliances were intended to facilitate AT&T's entry into the European market, in which it had little experience.[47] Parenthetically, both of these early strategic alliances were dissolved because they failed to live up to their partners' expectations. Seventh, strategic alliances can be driven by market-share considerations. An alliance, for example, may reduce the number of potential competitors or increase the overall market shares of the two or more partners in a nation or region. Finally, strategic alliances may be defensive in nature. If your rival does it, you must do the same in order to compete effectively.

Canada, whose cross-border long-distance traffic with the United States is the largest in the world, provides an example of some of these considerations in practice. Initially, as we observed, Canada restricts foreign ownership quite severely; many countries do. Nevertheless, in September 1992 MCI entered into a strategic alliance with Stentor, the major Canadian long-distance company. In January 1993 AT&T entered into a parallel alliance with Unitel, the second largest Canadian long-distance carrier. Inevitably, Sprint then allied with Call-Net, another Canadian long-distance carrier, in August 1993. Each of these alliances were within the permitted level of voting shares allowed to non-Canadians. Each alliance was based on other considerations as well as market ones. Stentor acquired MCI's intelligent network software, which could enable it to develop new services. Unitel obtained switches, transmission equipment, and software in exchange for AT&T's 20 percent share of the company. Additionally, Unitel was able to appoint senior AT&T operating personnel and was provided access to AT&T's extraordinary research and development prowess. Call-Net received the rights to Sprint's network and billing technology as well as other Sprint products. Additionally, Call-Net could undertake marketing programs using the name "Sprint Canada."[48]

As the strategic-alliance structure developed, by late 1996 three such groups predominated among the many that have been formed. The oldest of these is Concert Communications, the members of which were BT and MCI. Announced in June 1993, it allowed BT to purchase 20 percent of MCI's shares and was intended to offer customers a full complement of voice, video, data, and multimedia services. Analysts saw BT's cash investment in MCI as quid pro quo for MCI's marketing prowess in obtaining global corporate customers and technical skills. At the time of the investment MCI was expected to use the new cash to make other alliances and acquisitions in the cable, television, cellular, and multimedia industries in the United States and elsewhere. Most importantly, the two companies intended to create a seamless telecommunications service throughout the world with one-stop billing and ordering for its customers. Notwithstanding AT&T's regulatory objections, the United States Justice Department approved the agreement in June 1994. The Concert arrangement did not preclude BT from establishing other alliances in Europe and Asia. On November 4, 1996, BT-MCI's ties moved even closer when BT agreed to acquire MCI.[49]

The second major alliance, dominated by AT&T, is very different in structure from Concert. Called World Partners, it is a complex arrangement consisting, first, of Unisource, a European consortium of Dutch, Swedish, and Swiss PTTs. Unisource is linked with AT&T and Unitel as well as other carriers in Asia, most importantly KDD in Japan. The alliance between AT&T and Unisource, which was preceded by some of AT&T's Asian alliances, completed AT&T's global system in June 1994. Again, the underlying idea was to create seamless, one-stop global shopping for telecom services. The arrangement was to some extent defensive on AT&T's part. John Finnegan, AT&T's international-alliances vice president, conceded that AT&T would have lost key corporate customers if it had not constructed a strategic alliance that embraced Europe, North America, and Asia.[50]

Different from both AT&T's and British Telecom–MCI's ventures is the alliance into which Sprint has entered. Originally called Phoenix (later Global One), it includes France Télécom and Deutsche Telekom, the PTTs in their respective countries. Each of the PTTs agreed to take a 10 percent stake in Sprint. Unlike the other alliances, Phoenix was greeted with considerable dismay by analysts and the stock market on the ground that Sprint's aggressive corporate culture could not be blended with the stolid PTTs that, unlike BT, were still state-owned at the time of the alliance's formation. The alliance was conceived largely as defensive on Sprint's part. Nevertheless, Sprint's chairman was extremely enthusiastic, envisioning worldwide voice, data, and video transmission services for multinational companies, as well as international consumer services, such as calling cards. Sprint received a huge cash injection while its PTT partners received access to the world's largest market. Again, American and European regulators and antitrust authorities eventually approved the alliance.[51]

There are many other alliances, mergers, and arrangements as we move irrepressibly forward into the global economy and, of course, there will be yet more. No industry has made more rapid strides in this direction than telecommunications, beginning in 1984 when the industry was largely a collection of state enterprises that did not reach beyond their borders. Tele-communications has been both a cause and effect of the trends that we examined in this chapter. But as the three grand alliances illustrate, the rest of the world appears to be mirroring the American model in the telecommunications sector. One conclusion is clear as the firms form and re-form alliances. The major players will attempt to offer virtually all services and will employ all transmission systems that are economically viable. Because mistakes can be very costly, each alliance will attempt to cover all bases in the converging international hypercommunications marketplace.

7

The Wireless Revolution

The Origins of Wireless

Less than twenty-eight years after Samuel F.B. Morse invented a practical telegraph in 1837 and thirteen years before Alexander Graham Bell patented the telephone in 1876, James Clerk Maxwell, the greatest nineteenth-century physicist, presented a paper that would revolutionize the world. Addressing the Royal Society, Maxwell presented a theory showing that electromagnetic fields could be propagated through space as well as through conductors. Moreover, they could travel as waves with the speed of light (186,252 miles per second). In his view, light itself was electromagnetic radiation within a certain range of wavelengths. It followed that it was theoretically possible to propagate light as well as electromagnetic waves of other wavelengths. It was not until the experiments of Heinrich Hertz in 1887–88 that electromagnetic waves were generated, detected, and measured. Hertz, however, was concerned only about scientific discovery, eschewing any interest in the economic implications of his research. Based on Hertz's research, the English physicist Oliver Lodge undertook the next step, demonstrating in 1894 an effective and practical system of wireless transmission and reception. But Lodge, too, failed to see the commercial possibilities—although he later did participate in such ventures. The early technology of wireless was then in place.[1] Physicists would continue to investigate the theoretical basis of radiation; but the theory of the electromagnetic spectrum was now ready, and the world awaited the insights and business acumen that would develop the practical application of radio waves.

Guglielmo Marconi was the visionary who saw the commercial opportunities of radio. In 1896, at the age of twenty-two, he was granted the first radio patent and soon demonstrated that it had a practical application for ship navigation. But the crucial step occurred in December 1901 when Marconi transmitted the letter *s* in Morse code from Cornwall, England, across the Atlantic Ocean to Newfoundland. Confounding many critics Marconi's effort demonstrated, first, that radio waves, transmitted without the aid of wires, produced and detected by electrical circuits, could travel great distances. Second, he showed that such waves could be translated into intelligible information.[2] Marconi's success led to the postulation of the ionosphere (or Kennelly-Heaviside layer), atmospheric layers of ions that refract waves back to earth. Marconi's success and the commercial possibilities it opened induced many other inventors and entrepreneurs to focus their efforts on radio. Among the most important set of discoveries associated with inventor Lee de Forest was the development of vacuum tubes that could be used in voice-frequency amplifiers, among other purposes.

It is a long way from transmitting the letter *s* in Morse code to transmitting music and intelligible speech. AT&T was to play a major role in this progress because amplification, modulation, and other technical problems were conceived as common to wireless and long-distance wire communication, to which AT&T had become committed. In fact, when Alexander Graham Bell, seated in New York, replicated his famous statement to Thomas Watson, seated in San Francisco, "Mr. Watson, come here, I want you," a modified version of de Forest's vacuum tube was used to fulfill modulation and amplification functions. Nevertheless, early on AT&T did not seriously consider that wireless would become a serious competitor to wire communication for point-to-point conversation because of the ease with which third parties could eavesdrop on private conversations. Accordingly, wireless was conceived as a supplement to wire in point-to-point communication. Additionally, transmitting long-distance radio entailed enormous power requirements compared with wire communication, imposing major economic as well as technological difficulties.[3]

The Rise of Radio and Television

Nevertheless, broadcasting and point-to-point communications across areas that wires could not practically traverse were sufficiently potentially large markets to encourage considerable research in radio. There was still a pot of gold to be had. Pittsburgh, Pennsylvania, was the home of two major developments that led to broadcasting becoming a major new industry in the 1920s. In 1906 Reginald Fessenden of the University of Pittsburgh developed a continuous-wave generator in which voice currents were superimposed on a carrier wave. (Continuous waves are those generated by pure tones.) Demodulation would, therefore, allow the sending voice to be received and understood. On Christmas Eve, 1906, Fessenden broadcast a music and speech program that was picked up by several ships in the North

Atlantic. Capitalizing on Fessenden's work, Frank Conrad, the engineer in charge of Westinghouse's wireless research during World War I, innocently began broadcasting phonograph records in the Pittsburgh area during spring 1920. Soon, a growing number of listeners began making musical requests. Next, Conrad devised a regular schedule for broadcasting records. Exhausting his personal collection, Conrad borrowed additional titles from a local record store in exchange for which the store's name and location were mentioned on the air.

The commercial possibilities became clear when the record store discovered that its sales of recordings played on the air far exceeded those that were not. Part of the explanation for this development was that a local department store advertised amateur radio sets for ten dollars in Pittsburgh newspapers. Horne's Department Store had set up a demonstration receiver in the store, which led to great sales success. Some of the lessons of these events were not lost on Westinghouse, Conrad's employer, which had been looking for a way to enter the wireless business. Accordingly, Westinghouse began operating a station in East Pittsburgh on November 2, 1920. Westinghouse's objective at that time was to sell nationally radio receivers that it would manufacture. KDKA, the station, was seen as an adjunct to the manufacturing enterprise. Even though from a contemporary perspective the economic potential of radio advertising was another lesson that could have been drawn from Conrad's experience, the culture of early 1920s America would have viewed such an effort as an affront to privacy.[4] Nevertheless, KDKA ushered in the 1920s radio boom.

Westinghouse was not to play the dominant role in shaping the structure of American broadcasting, the nature of government supervision, and its gradual complete divorce from wire communications into a discrete market. Not until the end of World War II would wireless technology become important again in point-to-point communication. And while AT&T attained the dominant position in wire communication, three networks presiding over a large number of affiliated radio stations would dominate radio, although not as fully as AT&T controlled wire communications. Entertainment, broadly defined, would become the principal purpose of radio. Stations would be privately owned, in contrast to the European system of public ownership. The most important stations would be tied together into nationwide networks. Radio advertising would become the stations' and networks' principal source of revenue. While rate regulation became the most important government activity in the realm of wire communication, there would be no rate regulation in the radio market. Rather, licensing would become the crucial activity in that market. Radio and television broadcasting would grow into enormous businesses with vast audiences. All of these developments occurred within the short period between KDKA coming on the air and Franklin D. Roosevelt's assumption of the presidency in 1933. And while many individuals played roles in shaping the exploding radio business, two were paramount: David Sarnoff and Herbert Hoover.

Sarnoff's life is the quintessential rags-to-riches story. Born in a dismal Jewish ghetto in Russia in February 1891, he emigrated to the United States in 1900. Almost immediately Sarnoff began work selling Yiddish-language newspapers, while in his remaining time studying a variety of topics and mastering English. By 1906, his father's imminent death ended his education at the eighth-grade level and forced him to become the chief breadwinner for his family. An error Sarnoff made in applying for a job changed his life and the history of American wireless communication as well. Instead of applying for an office-boy job at a newspaper as he intended, Sarnoff mistakenly applied for similar employment at the Commercial Cable Company located in the same building. Offered a job, Sarnoff soon rose to become a Morse-code operator. After, moving to the American Marconi Company as an office boy, Sarnoff remained with the company and its successor, the Radio Corporation of America, for more than sixty years.[5]

Sarnoff rose rapidly in American Marconi. His energy, his vision, and not least his friendship with Guglielmo Marconi assured this. As early as 1915, when he was assistant traffic manager, he wrote, "I have in mind a plan of development which would make radio a 'household utility' in the same sense as the piano or phonograph. . . . The receiver can be designed in the form of a simple 'radio music box' and arranged for several different wave lengths."[6] The Woodrow Wilson administration, which had seized control of radio during World War I, was anxious that an American firm, not a British subsidiary, should control radio in the United States. Hence it arranged for General Electric and other wireless patent holders to create RCA in 1919, which in turn would purchase American Marconi from its British parent. When the broadcasting boom began it took the various RCA shareholder firms, including AT&T, by surprise. When AT&T disposed of its RCA stock and established several radio stations in competition with the RCA group, a complex battle between the two groups ensued. The end result was that AT&T bowed out of radio in 1926, selling its stations to RCA.[7] At that point RCA was well on its way to constructing a network. The National Broadcasting Company (NBC) was established in 1926 and reorganized into two semiautonomous networks (Red and Blue) in 1927. By 1930 Westinghouse and General Electric had relinquished control of NBC and in 1932, pursuant to an antitrust decree, it became a wholly owned subsidiary of RCA. The Blue network was sold in 1943 under pressure from the Federal Communications Commission and was renamed the American Broadcasting Company (ABC) in 1945.

The final step in setting up the basic structure of the American broadcasting industry was the creation in 1927 of the Columbia Broadcasting System (CBS). Several stations excluded from the NBC networks, seeking syndicated programming that could fill their time, established the United Independent Broadcasters, which was then transformed into CBS. Just as Sarnoff dominated the affairs of NBC, William S. Paley dominated CBS from the time he bought controlling interest in September 1928. Not until 1977 did Paley step down as chief executive, having transformed CBS and its member stations into an enterprise incomparably more valuable than what he had paid for the network and its directly owned stations. While Sarnoff had a larger vision of broadcasting and far more technical knowledge than Paley, the latter's marketing strategies were extraordinarily innovative. Although AT&T had devised radio advertising in 1922, when Paley took over CBS the network's sales and techniques of advertising were greatly expanded so that it gradually became the principal source of network revenue.[8]

The most important focus of wireless communications by 1930 became AM broadcasting, and the American pattern differed sharply from that of other developed countries. The private ownership of competing networks and stations financed primarily by commercial advertising contrasted with the advertising-free publicly owned stations in other nations, where government subsidy and fees imposed on owners of radio sets (and later television sets) were the principal sources of revenue. Second, in contrast to the few stations in other nations, the United States developed a large number of independent stations, some of which became linked together in networks smaller than ABC, CBS, and NBC. Third, although wireless was employed in safety, dispatch, and a few other specialized services, the dominant use was in commercial broadcasting. Fourth, the star system that had been developed in the movies was adopted in AM radio with great success; millions of listeners week after week heard Jack Benny, Amos 'n' Andy, and other stars' shows. Fifth, as a result of telephone hookups and national advertising, the networks were able to successfully syndicate programs throughout the country.

But one of the most interesting characteristics of American broadcasting occurred because the AT&T model was rejected when that company withdrew from broadcasting.[9] Perhaps the best way to understand AT&T's concept of toll broadcasting is to compare wire communication and network broadcasting. In the former case, telephone companies distribute information (including switched) between communicating parties. The telephone company cannot censor messages or determine who can use the system, subject, of course, to the payment of fees and other moderate regulations. In contrast to telephone, radio transmission equipment was very expensive and could not be supplied to subscribers on the same basis. Thus, unlike two-way telephone usage, the radio was one-way and effectively barred would-be users from transmitting what they wanted to communicate. They could receive messages because receiving equipment, even in the primitive stage of radio, was very cheap relative to transmitting equipment. Radio, from the perspective of one seeking to communicate with others, had only half the capability of wire telephony. Instead of intercommunication, broadcasting consisted of active transmission and dumb reception. Moreover, persons controlling transmission can effectively exclude anyone they want from providing messages or can censor what is transmitted. Toll broadcasting was intended to partly redress the differences between wire and wireless. Under toll broadcasting the station sold blocks of time to purchasers who could use it in any way they saw fit, subject, of course, to prevailing canons of decency. Nothing prevented the further subdivision of time, or reselling it for that matter. AT&T envisioned a network of local stations connected by long-distance wires so that the same program could be heard simulta-neously in many places. But, unlike the present permanent system of affili-ates, such networks could be constructed on an ad hoc or temporary basis. Finally, allocations of time would be reserved for public service and cul-tural programming.

Toll broadcasting ended with AT&T's withdrawal from the industry. Instead we have had a system in which stations and, most importantly, a few networks control not only the distribution of information but its content as well. Much of the current resentment against the media elite and their control of information might have been averted if toll broadcasting had taken hold. The network system that developed in AM radio continued when the VHF monochrome television boom began its takeoff after World War II. The three networks came to dominate the new medium, with a scattering of local stations offering less popular programming in many mar-kets. And the same pattern persisted in color television after the F.C.C. ultimately resolved a bitter dispute between CBS and RCA, known as the color wars, over which system would be employed, in the latter's favor. Commercial color television broadcasting was authorized to begin in Janu-ary 1954. Sarnoff's faith in color television was not, however, justified until 1964, when at last color television sets began to sell in great numbers. From that time until the cable television explosion, the commercial system that Sarnoff envisioned from the advent of primitive commercial radio pre-vailed just as broadcasting, not point-to-point transmission, was the domi-nant use of wireless.[10] Ironically, as cellular telephony and cable television grew dramatically, wireless became more widely used in point-to-point communication, while cable began to break the long-standing network dominance.

Before turning to the point-to-point wireless market, two additional markets should be briefly examined. FM radio and UHF television, different as they are, were both expected to challenge network dominance and reduce concentration in the broadcast industry. The story of FM is a very complex and detailed one. Major Edwin H. Armstrong, a brilliant engineer and holder of many telecommunications patents, more than any other person was responsible for FM's development. Originally a close friend of Sarnoff, the two men became bitter enemies as Sarnoff perceived FM as a threat to the network system that had evolved.[11] In 1945, reversing a prewar decision on where to locate the FM broadcasting band, the F.C.C. effectively wiped out the market for FM sets already made; the FM industry had to start from scratch. Coupled with network focus on AM and television and a lack of programs, FM stagnated until 1957, when at last the industry gradually took off. Not only do the three major networks provide service, but other successful networks have thrived as well. UHF television's story has not been as fortuitous. Plagued by generally poorer reception than the VHF band, UHF was unable to make major inroads in the market notwithstanding a 1963 law requiring all television receivers made thereafter to be able to receive both VHF and UHF channels. Because of UHF's poorer reception, it had generally not been able to obtain popular programming. The rise of cable systems, which created a more level playing field in reception, has aided UHF prosperity.[12]

The Rise of Spectrum Regulation

As the foregoing section shows, entertainment became the dominant use of wireless transmission after the radio boom began in the 1920s. But it was not the only use. Ship-to-ship and ship-to-shore use for safety and navigational purposes preceded the employment of radio frequencies for entertainment. World War I triggered military applications, most importantly the United States Navy's deployment of radiotelephonic communications for quick and flexible strategic and tactical decisions. That war was the first in which aviation played a major role. At the request of the U.S. Army Signal Corps, the Western Electric division of AT&T began work on the aviation radio problem in 1916. In July 1917 Western Electric was able to develop the first air-to-ground and ground-to-air transmissions (about two miles), and in August it successfully tested two-way communication between planes in flight. These wartime developments would have obvious peacetime applications, especially in commercial aviation and ocean shipping and travel. The next important application occurred in 1920 when AT&T developed a radiotelephone link between Catalina Island and the California mainland at Long Beach. Under normal circumstances, AT&T would have laid cable over this relatively short distance, but wartime conditions created a severe shortage of the requisite materials. Thus, for the first time wireless became a direct rival to wire. Notably, AT&T by that time had made substantial progress on the security issue to assure the privacy of point-to-point communication.[13]

The 1920s radio explosion coupled with the other uses found for wireless transmission and the likelihood that yet more would be found placed the issue of allocating the scarce resource of spectrum high on the agenda. Allocation through regulation was the method chosen as early as the 1912 Radio Act, when broadcasting was unknown and safety at sea was Congress's primary focus. Under that statute the secretary of commerce and labor (later secretary of commerce) was given authority to issue licenses. After the broadcasting boom began, Secretary Herbert Hoover frantically tried to deal with the rampant interference problem, but was essentially prevented from doing so by a United States Court of Appeals for the District of Columbia circuit decision holding that under the 1912 act, the secretary lacked power to refuse a license to an otherwise qualified applicant, regardless of the interference created. Fruitless attempts at voluntary allocation and other Commerce Department court losses wreaked havoc in the system as more and more stations went on the air, using any frequencies and power they chose, regardless of interference.[14]

Hoover's efforts bore fruit in the form of the Radio Act of 1927, which created the five-member Federal Radio Commission (FRC). The act provided that the agency could grant federal licenses to individuals or business organizations for limited periods of time. The statute's test for a license award or renewal was whether the applicant's service (in both the technical and nontechnical senses) would serve "the public interest, convenience and necessity." Thus, the federal government surreptitiously got into the business of assessing content and effectively censoring speech—dangerous precedents in a free society and in complete contrast to the greater freedom of the print media. Wireless, in contrast to wire communication, was not treated as a public utility. Therefore rates were not regulated. The agency was also granted the powers to classify stations and prescribe the services to be provided by each class, and to assign frequencies, power, operating hours, and location. The licensing system created in the Radio Act carried over to the Communications Act of 1934, which absorbed the telephone functions of the Interstate Commerce Commission and the FRC's wireless regulation, thus establishing a unified agency with regulatory powers over all means of communications.[15]

Before leaving the subject of radio regulation and the establishment of the FRC and the F.C.C., it is useful to compare alternative paths that might have been taken to the one constructed in 1927 (and even earlier, if one considers Secretary Hoover's previous attempts). Continuing government licensing is based on the spectrum-scarcity principle; only government can be the umpire. But a landmark article in 1959 by R.H. Coase clearly shows that even at the time of the 1927 Radio Act there was an alternative.[16] Coase argued that, prior to the act, the courts were in the process of creating a system of property rights for spectra in the same way they had created property rights for tangible property (such as land) and representational property (such as stock certificates and negotiable instruments). Had the government followed that route instead of licensing coupled with regulation, it would have auctioned off spectra in such a way that interference would have largely been avoided. A market would then have been created in spectra in the same way that land or stock certificates are subject to market operations. Coase belittled the viewpoint that spectra are physically limited in a way that land is not. After all, he asserted, the number of original Rembrandt paintings is even more limited, yet the market satisfactorily deals with their sale and use without a need for government regulation. He similarly rejected the interference argument, since one person's use of land would interfere with another's proposed use of that same land if a property system did not exist. Indeed, one of the major functions of the private legal system is to devise rules regarding interference, and one of the most important conceptions it has devised is property rights protecting exclusive use. Precisely the same principle could have been employed in the novel case of spectra during the 1920s.

Coase and others who accept this argument have concluded that a system of auctioning off spectra would have been far more efficient than a government regulatory apparatus. First, of course, there is the deadweight loss attributable to regulation and the apparatus designed to enforce it. Second, the danger of government censorship and arbitrariness is always present when an agency has broad discretionary authority. More important, a market system with property principles would lead to more efficient use of spectra, according to this view. But that was not the path taken.

The F.C.C., carrying on the work of the FRC, began early to allocate the radio spectrum. The process is a complex one. First, engineering issues must be addressed. Standards are devised for different frequency bands, the number of channels each will contain, their bandwidths, geographical locations, and power. The political part of the process constitutes assigning channels in specific locations to users for designated purposes. In this part of the process, the F.C.C. traditionally used a comparative hearing in which applicants provided evidence that reflected favorably on them, pursuant to the broad "public interest" standard. They could also provide information about an opponent's adverse factors.[17] As the 1930s proceeded the F.C.C. allocated frequencies for the so-called fixed services, including those concerned with safety (aviation, fire, police, forestry conservation, and so on), land transportation (automobile emergency, highway truck, railroad, taxicab, and so on), and industrial services (forestry, petroleum, power, motion picture, and so on). Finally, the F.C.C. allocated frequencies for amateurs' and citizens' uses. By 1954 the agency could justifiably claim that "usage now extends from the cradle to the grave. There are radio facilities for calling doctors and ambulances to the homes of expectant mothers. . . . At the omega of life, radio is utilized to dispatch vehicles in connection with death and burial."[18]

Microwave Transmission

World War II and the period immediately preceding saw research that greatly enlarged the usable spectra. As we saw in Chapter 3, the use of microwave transmission (frequencies from 1 GHz to 30 GHz) greatly expanded the available spectra and undermined AT&T's position. Such frequencies increase the communications capacity (bandwidth, or the rate at which information can be exchanged between two points in an analog network). As we saw in the *Above 890 Mc* decisions, the F.C.C. adopted a newly liberalized licensing policy for private microwave systems, rejecting the AT&T argument that such licenses should be granted only in exceptional cases. Virtually every big-business interest was, for the first time, arrayed against AT&T and the other common carriers, demanding the "free choice" to operate their private microwave systems. For example, the Automobile Manufacturers Association urgently claimed that "the highly competitive nature of the automobile industry makes it mandatory that privately operated systems be considered in comparison with common carrier charges."[19] Such arguments prevailed and the opportunities of private carriers for using the microwave portion of the spectrum were gradually expanded. In turn, as we have seen, this led to the applications of MCI and others to provide microwave service to customers, gradually leading to the offering of full-scale alternative long-distance services. Wireless transmission for point-to-point communication was on the road to becoming as important as it was in broadcasting.

The assumption that microwave would dominate long distance and find increasing application in local loops underlay policymaking in the AT&T

Modification of Final Judgment and many F.C.C. decisions. In the case of local-loop communications, there were two reasons. First, microwave required no rights-of-way, a major problem in urban areas. Second, microwave was the most flexible way to add new communications points in the least time. More generally, digital technology was being applied to microwave; indeed, one study indicated that digital microwave transmission had "exploded" in the six years prior to 1983.[20] Digital transmission essentially freed microwave of the major problems with which analog transmission was associated, including cross talk and inconsistent signal level noise. Moreover, going digital reduced short-haul (under 250 miles) costs compared with analog because of lower terminal equipment costs. For these reasons, the F.C.C. commented in a 1973 proceeding that "digital modulated systems should be the rule rather than the exception."[21]

Accordingly, the ascendancy of digital microwave was widely conceived as inevitable. From digital microwave's introduction in the mid-1970s until the AT&T breakup, it triggered rapid deployment of microwave. For example, in the five years preceding 1980, use of terrestrial microwave in the United States tripled from approximately 165,000 to 500,000 installed miles, with other industrialized nations experiencing similar growth.[22] Two important policy implications were presumed to flow from microwave's ascendance. First, as economist Leonard Waverman argued in 1975, the advent of microwave as a long-distance transmission medium dramatically altered the industry's economics, so that the natural-monopoly justification for AT&T's long-distance monopoly no longer existed as it had when open wire pairs were the principal medium for intercity traffic, which was the case until the late 1940s. Accordingly, he urged in an influential paper, increased competition was in the public interest.[23] Breaking the AT&T long-distance monopoly was the inevitable consequence of this view. Second, at the time of the breakup the fear that microwave would allow large business subscribers to bypass the local loop was widespread. A 1984 *Fortune* article summarily conveys what was then the conventional wisdom: "Bypassing, which promises to grow fast and large, will mean reduced growth and diminished profitability for the local phone companies. Much of their revenue comes from a few large clients. . . . If several large customers set up bypass networks, profits are penalized because phone companies usually cannot cut costs as quickly as bypassing siphons off revenues."[24] Lower local rates for large customers and higher access charges from long-distance companies to local telephone companies were conceived as the most effective response to the threat, which would inexorably take its toll on the local operating companies.

In order to evaluate the impact of the alleged threat, it is initially important to distinguish between two kinds of bypass. The first is facility bypass, in which users build a microwave link or lease a line from a bypass vendor that connects the user directly to a long-distance carrier's point of presence. Service bypass involves users purchasing private lines from the local operating company. In facility bypass the customer is completely lost to the local carrier, but in service bypass—use of which has been much greater than the former—the operating company still obtains considerable revenue from the customer. Operating companies have compensated for the loss by raising network access fees to residential subscribers.[25] Aiding local operating companies, access charges that long-distance carriers must pay them amounted to about 40 percent of long-distance costs in 1991. By 1995 access charges accounted for almost $30 billion of local carriers' $115 billion revenues. Further, service bypass and special rates for dedicated lines have enabled local operating companies to counter—or at least blunt—the bypass threat.[26]

Nevertheless, the bypass threat is a real one and likely to get worse as personal communications services, at which we look later, and other technologies come on line later in the 1990s. To date, however, the threat has not been as great as the doomsayers and prognosticators were suggesting in the immediate post-AT&T-breakup era. The past is, however, not necessarily a guide to the future for two reasons. First, bypass has, indeed, been increasing. For example, even though AT&T's long-distance revenues decreased between 1984 and 1990, from $34.9 billion to $33.9 billion, the access charges it paid declined at a much greater rate, from $20.6 billion to $12.2 billion. The erosion continues as long-distance carriers encourage the growth of local bypass carriers.[27] More importantly, the sound quality and reliability of wireless technologies have improved, and digital technologies will accelerate further improvements. At the same time, consumers have become more comfortable using wireless technologies. Typically in telecommunications, then, there are significant threats to wire communications, but the expectation that microwave would constitute the major one turned out to be wrong.

What then is the future of microwave transmission? First, some entrepreneurs have rediscovered microwave and are devising new technologies to deploy portions of the microwave spectrum competitively. For example, Associated Communications, a small firm, developed microwave transmitters that use the 18 GHz to 19 GHz band to transmit video, Internet, and data information. While its transmitter-receivers are fixed on buildings and must be in sight of each other, the equipment is relatively inexpensive to install and provides excellent data-transmission capability. Second, several telephone companies, instead of building expensive cable television systems to compete with cable providers, have acquired so-called wireless cable companies that use microwave frequencies to broadcast a limited number of television channels over the air. Third, cellular radio companies often use microwave radios in short-haul applications. Fourth, because of microwave's reliability in disaster situations, it is commonly used as a backup system when the wire system goes down. Fifth, in situations where fiber-optic cable cannot be laid down or is extremely expensive, microwave is a typical substitute. Finally, short-haul digital microwave can provide superior transmission quality and reliability to large users than T1 transmission lines (lines that carry digital signals at a rate of 1.544 megabits per second) under some circumstances.[28] Nevertheless, the bright future for microwave on which the *Western Electric* Modification of Final Judgment was based has not come to fruition. By late 1994, 95 percent of AT&T's traffic was carried by fiber-optic cable. From the time of the consent decree forward, the wireless growth sector was cellular telephones.

The Cellular Revolution

World War II accelerated the development of wireless transmission. Motorola developed two wireless transmission devices—the Handie-Talkie and the Walkie-Talkie—that facilitated military communication, most importantly on the battlefield. Millions of veterans saw firsthand the effectiveness of wireless communications and many would-be entrepreneurs envisioned civilian uses. AT&T received regulatory approval to operate a commercial radiotelephone service in 1946. The service was fully subscribed quickly, and within one year similar systems were available in twenty-five other cities. But the central problem with land mobile systems was far too little spectrum available for the large number of potential users. In 1984 less than one-tenth of one percent of all motor vehicles was equipped with mobile telephone service, and the quality of that service was very poor. In New York City, only twelve vehicles could then engage in mobile telephone communications simultaneously.[29] Like citizens band (CB) radio, the insurmountable problem with traditional mobile telephone was that a large number of users had to share a small number of frequencies.

The solution to the problem, like so many in the telecommunications field, was developed at Bell Labs. What triggered the development was the observation that television stations often used the same frequencies but were situated far enough apart to avoid or greatly reduce signal interference. The same principle might be used in much smaller areas for mobile telephony. In 1947 work began on cellular radio. In 1960 H.J. Shulte and W.A. Cornell, two Bell Laboratory scientists, proposed the first cellular concept, which notwithstanding increasing technological complexity still provides the basic cellular model. In their concept a metropolitan area is covered by adjacent hexagonal cells so that the entire region is included. The available mobile telephone channels are divided into groups, with each group assigned to specific cells. The same group of channels can be used in different cells if the cells are separated by a distance (reuse distance) so that cochannel interference in each cell is tolerable. Further, more channels can be assigned to higher-traffic cells.[30]

The breakthrough can best be understood by contrasting older mobile radio systems to the newer cellular radio (also called cellular telephone) system. As we saw, mobile radio was first employed in ship-to-shore and ship-to-ship transmission. By 1920 mobile radio was adapted for use in land vehicles and was used in police and public safety work. Spectrum shortage and the sheer bulkiness of the equipment largely precluded its use for other purposes. The World War II technological breakthroughs led AT&T to propose the commercial mobile radio system in 1946. The initial system was deployed in St. Louis, Missouri, but available technology limited the experiment to three one-way channels. The units employed a push-to-talk switch with all calls routed through a mobile operator. Because only three channels were available, subscribers had to have the patience of Job to get on line. Nevertheless, waiting lists to use the service were very long.[31]

Improvements occurred in the service to meet the enormous demand, while the F.C.C. established a competitive regime in 1949 by authorizing the new class of radio common carriers (RCCs) to compete with the established telephone companies on a different set of frequencies. By 1956 demand for the service led the F.C.C. to authorize seventeen more channels for the mobile telephone service. Technological developments in the 1960s allowed a customer to use any available frequency that might be unoccupied, thereby greatly reducing waiting time. In the same period the new "Improved Mobile Telephone Service" (IMTS) allowed automatic dialing without operator assistance and conventional two-way telephone conversation without the need to push a button. Increasing demand compelled the F.C.C. to allocate considerably more bandwidth to the mobile service in the mid-1970s. Nevertheless, as conventional mobile radio's day was coming to a close, the consensual view was that it had provided an inferior service. "At the end of 1983 there were only 12 channels in New York City to be shared by 730 radio-phone subscribers, with a waiting list of at least 2,000. Even the lucky 730 often had long waits for a free circuit during rush hours. And quality was poor; callers sometimes sounded as if they were at the bottom of a well."[32]

The traditional mobile phone service was based on a system in which the signals transmitted were strong enough to interfere with others. Therefore, just as in conventional radio, channels assigned to one area could not be used in nearby ones, sharply limiting the number of channels and, therefore, subscribers. In a metropolitan area all signals are transmitted to a central antenna. In contrast, under the cellular concept, a metropolitan area is divided into small areas—called cells—each with antennae and switching centers. Although any one frequency within a cell could handle only one call, the same frequency could be used for a different call in another cell because there is no interference between calls in different cells using the same frequency. Transmitters are very low powered and sufficiently distant from each other. Further, cells can be divided when call volume at any site becomes very heavy. A highly sophisticated switching system, handing off calls from cell to cell, prevents conversations from being interrupted as the cellular caller moves from cell to cell. As a caller moves along roads, the cellular system continuously monitors signal strength and direction. This allows a computer at the central switching office, with which the equipment at each cell is connected, to switch the call to another channel or cell or both. The cellular system allows the transmission of data as well, but in that case an add-on device is necessary to prevent loss of data during a handoff.[33]

Both businesses and individuals grasped cellular's possibilities immediately. For businesses it transformed travel time into work time; cellular telephony, in short, became a major productivity tool. A widely publicized AT&T study on a matched sample of salespeople, half with cellular phones and half without, showed that the group with phones averaged $11,000 more in sales per year than the group without them. Ameritech, through its mobile phone subsidiary, began commercial cellular service in Illinois on October 13, 1983. In 1984 there were approximately 100,000 cellular subscribers. Five years later the number had skyrocketed to 3.5 million. But even that spectacular growth paled before the increases from 5.3 million in 1990 to 23.2 million in 1994, with the expectation that the number would reach 46.9 million in 2000.[34] The only dark spot was that in the 1990s subscribers were on average making fewer calls. Finally, cellular's spectacular record was not just an American phenomenon. Cellular use was rapidly expanding everywhere, most dramatically in Latin America and Southeast Asia.

As one would expect, the battle to enter this lucrative arena, whose growth was foreseen at the outset, was a particularly intensive one. On the demand side, at the outset prices of equipment and service initially precluded widespread use. But as early as 1988 prices had dropped to levels that most analysts had not expected to occur until much later. As *Business Week* summarized, "Cellular phones already are becoming a shelf item for mass retailers."[35] Economies of scale and widespread foreign-equipment competition contributed to the decline. At the same time newer entrepreneurial companies, like McCaw Cellular, developed novel marketing strategies, such as paying a bounty to retailers who signed up customers for cellular service. Universally held early expectations of a booming industry had not only been met; they had been surpassed.

The F.C.C.'s early responses to the booming industry were criticized in some quarters, but an examination of how the agency shaped the structure of the industry indicates that the actions taken were at least plausible, and arguably better (or not worse) than alternatives not taken. Under the 1934 Communications Act, the agency was empowered to make spectrum allocations for a new technology and to construct a licensing system to determine which applicants would be awarded franchises. The F.C.C. was also empowered to impose technical standards for the equipment employed and how such transmitters and receivers are used. While the United States Supreme Court had admonished the F.C.C. that competition is the general preference in the use of wireless frequencies (in contrast to the preference then, but not requirement, for monopoly in traditional telephone service), the shape and nature of that competition was in the hands of the agency.[36] Moreover, the agency's structural options were complicated during the period that cellular policy was being considered by three other factors. The first is the advent of cable television and the beginnings of the traditional breakdown between wire and wireless service, with the former governed by public utility principles. The F.C.C., as we shall see in Chapter 9, was getting mixed signals from courts on how to treat cable. Second, during much of the period in which cellular's fate was being decided, the more important issue of the ultimate structure of the Bell system was pending in federal district court. That the F.C.C. took a long time to make a final determination and that it changed course should not come as a surprise when we take into account the complexity and the stakes involved. Third, add to this the fact that every state public utility commission could play a role in the eventual outcomes. Because many states had regulated traditional mobile telephone service, the reasonable assumption was that they would assert jurisdiction over cellular.

As we saw, the cellular concept was first proposed in a 1947 internal Bell Labs memorandum. Formal publication of the basic ideas occurred in 1960. By 1970 two Bell Labs scientists had developed computer models of dynamic channel assignment. In 1971 further refinements were made in the engineering of channel assignment. AT&T continued its research into cellular problems through the 1970s. AT&T was, of course, anxious to exploit commercially the new technology that its Bell Labs had developed as soon as it became feasible. Accordingly, as early as 1970 AT&T proposed building the first high-capacity cellular system, which it called Advanced Mobile Phone Service (AMPS). AT&T's proposal was submitted to the F.C.C. in

1971. AT&T's submission was, in part, a response to the F.C.C.'s 1968 invitation to develop an "efficient high capacity" mobile system that would alleviate the worsening congestion taking place under the older system.[37] In 1970 the F.C.C. authorized AT&T to test the system in Newark and Philadelphia, two densely populated cities with considerable traffic. In 1971 Bell Labs reported that the new system worked very effectively. In 1974 the F.C.C. approved the cellular telephone concept and allocated 40 MHz to it, adding that it would require cellular systems to be compatible. In this way cars would be able to roam from city to city and customers would continue to use their sets regardless of location.[38]

In its 1974 order the F.C.C. limited the awards of cellular licenses solely to telephone companies on the grounds that cellular was an adjunct to regular telephone service and that AT&T had incurred virtually all of the development costs. Further, the agency concluded that only telephone companies had the technological prowess to resolve the complex installation and operation problems. A court of appeals in 1976 upheld the F.C.C.'s decision to limit the new technology to wireline carriers. Between 1974 and 1979 the F.C.C., adopting a cautious approach, granted construction permits in a number of cities. Meanwhile, developments in other countries were moving more rapidly. Japan instituted a cellular system in the Tokyo metropolitan region in December 1979, while L.M. Ericsson, a Swedish equipment manufacturer, deployed major cellular systems in the Scandinavian countries shortly afterward.[39] The standards in these systems were incompatible with the U.S. system.

The F.C.C.'s long-awaited decision was issued in 1981 after examining an enormous volume of findings and considering the views of numerous participants and commentators. Taking into account the argument made against a wireline company monopoly in each market that such a structure would thwart cellular development and eventual competition with conventional telephone service, the agency decided to award two franchises in each market. As we noted, the F.C.C. allocated 40 MHz of spectrum to cellular radio. Because technology then precluded splitting the allocation into less than 20 MHz blocks, only two systems could effectively operate in each market. One company would be a separated subsidiary of a telephone company operating in the area, while the "nonwireline" franchise would be awarded to one among competing applicants. Finally, since the telephone company franchise would be able to operate before the nonwireline carrier, the F.C.C. would consider delaying the head start.[40] In order to move quickly, AT&T and GTE agreed not to compete with each other in the license awards, allocating markets between them. The F.C.C., similarly, encouraged the nonwireline companies to engage in such market division wherever feasible.

The next major event affecting the structure of the cellular market was the AT&T breakup on January 1, 1984, leading to the issue of whether AT&T or the new Bell operating companies should run wireline cellular service. Since a fundamental division in the settlement was between local service and all other services, cellular communication was obviously on the local side. Consequently, the seven RBOCs inherited the AT&T wireline cellular subsidiaries. Nevertheless, the overlap between the RBOC territories and the market areas in which the cellular carriers would operate was far from congruent. For example, northern New Jersey is part of the New York metropolitan area, but the area is divided between two different RBOCs. Accordingly, Judge Greene's approval was required in such situations—a process that delayed operations for a considerable time after applications were made. But the new RBOCs went further. Since as we have seen the general expectation was that the cellular market would grow rapidly, and each RBOC was now independent of the others, the Bell companies began acquiring nonwireline cellular carriers outside their areas, which was permissible under the consent decree.[41]

The final issue at which we look is the method by which the F.C.C. would award the nonwireline franchises. The agency had traditionally used a comparative-hearing method in wireless situations—most importantly the award of local radio and television station licenses. Under this system the F.C.C. examines comparative financial data, experience, technological facility, and other factors in determining winners. This process has three major drawbacks. First, it delays awards that are contested by several applicants for a considerable time. Second, such proceedings are often so lengthy and complex that enormous resources are expended on lawyers, experts, and so on, rather than on the service itself. Third, the procedure discourages smaller start-up firms and those willing to take risks. Who, after all, is willing to enter a battle against a huge company with extensive technological experience and resources? But it was primarily the first drawback that led the F.C.C. to abandon the notion, envisioned in its 1981 decision, of comparative hearings. Instead, in an important 1984 ruling, the agency adopted a lottery method for nonwireline carriers.[42] Since the competent and incompetent had equal chances to win the lottery in any market, the method led to an explosion in the number of applicants. Some successful applicants had no intention of entering the cellular business and promptly turned around and sold their franchises for enormous profits.

One successful applicant that retained its franchises would radically alter the conception of cellular telephony.

McCaw Cellular and the Growth of Hypercommunications

In our look at the early development of the Bell system we saw the gradual shift of telecommunication from isolated local markets to transcontinental long distance. Theodore Vail's vision and leadership triggered this dramatic change and the technological improvements that it demanded. In more recent times, the conception of telecommunications has become global. When cellular telephony began it was primarily conceived as local in nature. But just as Vail broadened horizons in wire communications, Craig McCaw, who led McCaw Cellular Communications from its infancy until its acquisition by AT&T, was one of the leaders in expanding the horizons of wireless communication. McCaw grew up in telecommunications. His father founded Centralia, Washington's, first radio station in 1937 and began operating one of the nation's first cable television systems in 1952. Until his death in 1969, John E. McCaw bought, sold, and operated numerous radio and television properties. In 1966 John McCaw began Craig's communications career by selling Craig and his three brothers the Centralia cable franchise for no cash, taking back preferred stock. Craig was then sixteen years old. Young McCaw successfully operated the cable television system, but in 1981 the company's revenues were about $5 million—a far cry from the $11.5 billion that AT&T paid to acquire McCaw Cellular in the deal that concluded in September 1994.

McCaw's interest in cellular radio was piqued when he read in 1981 an AT&T filing with the F.C.C. that projected 900,000 cellular subscribers by 2000—a figure that, of course, turned out to be absurdly low.[43] When the F.C.C. began its process of awarding cellular franchises, McCaw was awarded licenses in six of the top thirty markets in 1983. This was only the beginning. McCaw undertook a huge buying spree between 1983 and 1987, largely financed by borrowed money and the sale of the cable television properties. Debt in 1989 approached 87 percent of capital—an extraordinarily high figure. But McCaw Cellular continued buying and selling cellular franchises. In that year McCaw Cellular outbid BellSouth for a controlling interest in Lin Broadcasting, a major cellular operator with licenses in Dallas, Houston, Los Angeles, and New York. Behind the buying and selling, McCaw had a strategy to completely transform the cellular telephone industry from one with a local focus to a national network. Its operations were shaped in the form of market clusters that were intended to eventually form a national wireless network in the same way that AT&T had been gradually transformed from local systems into a national wireline network earlier in the century. Under the Cellular One system that McCaw devised, a person calling a San Francisco subscriber is automatically switched to that subscriber, who might be visiting in Miami. McCaw, in a word, was implementing a vision of primarily reaching people, not places. His grand plan, called the North American Cellular Network (NACN), would, like AT&T earlier in the century, invite companies that McCaw did not own or control to enter into the network that he hoped would embrace all of North America.

In order to implement the NACN vision, McCaw would have to install a more modern system than the analog one that characterized the first phase of cellular communication. At the same time the commitment to primarily reach people not places implied two other undertakings. First, McCaw would have to be able to reach people in places that cellular did not ordinarily reach, such as in airplanes. Second, McCaw would have to offer not just cellular voice communications but a full range of services that corporate customers would require, including paging, voice mail, and data communications. Corporate customers, McCaw realized, would be attracted to the idea of one-stop shopping for the full gamut of their communications needs. In order to carry forward the first leg of its strategy, McCaw announced in 1990 that it would replace existing switches (largely made by Motorola or AT&T) with new digital ones made by an Ericsson–General Electric joint venture. The uniform digital switching structure would allow information to move rapidly through the homogeneous system. At the same time the system would link with Rogers Cantel, the powerful Canadian cellular operator that already used such switches.[44] Underlying this move was, of course, the idea that the company that controls an industry standard has a better—although far from certain—chance to dominate the industry than its competitors.

McCaw saw the need generally to move to digital transmission from AT&T's AMPS concept that was devised in the 1970s. Only in this way would it be possible to achieve the goal of reaching a person anywhere in North America, wherever he or she might be temporarily located. During the 1980s, the AMPS networks were reaching the limits of their capacity. To provide extra capacity, D-AMPS (Digital Amps) was developed and brought into service in 1992, initially in Hong Kong. Ericsson gained an early lead in D-AMPS, one advantage of which was that it could be integrated into an AMPS system rather than having to fully replace it. D-AMPS and AMPS could coexist because they used the same radio frequencies. But in contrast to AMPS, D-AMPS is transmitted as a series of digital pulses with technology that allows far more information to be squeezed into the same frequency. By 1993 McCaw was offering the digital service in south Florida with conversion in other clusters following apace. Digital cellular not only permits distortion-free calls and raises wireless signal quality up to wireline standards, it also allows the wireless service to offer a full range of value-added services, such as paging, through the same customer equipment. McCaw was also a leader in transmitting data employing the cellular digital pocket data (CDPD) system. This system employs existing D-AMPS/AMPS networks, allowing wireless data and voice cellular service to be combined within the same frequency bands and channels. CDPD is able to detect and utilize the approximately 30 percent of the actual airtime when a voice channel is unused and send data in small packets and short bursts during these periods.[45]

As cellular phones became truly mobile and could be used away from vehicles, even while walking or riding a bicycle, another link in McCaw's dream of being able to telephone anywhere at any time was communication between an airplane passenger and a ground station. Air-to-ground communication was pioneered by In-Flight Phone Corporation. This innovative company offered not only air-to-ground service, but a viewing screen and keypad with the telephone, allowing fax transmission, the ability to listen to radio stations and play games, and other information services as well. GTE Airfone, a division of GTE, also entered the airphone market and was soon joined by Claircom Communications, at first a joint venture of McCaw and Hughes Electronics but later a subsidiary of McCaw alone. The digital service was made available not only for commercial airlines but for corporate jets as well. The three companies then undertook the next step of linking their systems with satellites to provide worldwide access and making their systems compatible with the European flight telephone system. While doubts remain about the commercial viability of airphone service, the significance lies in the promise of wireless communication that can reach anywhere.[46] The development of higher-quality cordless phones in the 900 to 928 MHz range with greater range and clearer sound than 1980s models reinforced McCaw's vision that wireless was not simply an addendum to wireline transmission but a full-scale complement and competitor.[47]

The inexorable next step in the drive toward market convergence was the marriage of a major wireless carrier to a major wireline one. Wireline had many more subscribers, but wireless had a far greater rate of growth. The first—and eventually rejected—engagement was Nextel Communications and MCI. Nextel was founded in 1987 by a former F.C.C. attorney and a CPA under the name Fleet Call. Their idea was to establish specialized mobile radio (SMR) services in major metropolitan markets. SMR's initial use was for dispatch service with which dispatchers are able to maintain contact with drivers in vehicle fleets, such as trucks or taxicabs. Nextel, like McCaw, had plans to use its frequencies for much more than what the

F.C.C. initially intended the assigned frequencies to do. After a purchasing spree of dispatch frequencies through the fall of 1993, Nextel was ready to make its biggest move. By acquiring approximately twenty-five hundred frequencies from Motorola in exchange for stock, Nextel had the potential to serve 180 million customers in twenty-one states, including forty-five of the fifty largest cities. At that point, Nextel had access to three times the customers that McCaw had.[48]

Nextel's move was based not so much on enlarging its dispatch service, but much more importantly on becoming a full-scale competitor in all wireless services. Its ambition was premised on converting its service to a digital one using Motorola technology and equipment, thereby being able to transmit far more information over each frequency than its analog system could. The green light to fully use SMR frequencies for paging, cellular, and data uses came out of a 1992 General Accounting Office study that concluded the F.C.C.'s duopolistic cellular radio structure provided insufficient competition. Congress reinforced this finding in the Omnibus Budget Reconciliation Act of 1993, which authorized the F.C.C. for the first time to use competitive bidding in the form of an auction to award spectrum licenses. These steps compelled the F.C.C. to allow Nextel and other "wide area" SMR carriers to modify their networks in order to provide a full range of wireless services.[49] The inevitable next step in market convergence stemmed from wireless's increasing ability to compete effectively with wireline services. That was, of course, attempts to form either tight-knit or loose-knit combinations of wireless and wireline companies. In the case of Nextel and MCI, the engagement never turned into a marriage, but in the case of AT&T and McCaw Cellular the sacred rites were performed. Ironically, however, Craig McCaw, after becoming AT&T's largest shareholder, agreed in 1995 to invest heavily in Nextel.

Why was one marriage consummated but not the other? When MCI announced in March 1994 that it would invest $1.3 billion in Nextel, most analysts viewed the alliance as a necessary defense to the pending AT&T–McCaw Cellular alliance. MCI's expected acquisition of 17 percent of Nextel's stock would provide Nextel with an enormous cash investment to fulfill its ambitious plans. MCI would be in a position to remain competitive with AT&T, which contemplated constructing a seamless wireless-wireline network that would take market convergence to a still higher level. Not only would every telecommunications service be provided, the service would be available everywhere. For example, the Nextel acquisition would allow MCI entry into local telephone markets. Comcast Corporation, which offered cable television and cellular service in the Northeast, then owned 17 percent of Nextel, offering the promise of providing entertainment, as well.

At the time of the proposed acquisition Nextel already offered combined paging, cellular phone, and dispatch service in Los Angeles and planned to extend such service to other locales soon.[50]

MCI's $1.3 billion investment was considered a bargain compared to AT&T's more than $15 billion acquisition of McCaw Cellular and Lin Broadcasting. But alas, either because of technological difficulties with Nextel's digital technology, Nextel's stock price, or the advent of newer and better technologies that we will examine in the next section, MCI canceled its preliminary agreement in September 1994, later pursuing other wireless moves.[51] In contrast, the AT&T acquisition of McCaw announced in August 1993 was consummated, notwithstanding difficult legal hurdles stemming from a bitter battle conducted against the merger by AT&T's former children, the regional Bell operating companies. By late September 1994 the acquisition was complete, with McCaw Cellular becoming the AT&T Wireless Services Division. AT&T president Robert E. Allen emphasized that market convergence was the underlying reason for the acquisition: "By joining forces with McCaw, we are taking a giant step forward in 'anytime, anywhere' communications. . . . Together we will not only satisfy customers' growing appetite for mobility, we will serve up that mobility with a range of wireless services that goes beyond anything most of us have ever imagined."[52] In October 1996 AT&T was on the way to fulfilling its expectations, unveiling a national digital wireless service combining phone, data, and paging functions in one single piece of equipment. AT&T called its new offering AT&T Digital PCS, but whether it, in fact, deserved to use the acronym PCS—the newest technology—was heatedly contested by its rivals. Enlarging its offerings further, in February 1977 AT&T announced a wireless local phone system using a radio transceiver box attached to internal phone wiring.[53]

Personal Communications Services (PCS)

Interest in personal communications services (PCS), a term that is sometimes used ambiguously to cover every future wireless technology, was triggered by a 1989 British report that called for the United Kingdom to become the world's wireless leader. The British government responded to the report by licensing four companies to provide "telepoint services"—essentially cordless pay phones that allow subscribers to originate, but not receive, short-range telephone calls with base stations in areas such as shopping malls and airports. Telepoint service never took off, but its introduction stimulated the F.C.C. to issue experimental licenses based on its promise.[54] The agency (as well as new and old industry players) began the PCS inquiry, not on the basis of a new and explicit technology as in the case of cellular radio, but rather on the basis of a set of expectations, or perhaps hopes. For this reason various PCS definitions have been ambiguous and sometimes inconsistent.

Because of this ambiguity, it is best to begin with the expectations to which all interested parties subscribe, rather than the definitions. No one has summed up the expectations better than attorney Thomas A. Monheim:

> Imagine having one, permanent telephone number and a small, wireless telephone that you could carry and use everywhere—at home, at the office or in the car. Imagine having a laptop computer that had built-in radio functions and was connected to a wireless local network. Imagine having a sensor in your car that was part of an intelligent vehicle highway system that kept you apprised of traffic conditions and ideal commuting routes. These are just a few of the scenarios that may become everyday reality with the development of advanced personal communications services (PCS).[55]

One important goal of PCS, then, is to establish a system of person-to-person, in addition to station-to-station, communication—a system of location independence.[56] Of course, cellular radio provides some location independence, but as the above quote indicates, considerably more is expected of PCS. Cellular systems, which are analog or mixed analog and digital, have a range of about twenty miles from transmitter stations and operate best in open spaces. In contrast, PCS systems will operate at higher frequencies; will transmit all calls digitally; have (at present) a range of about one thousand feet from a transmitter station; operate equally well in homes, offices, even tunnels; and have consistent wireline voice quality or better. PCS is also expected to solve two of the major interconnected problems that cellular transmission presented, by greatly enlarging the available message capacity and increasing the number of competitors in each market.

One should also note that the future holds in store the prospect of at least two satellite phone services using low-earth-orbit satellites (LEOs) that are now under construction and also promise person-to-person or point-to-point service anywhere on earth. These projects, whose estimated construction costs are about $6 billion each, are Iridium, a consortium of companies led by Motorola, and Globalstar, a consortium led by Qualcomm. At some stage it is anticipated that prices for satellite phone service will fall rapidly and the number of subscribers will commensurately increase.

With this background, we can now examine the definitions of PCS. We begin with the F.C.C.s—a family of mobile or portable radio communications services with the ability to provide services to individuals and businesses virtually anywhere and anytime.[57] Accordingly, the broad PCS concept embraces a new generation of cordless telephones, paging services, car telephones, portable facsimile devices, and so on that can send and receive voice, video, data, and any other conceivable kind of information. The F.C.C. began its policymaking in 1990 and by January 1992 instituted a proceeding that allocated 220 MHz of spectrum in the 1850 to 2200 MHz range. Additional frequency allocations occurred, including the 900 MHz band that, as we have seen, has been allocated to cordless phones that can be used for PCS' and the 2 GHz portion of the spectrum. In 1993 that year's budget statute called for a competitive spectrum auction process for which the commission had to provide rules in 1994.[58] To suggest that the auction process has been a financial success would be an understatement. As the auctions proceeded, the United States government took in more than $1 billion by late September 1996. Notably, the successful bidders included both established companies, such as AT&T and Sprint, and relative newcomers.[59]

But will the PCS future be fulfilled economically or technologically? As we have seen in every chapter, the number of variables makes it impossible to confidently predict the future. We are always surprised by outcomes as well as winners and losers. We can, however, look at the major difficulties that will be faced. First, cost estimates to build the PCS infrastructure range as high as $25 billion, in no small part because the microcell structure and short transmission range require many more towers than cellular does. But not every technological advance, as we know, meets with consumer acceptance. Will PCS be viewed as just another competitor with cellular and, therefore, get into a bidding war? Or will consumers view it as something significantly different?[60]

Even the kind of digital technology that will provide the PCS standard has not yet been determined. In one corner are AT&T, Ericsson, and other telecommunications giants who are advancing time division multiple access (TDMA), in which signals from several sources share a single channel by using the channel in discrete time slots when the channel is unused, as we saw in our discussion of CDPD. In the other corner is code division multiple access (CDMA), a more revolutionary technology associated with Qualcomm, Inc., that purportedly offers much greater capacity and security than TDMA. CDMA breaks the data in a call into digital packets and assigns a computer code to each one. These packets are intermingled with calls from other packets and unscrambled at the receiving end. And there are yet other technologies that compete with TDMA and CDMA. The exceptional potential of CDMA to increase capacity and enhance security, as well as successful tests in Korea and Hong Kong, may eventually make it the dominant PCS technology.[61] Whatever the outcome, the once sharp division between wire and wireless has now closed. The markets have converged.

8

A Marriage Made in Heaven: Computers and Communications

Introduction—The Computer Comes of Age

On February 14, 1996, Vice President Al Gore flew into Philadelphia to cele-brate the fiftieth anniversary of the ENIAC, or Electronic Numerical Integrator and Computer, the world's first general-purpose digital computer. (The claim, as we will see, is disputable.) The thirty-ton machine was constructed under contract to the United States government. The machine, which had actually been used prior to the 1946 unveiling, was built to meet the needs of the U.S. Army Ordnance Corps to compute all army and air corps artillery firing tables. While in some respects ENIAC was a beginning, in other respects it was a culmination of many steps, frequently traced to Joseph-Marie Jacquard's 1801 invention of a loom programmed by a continuous belt of punched cards that controlled and could change the patterns designed. While other important con-tributions occurred before 1876, when the telephone was invented, clearly the most important was the work of Charles Babbage (1792–1871). His two differ-ence engines were the first automatic calculating machines. At the same time, he developed the use of punched cards for computation and as a storage de-vice—a prophetic achievement.[1]

As advances continued after the invention of the telephone, develop-ments were focused largely on the process of rapidly and accurately calcu-lating—as the eventually adopted term computer implies. For example, in 1911 Elmer Sperry invented a computer that made automatic corrections to his gyrocompass. Five years later Sperry produced another analog computer that plotted both a warship's and its target's course and speed.[2] Sperry's ingenuity, like that of so many others before and after, was focused on the

economic exploitation of his ideas. Accordingly, in 1910 he founded the
Sperry Gyroscope Company to exploit his past and future achievements.
That company was one of the ancestors of computer giant Unisys Corp. In
similar fashion IBM can trace its lineage to Herman Hollerith, who won a
Census Bureau contest with a method to collect, count, and sort 1890 census data. Hollerith developed the idea of storing the data on punched cards
in which holes represented number of people in the family, occupation, and
so on. The cards were placed in a card-reading machine that used an electric
current to determine whether holes were punched in each entry. The machine tallied each entry and displayed the results on dials on the front of the
machine. In 1896 Hollerith formed the Tabulating Machine Company, one
of the ancestors of International Business Machines—IBM.[3]

The path from calculators to the computer—a system consisting of a central
processor, memory, and input-output peripheral equipment (such as disk
drives) that is capable of manipulating data in many forms (such as numbers, symbols, graphics, and so on)—was a long one marked by many
scientific and technological breakthroughs. We will now consider some of
the most important early breakthroughs that had important bearing on the
integration of computing and telecommunications. Some of these developments occurred as abstract contributions, while others were in response to
economic needs.

We begin in 1929, a year that saw both the crest of the post–World War I
boom and the onset of the Great Depression. No industry more characterized that boom than electricity. Lamps, refrigerators, radios, and a host of
other appliances boosted the demand for electricity dramatically in the
1920s. In turn this called for the design and construction of huge generating
stations and transmission networks. And this created complex problems to
balance the supply and demand of electricity in a network. Engineers had to
know how load changes in any part of the network would affect other parts
of the network as well as the connections between adjacent networks. The
differential equations that had to be solved grew so complex that electrical
engineers could not solve them. Given the anticipation that electric-power
consumption would continue to grow, solving the mathematical problems
rated as a very high priority. In 1929 General Electric Company and the
Massachusetts Institute of Technology introduced the A-C Network Analyzer, a special-purpose machine capable of solving the complex differential equations raised by electricity distribution. Based on the efforts to
produce the A-C Network Analyzer, MIT's Vannevar Bush built the Bush
Differential Analyzer, an all-purpose machine that could solve long, intri-
cate differential equations previously considered unsolvable. Bush's machine, which he conceived as the precursor of larger ones that could solve

even more complex differential equations, computed mechanically, but used vacuum tubes as storage devices. The machine, nevertheless, was an analog one that largely used mechanical parts to perform calculations. It triggered further interest in the development of machines that could solve complex mathematical problems, especially those associated with military applications.

Bush and his group were not the only team working on the development of a computer in order to solve economic problems in the pre–World War II period. AT&T, too, was faced with mathematical issues that impeded growth just as the electricity industry did. AT&T's major problem concerned relays, which are small, glass-encapsulated electromechanical switching devices that are closed in response to the number dialed and that send pulses through coils wound around the relay capsules. Relays automatically convert phone numbers into routing instructions. In the mid-1930s, the mathematics concerned with relays and transmission had become sufficiently complex that telephone engineers found ordinary desktop calculators inadequate to perform the calculations necessary to satisfy the company's growth expectations. In 1937, George Stibitz, a Bell Labs mathematician, experimented with relays that he brought home from an AT&T scrap heap. His fundamental insight was that the ones and zeroes used in the binary numbering system correspond to the two-state quality—on and off—of the relay. The homemade device that Stibitz constructed attracted the attention of his Bell Labs' superiors, who in 1938 commissioned a team to construct a machine based on Stibitz's ideas. The Complex Number Calculator, fully operational in 1940, did not have a stored program but could rapidly add, subtract, multiply, and divide complex numbers. More importantly for the development of the computer-telecommunications interface was that the Complex Number Calculator was the first machine to be used from a remote location. In 1940 Stibitz, attending a meeting of the American Mathematical Society in Hanover, New Hampshire, arranged for a telephone connection between a teletype machine in the meeting area and the calculator in New York. Conference participants entered problems and the machine answered in less than one minute. Later variants of the Bell Labs machine could also engage in multitasking.[4]

While practical problems triggered research at various locations, two mathematicians made theoretical contributions that paved the way for the remarkable progress coalescing various programs that took place during World War II. In 1937 Claude E. Shannon earned his master's degree from MIT by using Boolean algebra to describe the behavior of circuits. George Boole (1815–64) had developed the algebra of logic in which different classes can be divided into the absence or presence of the same property—

that is, zeroes and ones. Shannon drew a parallel between switching circuits and the algebra of logic. True and false values are analogous to open and closed circuits. Similarly, the binary system can correspond to high or low voltage, a punched hole or a nonpunched area on a tape, or any other duality that corresponds to the simple operations of a machine. The superiority of digital techniques to analog ones for directing information through switches and circuits became apparent as a result of Shannon's work; building a reliable machine the circuits of which could tell the difference between a one and a zero was clearly much easier than the task of designing circuits that would be compelled to distinguish between a larger number of digits. For the same reason, a digital machine would be far more accurate. Shannon's conception "that information can be treated like any other quantity and be subjected to the manipulation of a machine" had a major influence on the general-purpose computers that were soon designed.[5]

In 1937 British mathematician Alan Turing published another seminal paper that shaped the conception of the computer. Working in the area of mathematical logic, Turing sought to prove that there was no mechanical process by which all provable assertions could be proved, then a topic of considerable debate among mathematical logicians. In the course of his proof, Turing invented what is called a "Turing Machine," an abstract machine that "could recognize and process symbols, including arithmetic, according to a 'table of behavior' with which it was programmed."[6] Using the "machine" to compute numbers, Turing showed that there was a universal machine that with appropriate programming could do the work of any machine designed for special-purpose problem solving. The machine processed not numbers but symbols, and was therefore capable of processing any kind of information for which instructions could be written. Turing, in a word, invented a theoretical computer.

By about 1940 many of the intellectual and practical elements were in place for the development of the computer. Considering these developments will help us understand the later interface of computing and telecommunications and the important role that digital technology has played, and will continue to play, in that marriage. While computers would eventually have been built based on the foregoing developments, there is no doubt that World War II clearly forced the pace. As we saw, the U.S. military faced major trajectory problems that could not be solved with machines available in the early 1940s. In 1942 the U.S. Army Ordnance Corps commissioned a group of scientists and engineers centered at the University of Pennsylvania to create a machine that could rapidly solve trajectory problems. Dr. John Mauchly and his chief assistant, J.P. Eckert, Jr., headed the group and collected the requisite information and talented people to do the job. One of their early decisions was to construct a machine with as many electronic parts (and as few mechanical parts) as possible. John Antanasoff, a professor at Iowa State University who had designed large-scale calculating machines, influenced Mauchly's vacuum-tube design. By the time the ENIAC was completed in February 1946, it was the largest and most complicated electronic device ever built. It contained 18,000 vacuum tubes of sixteen basic types, 70,000 resistors, 10,000 capacitors, and so on. The machine was eight feet high, three feet wide, and almost one hundred feet long. It weighed thirty tons and consumed 140 kilowatts of power. By the time the machine was constructed, the total cost was almost $487,000.

Because vacuum tubes generate considerable heat, draw enormous amounts of power, and have a high failure rate, they imposed a serious limitation on the postwar utility of computers. At this point center stage is once again occupied by AT&T, for in 1947 three Bell Labs scientists invented the point-contact transistor—the first kind of transistor. AT&T had long undertaken research that it hoped would develop technologies to supplant the vacuum tube for the reasons cited above. The research focused on semiconductors, which have different characteristics than either insulators (such as glass) that resist the flow of electricity or conductors (such as copper) that allow electricity to flow. Semiconductors, such as silicon, can be altered to be either a conductor or an insulator. Transistors are semiconductor devices designed to simulate the functions of vacuum tubes, but they are much more efficient, reliable, and compact than vacuum tubes. In addition, they switch on and off much faster than vacuum tubes, an obviously important need for computers. In contrast to vacuum tubes, transistors stand up well to mechanical shock and do not require a warm-up period. Transistors can also serve as memory devices. It is no exaggeration to assert that computers would not have developed as a large-scale business without the advent of the transistor. Indeed, the power requirements alone of vacuum tubes would have precluded it.

While the transistor's potential importance was recognized quickly, it was not until 1954 that Texas Instruments, under license from AT&T, produced the first commercial silicon one. In that same year Texas Instruments designed the first marketable transistor radio.[7] By 1960 all significant computers used transistors for their logic functions. But in the meantime ENIAC, even though initially based on vacuum tubes, signaled the beginning of the new computer industry. And important events occurred quickly that would have major implications for the connections between computers and telecommunications. In June 1948 a team at Manchester University in England produced the first computer with a true stored-program capability, a conception for which American mathematician John von Neumann was partly responsible. Because the rapid developments and technological breakthroughs that, in fact, occurred were reasonably anticipated and the National Bureau of Standards promised orders, Eckert and Mauchly, ENIAC's two leading figures, established the Electronic Control Company in September 1946, and set up shop over a clothing store in Philadelphia. Other orders and promises followed as Eckert and Mauchly developed an all-purpose machine that they called the Universal Automatic Computer, or Univac. Nevertheless, financial and engineering difficulties (especially with vacuum tubes) as well as missed deadlines compelled the founders to sell their company to Remington Rand in March 1950.

At the time of the Remington Rand buyout (which became Sperry-Rand after a 1955 merger), the Univac machine was under construction. In 1951 the Univac was completed for the Bureau of the Census, and in 1954 the first commercial installation took place at a General Electric plant in Louisville, Kentucky. But it was earlier, in 1952, that Univac became a household word when it was used by CBS to predict the outcome of the 1952 presidential election.

It was not Sperry-Rand, however, that was destined to dominate the mainframe computer industry and to move the product to new uses, including telecommunications. The company that came to dominate the mainframe industry was, of course, IBM. Shortly after communist armies invaded South Korea on June 25, 1950, IBM wrote a letter to President Harry S. Truman indicating the company's intention to support the American war effort in any way possible. The theme that persistently reached the company was that the military desperately needed more computing power. IBM had assisted a Harvard University team, led by Mark Aiken, on a computer project during World War II, but it was initially reluctant to enter the fledgling industry on the theory that few customers would be found to lease such a complex machine for a large rental fee. Notwithstanding IBM's success in developing computers that served well during the Korean War, the company's attitude was that "computers afforded limited opportunities and were a sideshow when compared to the punched card accounting machines . . . to meet the needs of . . . the ordinary businessman."[8] Nevertheless, as the 1950s advanced, it became apparent to IBM's leadership that the days of the accounting machine were coming to an end and would be supplanted by the solid-state (all transistor) computer. IBM's engineering talent, thus, became focused on the development of computers.

One of IBM's objectives was moving from building one-of-a-kind machines to fabricating many at a time. The company also focused on automating fabrication. Finally, it sought to establish a decisive advantage over its competitors—an endeavor it christened Project Stretch. Although it had considerable success beforehand, IBM's introduction in 1964 of its break-through product, the System/360—the research and development costs of which were more than $1 billion—allowed the company to attain its objec-tives. The System/360 was not a single computer but a family of compatible machines that allowed customers to move from smaller to larger ones as their needs dictated. At the same time, IBM introduced the 1403 printer, another decisive breakthrough, which allowed customers to print at the previously unthinkable rate of eleven hundred text lines per minute. IBM's domination of the mainframe market, although challenged, continued as it introduced each new generation of products.[9] That, of course, meant that when computers became integrated with telecommunications, the world saw the contests that would appear to be between two sumo wrestlers—IBM versus AT&T.

Computers Meet Communications

If the distinction between computing—the processing of information—and communicating could have been maintained as easily in practice as it can conceptually, the history of telecommunications would have been dramati-cally different. But technological advances tended to break down the bar-riers between one sector that was to be governed by the principles of open competition and the other sector that was governed by the public service principle and was heavily regulated by national and state agencies. Because the two markets eventually came to converge, policymakers were com-pelled to address the issues, first, of how to draw the line and, then, of what principles should govern the large border area of computing and communi-cations. AT&T, which already had many adversaries, now came in conflict with IBM and other computer companies. The problem was complicated by the fact that computer hardware devices with communicating abilities were only one type of interconnecting CPE. Consequently, the many interconnec-tion issues raised in *Hush-A-Phone* and *Carterfone* were fused with the computer boundary issues. Since the interconnection issue was tied to one concerning a crucial technology, the F.C.C. had to treat it with heightened sensitivity. The agency had a public-interest mandate to facilitate the prog-ress of the computer and its applications. AT&T had to fight against not only more traditional interconnecting companies but also computer compa-nies. AT&T's traditional CPE rivals now had powerful allies and their claim of standing for the public interest became more substantiated.

As we saw, IBM's 1964 introduction of System/360 marked its rise to preeminence in the mainframe industry. IBM's bold innovation, which al-lowed a single computer to perform both office management and engineering functions, and users to move upward in computers without the costly burden of developing new programs, paid off rapidly. From 1968 through the 1970s IBM held more than 65 percent of the world's general-purpose mainframe market.[10] Notwithstanding IBM's preeminence in computers, it would be a mistake to view the problem of delineating the respective terrains of computing and communications as simply a clash between IBM and AT&T. Clearly, there were differences in position between the two firms, but IBM was precluded under the 1956 consent decree into which it entered from engaging in the service-bureau business, except through a completely separate subsidiary. And it is precisely in the service-bureau part of the business that the initial difficulties arose. Service-bureau activities are those in which customer data are manipulated or changed. While IBM was able, in small ways, to circumvent this restriction, its major business was computer mainframes and other hardware. Nevertheless, it strongly supported the views of its many service-bureau customers.

The 1956 Western Electric consent decree appeared to prohibit AT&T from entering any industry except the regulated telephone industry, and Western Electric from manufacturing anything (with a few exceptions) other than equipment for telephone operations. Nevertheless, AT&T moved forward in the development of computers, peripherals, and software for its internal use. Computing capacity in the Bell system during the early 1960s grew exponentially with a doubling time of less than two years. By 1969 AT&T had developed the UNIX operating system, a major advance that allowed, among other advantages, programs to operate together smoothly. By the mid-1960s, AT&T was in an anomalous position—although a leading firm in virtually all phases of computer development, it was precluded from entering the business because computing was not a regulated public service. However, when researchers at MIT's Lincoln Laboratories developed a system in the 1950s for transmitting digital signals between air defense sites over analog telephone lines, a conflict was inevitable.[11]

AT&T and others engaged in programs to develop and improve modems that would be able to transmit and receive data over telephone lines through paths originally or principally devised for voice transmission. As early as November 1956, AT&T decided to begin the development of a commercial data service. An experimental program called Dataphone began in February 1958, demonstrating the feasibility of sending data at various speeds over telephone lines. In this period, IBM, too, undertook important developments in the field of data communications. As the 1950s came to a close, data transmission over private lines and through the switched network constituted a rapidly expanding market.[12] For this reason, AT&T became attentive to all matters that might establish a general principle. In particular, it remembered *Hush-A-Phone,* and the interconnection battles lost to small companies. The incident that triggered the F.C.C.'s major computer inquiries, which wrought such extraordinary changes in American telecommunications, was a relatively minor affair. The Bunker-Ramo Corporation, an early service bureau, had developed an information service for stockbrokers called Telequote III. Pursuant to this system, undertaken through arrangements with the New York and other exchanges, Bunker-Ramo gathered, updated, and stored in regionally located computers information important to stockbrokers. For example, a broker dialing a Bunker-Ramo computer could instantly obtain information about the last price sold, last price offered, and so on for any stock traded on the exchanges. The common carriers had no objection to Telequote III; indeed, one may surmise that they viewed it as the progenitor of many other lucrative dial-in services to computers.[13]

Telequote IV, which Bunker-Ramo sought to introduce in 1965, however, presented a problem to the carriers because it added a message-switching capacity that allowed any of the offices of the subscribing brokerage firms to communicate information to any other. Telequote IV, of course, took advantage of the fact that the same computer could not only store and transmit information but could switch it as well. Obviously, the speed with which information can be obtained and transmitted is critical to the brokerage business.

Before we consider the underlying reasons that Western Union, Bunker-Ramo's principal carrier, refused to provide Bunker-Ramo with private-line service for Telequote IV, we should first note that the refusal put Western Union and the other common carriers supporting the action on the defensive. Western Union, by refusing to supply private lines for Telequote IV, appeared to be blocking progress. Computers in 1965, as now, were considered important objects because of their extraordinary capacity to solve innumerable problems and make our lives better. Moreover, Western Union had taken on not only the computer service-bureau industry but, more importantly, the entire financial industry (including brokers and banks), which even then could foresee major uses for message switching. The distinction between message switching and circuit switching should be noted. The latter involves a carrier providing a customer with exclusive use of an open channel for direct and immediate electrical connection between two or more points. The traditional telephone system typifies circuit switching, whereas the telegraph industry uses message switching, which is indirect in the sense of a temporary delay or storage of information prior to forwarding the message to its destination. While the F.C.C. conceived of circuit switching by a computer as communications, message switching by a computer was the focus of controversy because it inexorably involved some processing by a computer.

Western Union and its ally AT&T must have been aware of the risks they faced, the potential affront to major communications users, and the fact that Bunker-Ramo would not abandon such a potentially lucrative service without a fight before the F.C.C. and, perhaps, the courts as well. It is therefore necessary to consider carefully the arguments of the public service companies. Western Union advanced two basic arguments to justify its refusal: (1) Bunker-Ramo was not entitled to switched service under the carriers tariffs; and (2) if Bunker-Ramo engaged in Telequote IV, it would be subject to F.C.C. regulation under the Communications Act. Under the then prevailing conception of private lines, they could not be connected to the general exchange system nor could switching be permitted between the stations. In 1942, the New York Public Service Commission stated: "Communication may be had between several stations and a central point but the different stations are not connected one with the other."[14] Thus, the switching of information through Bunker-Ramo's computers would be considered a common-carrier activity, in violation of existing tariffs, and subject to F.C.C. regulation. Further, the switching would be used by Bunker-Ramo to obtain compensation from customers—precisely the activity carved out for communications public service companies. Bunker-Ramo would, according to Western Union, become a retailer of common-carrier services with Western Union forced to become, against its will, a wholesaler. To follow the logic of Western Union's argument, there would be no obstacles preventing any large enterprise from leasing what purported to be a private line from the telephone company for computer services, and then adding switching capacity so that all customers in the network could communicate with each other. This issue had become a practical one when computer technology permitted, first, the installation of remote terminals that would transmit and receive data from computers, and, second, time sharing. Prior to the advent of time sharing in late 1961, a computer user had to deliver his or her problem to a computer's managers and then wait hours or days for an answer that would take the machine only a few seconds to generate. Until time sharing, the computer worked on one problem at a time. In 1959, British physicist Christopher Strachey proposed methods that would allow a computer to work on several problems simultaneously. Following through Strachey's suggestions, MIT's computation center developed a time-sharing system in 1961, which contained many direct connections to the computer. Moreover, the MIT system was connected into the Bell and Western Union systems so that access to the MIT computer could be had from terminals anywhere in the United States and abroad.[15]

The time-sharing concept virtually begs for connection not only between users and the computer but also between the users themselves. Users can carry on communication among themselves through the machine, cooperatively examining a set of problems and sharing information. Although there were early difficulties in large-scale time sharing, by the mid-1960s it was clear that it was growing, in part because Bell Labs endorsed the concept in 1964 by ordering General Electric computers that featured time sharing. The boom in time sharing lowered computing costs and drew more companies into computer use, which, in turn, stimulated the rapid development of service bureaus, some of which developed specialized software for a variety of business and scientific uses.

The Telequote controversy was settled through negotiation in February 1966. Bunker-Ramo devised a modified Telequote IV service that it transmitted over the telephone. But Bunker-Ramo's complaint to the F.C.C. and the more general questions that it raised about the appropriate terrains of computing and telecommunications, unregulated and regulated activities, cried out for comprehensive treatment. The F.C.C. hoped that by addressing the issues raised by the computer-communications interface early in the development of the field, it could resolve many of them before they became full-blown controversies. Little did the agency realize, when it adopted a notice of inquiry into the interdependence of computers and communications in November 1966, that major questions would still be unresolved into the 1990s.

After a staff investigation, the compilation of a lengthy record, a lengthy study by the Stanford Research Institute (SRI) commissioned by the agency, and voluminous industry comments on the SRI study, the F.C.C. issued its long-awaited tentative decision (known as the *Computer I* tentative decision) on April 3, 1970. Essentially, the agency concluded that computer-communication services should be governed by the principles of free competition except in circumstances of natural monopoly or where other factors "are present to require governmental intervention to protect the public interest because a potential for unfair practice exists."[16] Not only would the F.C.C. not impose regulation on most computer services, but the existing common carriers (with the exception of AT&T because of the 1956 consent decree) would be free to enter data-processing services for three reasons. First, they would add competition and, possibly, innovation. Second, they might exploit economies resulting from integrated operation. Third, computer services might afford an opportunity for Western Union to diversify in the face of its declining message telegraph business. However, to prevent the ills that could result from admixing regulated and unregulated businesses (including subsidizing unregulated business with the profits of regulated business, or disregarding the primary responsibility of the regulated activity), the F.C.C. required strict separation of the two sets of activities and nondiscriminatory treatment between the separate subsidiary and other customers.

AT&T was barred from computer services not only because of the 1956 decree but also because of the F.C.C.'s policy of favoring smaller competitors in newer technologically based fields. The agency's policy made the issue of what constitutes a "computer service" far more consequential than a matter of definitional craftsmanship. The niceties of definitional hairsplitting were now potentially worth billions of dollars, for if an activity was on the communications side of the boundary AT&T might be allowed to engage in it, but if on the computer side it could not. The agency invented the phrase "hybrid service" to describe the close cases, those that combined data processing and message switching to form a single integrated service. In such hybrid services where message switching was offered as an integral part of a package that was "primarily" data processing, it would be treated as data processing. But where the data processing feature or function was an integral part of and incidental to message switching, the entire service would be treated as a communications service subject to regulation. The Bell system was warned to stay on the correct side of the line. The presumption in a close case would be against allowing the Bell system to engage in a service. But could this decision rule be applied in practice?

In March 1971 the F.C.C. spoke again, generally endorsing the framework it had developed in the tentative decision, but going further. Communications common carriers would now be barred from buying data-processing services from their own affiliates. This harsh provision was adopted because the agency felt that it would be virtually impossible to investigate every dealing between a carrier and its data-processing affiliate. The maze of ambiguities guaranteed that appeals would be made. In February 1973 the Court of Appeals for the Seventh Circuit provided an anticlimax, holding that the F.C.C. lacked the authority to regulate data processing; therefore, the rules restricting dealings between common carriers and their data-processing subsidiaries were invalid. On the other hand, the rules requiring strict separation were upheld since these covered the structure of the common carriers only. The agency, however, could not concern itself with the structure or desirable behavior of the data-processing sector.[17] The commission amended its rules in March 1973 to reflect the appeals court's decision—almost seven years after the inquiry began. Although the agency still had not been able to arrive at a formulation clearly distinguishing computing from communications, something far more important had occurred. Because of the F.C.C.'s new thinking about interconnection in the post-*Carterfone* era that began in 1968, computers came to be considered as only one kind of interconnection—albeit a very important one—into the telephone network, and the rules applying to them had to parallel those for other interconnection devices.

The F.C.C.'s first important step in anticipating the post-*Carterfone* controversies was to commission in June 1969 the National Academy of Sciences (NAS), through its Computer Science and Engineering Board, to study the technical factors of customer-provided interconnection. The NAS report, issued in June 1970, concluded that uncontrolled interconnection could cause harm to telephone company personnel, network performance, and telephone equipment. It determined that harm might arise as a result of hazardous voltages, excessive signal-power levels, line imbalances, or improper network-control signaling. Finding that the electrical criteria in AT&T's tariffs relating to signal amplitude, waveform, and spectrum were technically based and valid, the NAS concluded that two approaches were acceptable to provide the required degree of network protection: (1) common carriers could own, install, and maintain connecting arrangements and assure adherence to the tariff-specified signal criteria; and (2) a program certifying appropriate standards for equipment and for safety and network protection could be instituted. The NAS warned that "No certification program . . . will work unless proper standards have been established. In the case of telephone interconnection, standards must be developed to cover certification for installation and maintenance of equipment and facilities, as well as for equipment manufacture, since all of these combine to determine the net effectiveness of the program."[18] In 1971 and 1972, the F.C.C. announced the establishment of advisory committees that would attempt to develop technical standards for protecting the network from harms that could result from customer-provided CPE. The committees included representatives from NARUC, the F.C.C., the common carriers, independent CPE manufacturers, suppliers and distributors, and others. Under the auspices of the committees, progress was made toward establishing standards agreeable to the various interests.

After appointing the advisory committees, the F.C.C. convened a joint board of state and federal regulators to report to the agency on whether customers should be allowed to furnish their own network-control signaling units and connecting arrangements and, if so, what rules the F.C.C. should institute. This body would provide crucial support for the direction that regulators would take at both the state and federal levels on interconnection issues, including those pertaining to computers. Between April 1975, when the joint board issued its report, and November, when the F.C.C. issued its First Report and Order, the agency clearly indicated the direction it would follow in interconnection. It would gradually break down the distinctions among types of interconnection equipment, leaving no exclusive preserve to the public service companies. Full-scale competition in all CPE would not take place all at once but gradually. Thus, in June 1975 the commission issued an order in which it rejected the distinction that it had earlier made between a substitution for telephone company equipment and an add-on to such equipment. The F.C.C. concluded that the distinction made no sense in terms of implementing the basic *Carterfone* policy. In view of the increasing complexity and integration of equipment within one shell, the distinction between substitution and add-on would have become unworkable.

In November 1975, the F.C.C. issued its *Computer I* First Report and Order. Complaining that the common carriers had failed to devise an acceptable interconnection program in the seven years that had elapsed since the *Carterfone* decision, the commission adopted a registration program for carrier- and customer-provided terminal equipment other than PBXs, KTSs,* main stations, party-line equipment, and coin telephones, which would be considered separately. The agency indicated, however, that it saw no reason to ultimately exclude such devices even though the joint board had done so, in that the technical concerns raised by the joint board about these classes of equipment had been mooted. The F.C.C. adopted a simple decision rule in the First Report and Order: If equipment was not shown to cause harm to the network, tariff provisions could not limit the customer's right to make reasonable use of the services and facilities furnished by the common carriers. Any device registered could be used by a subscriber, and registration was to be based on "representations and test data [that] . . . are found to comply with specific interface criteria and other requirements."[19]

During this period a technological advance that began quietly in 1958 would have a major impact on the eventual breakdown in the ability of regulators to sharply demarcate computing from telecommunications and, indeed, other interconnecting devices as well. The decision rule quoted above would become extremely difficult to apply. This was the development of the integrated circuit, the importance of which would not be realized until the 1970s. The first critical event was Fairchild Semiconductor's development of the planar process to manufacture transistors more cheaply. Jack Kilby, while at Texas Instruments (TI), was the first person to conceive of integrating transistors and other components on a single chip in 1958. Kilby, however, did not develop a chip on which the devices could be interconnected, except by hand. In 1959 Robert Noyce, then at Fairchild

---

*In key telephone systems (KTSs) a number of telephone lines are connected to each telephone set in a system and a line is selected by pushing a button corresponding to one line.

Semiconductor, led a team that conceived and developed the separation and interconnection of transistors and other circuit elements electrically, rather than physically. In 1961 the United States Patent Office granted a patent to Noyce, inaugurating a ten-year battle between the two companies and a battle for the honor of first development between the two men. Eventually both men were accorded the honor.[20] By the late 1960s, large-scale integration (LSI)—the placement of more than one hundred transistors on a single chip—had become possible.

One critical development to which integrated circuits led was the microprocessor, which in turn led to the personal computer revolution. The enormous impact of these developments will be considered later. At present, however, we are concerned about the impact of integrated circuits on the dull, dumb telephone that Western Electric had been manufacturing for AT&T. In 1967 TI invented the electronic handheld calculator. By 1971, TI was able to announce the release of electronic calculators at relatively low prices; these small calculators could be put into a pocket. The consumer electronics boom, largely dominated by Japanese firms, was based on the integrated circuit and its ability to miniaturize what were previously bulkier products. The introduction in 1972 of digital watches and smart 35 mm cameras triggered the equally dramatic growth of these industries as well, as prices came tumbling down.[21]

If integrated circuits can revolutionize performance in a host of other small appliances, why can they not do the same in the telephone and its peripheral equipment? The thought, obviously, was not lost on AT&T and entrepreneurs seeking opportunities in customer premises equipment. Planning was, of course, earlier than development, but the central theme that drove the movement to use integrated circuits to "smarten" telephones was articulated by ITT telecommunications expert Leonard A. Muller: "And when you put intelligence into devices, you begin to do things you never dreamed possible. . . . When you place in the hands of a homeowner a device that has electronic intelligence and can communicate with other electronic intelligence elsewhere only God knows what the applications could be."[22] Without minimizing the engineering difficulties that had to be overcome in order to develop such features as speed dialing, last-number recall, call forwarding, call waiting, and other more advanced features that chips within a telephone could perform, it is important to appreciate that the *vision* of such capabilities occurred during the period that the F.C.C.'s first computer inquiry was drawing to a close. New notions—that integrated circuits could allow the telephone to embrace computer functions, that the telephone was becoming a heterogeneous device with the possibility of performing a mix of many possible functions, and that the number of possibilities opened up was limitless—had a major impact on the F.C.C.'s thinking from that period forward. At the very least, these technological possibilities thoroughly undermined the idea that AT&T should own or strongly control the installation or design of customer premises equipment. This also encouraged the agency to open the interconnection market as wide as possible.

Computer II

As the foregoing shows, it became increasingly impossible to show in concrete situations whether computing or communications was the dominant activity in many applications. Thus, one of the central distinctions made in *Computer I* broke down. Further, as we have seen, post–*Computer I* computing equipment was capable of performing data processing and communications functions simultaneously: "Computer networks no longer followed the neat pattern of first processing information, and subsequently sending it over communications lines. Remote computer users could now receive raw or partially processed data at their locations and complete the processing themselves. In addition 'smart terminals' which were capable of performing some data processing functions were being developed."[23] *Computer II* also occurred as a result of a changing conception of the office during the 1970s. The office of the future would be equipped with such things as CPE that could exercise control functions for activities outside the office, and devices that allowed more kinds of information to be economically transmitted over existing telecommunications distribution facilities (such as wires, microwave, and satellite) and new kinds of facilities (such as optic fibers). Thus, control of robots in distant factories, electronic funds transfers, transmission and analysis of medical readings, and the appropriate CPE were components of the office of the future. The widespread transmission not only of data but of higher-quality video information and facsimile, holographs, electronic mail, and even complex engineering blueprints are other examples. Although not all of these advances would occur rapidly, the actors had to ready themselves for them.[24]

Among the many factors contributing to the onset of what the F.C.C. knew would be a massive inquiry in *Computer II* was AT&T's Dataspeed 40/4 filing in November 1975. The Dataspeed 40/4 terminal was a smart remote access device that could not only transmit messages but also store, query, and examine data. Errors that were detected could be corrected locally without the need to interact with a mainframe computer. IBM, the Computer Industries Association (CIA), and the Computer and Business Equipment Manufacturers Association (CBEMA) petitioned to have the Dataspeed 40/4 tariff revisions rejected on the ground that the service constituted data processing rather than communications, which was not permitted under the *Computer I* rules. The Common Carrier Bureau agreed that Dataspeed should be rejected because it was a data-processing service. Arguing before the F.C.C., AT&T pointed out that the Common Carrier Bureau's views would effectively remove the company "as a provider of data terminal services, whenever customers wish to update their service in order to communicate more efficiently with a computer without the need for an intervening operator."[25] That is, the Common Carrier Bureau required AT&T to be technologically backward and, therefore, uncompetitive. The F.C.C. rejected the Common Carrier Bureau's recommendation, holding that Dataspeed 40/4 was primarily a communications service. The agency also recognized that the existing rules were becoming increasingly inadequate since the capacity of terminal devices to engage in data processing had increased markedly since the *Computer I* rules were established. Accordingly, in 1976, during the pendency of the Dataspeed 40/4 proceeding, the F.C.C. launched its second computer inquiry. At this time, mini- and microcomputers as well as other devices that could compute at a user's premises and be readily interconnected into telephone lines had clearly rendered the old definitions and conceptions obsolete. Further complicating the issues was the ability of the common carriers to use some of their facilities to allow terminals to converse with each other. In addition, the common carriers had become capable of offering performance features that would otherwise be located in a smart terminal, including automatic call forwarding, restricted and abbreviated dialing, and special announcements. Accordingly, the F.C.C. proposed in its notice of inquiry a new set of definitions, which it hoped would make distinctions superior to those made in *Computer I.* A supplemental notice raised the possibility of common carriers having a data-processing subsidiary separate from the regulated entity.

After compiling a massive record and the filing of numerous corporate statements, including sharply conflicting ones from IBM and AT&T, the F.C.C. issued its tentative decision in *Computer II* in May 1979. Reversing the rules of *Computer I,* the new set of definitions recognized that technological advances had made the problem of defining the boundary between communications and data processing unworkable. The new framework focused "on the nature of various categories of services and the structure under which they are provided."[26] The F.C.C.'s tentative decision employed three basic categories: voice, basic nonvoice, and enhanced nonvoice services. Voice service was defined simply as the electronic transmission of the human voice, such that one person is able to converse with another. An enhanced nonvoice service was defined as "any non-voice service which is more than the 'basic' service, where computer processing applications are used to act on the form, content, code, protocol, etc. of the inputted information." Finally, basic nonvoice service was defined as "the transmission of subscriber inputted information or data where the carrier: (a) electronically converts originating messages to signals which are compatible with a transmission medium, (b) routes those signals through the network to an appropriate destination, (c) maintains signal integrity in the presence of noise and other impairments to transmission, (d) corrects transmission errors and (e) converts the electrical signals to usable form at the destination."[27] The central distinction that the basic nonvoice definition sought to convey was that the original information was not transformed in content. However, the definitions applied to basic and enhanced nonvoice services were sufficiently complex as to invite controversy and difficulty in application. Essentially, the new definitions would allow the public service companies to offer enhanced nonvoice services only through a separate subsidiary, which would lease telecommunications lines on the same terms and conditions available to information-processing firms without a common-carrier subsidiary.

While AT&T was not pleased with the F.C.C.'s new definitions or with the strict separate-subsidiary requirement, it was pleased with the F.C.C.'s discussion of the 1956 consent decree. Using Section V(g) of the decree, which permitted AT&T to provide services and products incidental to communications services, the F.C.C. decided that many enhanced nonvoice services may fall within the "incidental" category. Noting AT&T's technological prowess, the F.C.C. observed that the public interest would not be served if AT&T had to restrict internally developed computer hardware and software to the Bell system only. Accordingly, the commission tentatively decided to permit AT&T to market such incidental products and services through a strictly separate subsidiary in situations "where market forces promise to be adequate and where full regulation is therefore not required but the offering . . . would be in the public interest."[28] Thus, for the first time AT&T could enter the door of the unregulated computer business.

The F.C.C. conceded that its new general definitions were subject to reevaluation if necessary, that the new AT&T rules in particular would require case-by-case analysis, and that many issues remained unresolved. For these reasons, the F.C.C. decision was deliberately considered a tentative one and it called for further comments from interested parties.

Released on May 2, 1980, the F.C.C.'s final decision hardly sounded final. At virtually every turn the divided agency promised to review and reconsider its conclusions and rules. Six separate statements accompanied the 122–page decision, and the changes and supplements to the tentative decision were substantial. Instead of three categories of service, only two remained, basic transmission service and enhanced services. Basic transmission service was "limited to the common carrier offering of transmission capacity for the movement of information." Enhanced services were defined as offerings over a telecommunications network that add computer-processing applications and "act on the content, code, protocol and other aspects of the subscriber's information."[29] Conceding that its prior definitions were faulty, the F.C.C. was now satisfied that it had constructed workable categories that coincided with those used in the marketplace. It believed that an underlying carrier would now have clear guidelines on which services it could provide directly and which required a separate subsidiary. But the service distinctions, while having the merit of simplicity, would not definitively determine on which side of the boundary all of the new service offerings would be, especially those involving information storage.

Having decided that AT&T should form separate subsidiaries, the F.C.C.'s next step was to elaborate a complicated scheme of the activities that could be conducted jointly on behalf of parent and subsidiary and those that had to be separated. The subsidiary would have its own operating, marketing, installation, and repair personnel. Certain kinds of information could be shared, other kinds could not. To assure arm's-length dealings, the parent and subsidiary could not share space, and the implication was clear that any fraternization would be risky. The rules were so detailed and complex that they were tantamount to a deeper regulatory presence in the day-to-day operation of both businesses than had ever occurred. The final blow dealt to AT&T followed from the series of post-*Carterfone* interconnection decisions. Not just computer communications devices but all CPE, including the basic telephone, were to be deregulated pursuant to calendar schedules. Subscribers would now be able to own or lease any CPE—and pay for the cost of repairs. CPE would be removed from tariff regulation (detariffed) and would have to be offered through the separate subsidiary. In this way, CPE provision and transmission would be unbundled.

Almost every major participant in *Computer II* filed notices of appeal with the U.S. Court of Appeals for the District of Columbia. The court upheld the *Computer II* rules in 1982. But the story is far from finished, for the F.C.C. then had to consider the *Computer II* rules in view of the massive AT&T divestiture and decision entered in that same year. This led to the third computer inquiry, launched in July 1985. The focus now would be on the separate-subsidiary requirement and the services that should be regulated.

Computer III

Recall that the events with which we are concerned here began when Bunker-Ramo sought to introduce Telequote IV in 1965. Thirty-two years later, in 1997, the dust had not fully settled. During this period, of course, enormous technological progress occurred in both the telecommunications and the computer fields, and their integration has continued apace in no small part because of the continuing development of integrated circuitry and semiconductors. Additionally, the AT&T breakup played a significant role and, more recently, the 1996 Telecommunications Act (which will be discussed in the next chapter) raises still further considerations. While many considerations contributed to the opening of the *Computer III* proceedings in August 1985, the most important was the F.C.C.'s growing doubts about the efficacy of the separate-subsidiary requirement that was the centerpiece of the *Computer II* rules, especially after the dramatic restructuring of the old AT&T after January 1, 1984.

In order to understand the dramatic changes that the *Computer III* rules have wrought, we begin with the unarguable conclusion that the old AT&T, largely through the extraordinary efforts of Bell Labs, had compiled an amazing record of scientific and technological progress. Much of it had been in the field of pure science for which important applications were found a considerable time after the scientific discoveries. As we have seen, some of the most important developments in the computer and related fields, including the UNIX operating system, the transistor, computer movies, and a variety of programming languages, occurred in the Bell system. The 1984 breakup thrust AT&T into a new competitive environment in both long-distance and the various equipment markets. While Bell Labs remained a component of AT&T, many observers feared that the new short-run profit considerations would undermine the scientific and theoretical work of Bell Labs, the resources of which would be largely directed toward marginal product improvements. At the same time, part of Bell Labs was spun off to the regional Bell operating companies in the form of Bellcore, further ruining what most observers held was a national treasure in the form of the old Bell Labs. If one accepted these premises—as many observers did—it became necessary to keep AT&T and the RBOCs occupied in technologically advanced markets. Impediments to their engaging in competing in leading-edge technologies and enhanced services should be removed. It is within this context that we must understand the dramatic changes in the *Computer II* rules that *Computer III* sought to bring.

AT&T and the RBOCs, not surprisingly, sought to capitalize on these anxieties in an attempt to secure relief from the *Computer II* structural-separation requirements, under which the separated services had to be conducted in separate physical locations and with separate computer facilities. Their argument was based on the economies-of-scope conception employed unsuccessfully in *U.S. v. AT&T*. The *Computer II* rules, they claimed, imposed unnecessary costs on them by requiring duplication of staff, facilities, hardware, and functions. Further, the transaction costs in the forms of data and paperwork imposed on the arm's-length related firms could be substantially reduced if the requirement was lifted. Moreover, these firms would be deterred from realizing their potential for innovation by sharing technological information and integrating it in novel service offerings. The rules, they argued, also denied consumers the opportunity to engage in one-source shopping. All of the foregoing, they urged, injures consumer choice, unnecessarily reducing customers' options. "All the reasons [for separation] are gone. It's time to catch up with our customers," argued Alfred C. Partoll, an AT&T executive vice president.[30]

The focus of the campaign was, of course, in F.C.C. proceedings. At first, the RBOCs and AT&T sought waivers from the *Computer II* rules, which the F.C.C. largely granted in every instance. As this process developed, some of the commissioners felt that the waiver process was too cumbersome, slow, and uncertain. Virtually every other sector involved in the computer-communications interface opposed the waivers. When the accumulated impact of the waivers led to a call for reexamining structural separation, generally they opposed that as well.[31] The opposition of every segment of the computer industry as well as the segments of the telecommunications business that would face additional competition from relaxing the *Computer II* rules has been a consistent theme from the inception of the proceedings to the present day. Additionally, one must appreciate that the information-provision business was in its infancy when the *Computer III* proceedings began. But even then, CompuServe, one of the oldest on-line services, vigorously fought AT&T and its progeny.[32]

The pressures and dissatisfactions led to the F.C.C.'s August 1985 Notice of Proposed Rulemaking. The notice was a lengthy, complex document that, in essence, criticized the separate-subsidiary requirement, asserting that it imposed unnecessary costs on the RBOCs, to the ultimate detriment of consumers. Accordingly, the agency proposed that regulatory arrangements other than separate subsidiaries would better serve the public interest. Maintaining the long-standing distinction between basic and enhanced services, the commission nevertheless observed that there could be enhanced services that could most effectively be offered when integrated into the network. Since a basic service is conceived as traditional voice telephone service and enhanced services "use the telephone network to deliver services that provide more than a basic voice transmission offering,"[33] protocol conversion and voice messaging might be included within the basic service category, even though technically in the latter one. Voice messaging, which was the topic of one of the AT&T *Computer II* waivers, allows voice messages to be stored in the network and delivered later at the caller's or recipient's option. Protocol conversion concerns the fact that computer and computerlike devices do not necessarily speak the same language in the same way that you and I communicate in English. Protocols are sets of standards for exchanging information between two computers or computerlike devices. Protocol conversion involves the processing that permits communication between terminals or networks with different protocols. Thus, the notice devised three categories of services that might be governed by different rules. Withal, competition was to be preferred wherever possible.

In June 1986 the F.C.C. released its lengthy Report and Order in the *Computer III* matter.[34] The decision retained the basic/enhanced definitional distinction to determine whether a service should be regulated. Second, the agency decided that the *Computer III* regulatory scheme should apply only to AT&T and the RBOCs. Thus, GTE and all other telephone companies were exempted from the elaborate scheme that the decision devised. Third, the F.C.C. preempted the states from imposing their own separate-subsidiary or tariff requirements inconsistent with those on which the F.C.C. decided. Fourth, the agency decided to abandon the separate-subsidiary requirements in favor of a new set of conceptions that constituted the most important *Computer III* contribution to resolving the computer-communications issues. The two concepts are open network architecture (ONA) and comparably efficient interconnection (CEI). ONA was intended to allow enhanced-service providers to interconnect into the telephone network on a technically equal basis to AT&T and RBOCs operations. CEI requires that the telephone company offer enhanced-service providers (ESPs) equally efficient use of its basic service that it employs itself. If the telephone company offers an enhanced service, it must be required to offer equal network interconnection (called collocation) to competing or other ESPs. Lists of documents containing interface information and technical characteristics must also be provided.[35]

The key to the F.C.C.'s view that ONA could replace the separate-subsidiary idea and prevent abuse of monopoly power was the requirement that the RBOCs must unbundle their network services into individual cost-based elements that the ESPs could order as needed. The F.C.C. conceived unbundling (fragmenting) basic service "building blocks" into separate components as the centerpiece of the ONA plan. Unbundling services must be offered on the same terms to ESPs as to their own operations. In its order the F.C.C. required the RBOCs to file ONA plans indicating how they would comply with the requirements. Thus, the RBOCs had to show how ESPs could purchase various switching and transmission services so that a level playing field was created for each of the enhanced services. Until the acceptance of these plans, RBOCs had to maintain separate subsidiaries. The drastic overhaul of the *Computer II* structural separation rules was based on the RBOC arguments that they were hampered in introducing new services and that many new advanced services that had not appeared in the public network, such as voice messaging, were being employed in private networks operated by large businesses. Notably, in 1987 AT&T success-fully argued that because it faced considerable competition and did not have control of switching facilities that an ESP had to use, it should be exempt from most ONA requirements.[36]

While the F.C.C. thought that it had successfully shaped policies that promoted RBOC efficiency while at the same time encouraging innovative service providers, dissatisfaction among the RBOC opponents, who sought to impose higher costs on the telephone companies, was widespread. Ap-peals and further proceedings were as inevitable as night following day. The RBOCs had to overcome not just this hurdle but the additional one of Judge Greene's prohibition in the Modification of Final Judgment against provid-ing "information services," which partly overlapped the F.C.C.'s "enhanced services" concept. But the stakes were huge and well worth the fight. En-hanced services based on ONA were uniformly considered to be a major telecommunications growth area. Among the earlier network services on which ESPs can provide offerings are automatic callback, automatic recall, calling-number identification, selective call rejection, selective call accep-tance, selective call forwarding, distinctive ringing, customer originated trace, and so on.[37]

While such network services have clearly offered lucrative opportunities, these pale before the possibilities raised by three other ONA technologies undergoing development and refinement. Common channel signaling (CCS) is a network architecture under which call setup and billing data are transmitted through separate network facilities from those that transmit the actual communications between two (or more) parties. The services men-tioned in the last paragraph are available through CCS. But the new innova-tive technology is nonassociated CCS, which greatly reduces call setup time and enhances network flexibility because traffic resources are not wasted until signaling indicates that the call can, in fact, be completed. Since net-work capacity is becoming more and more taxed, especially during emer-gencies and through increased Internet use, the advantages of nonassociated CCS are eminently clear. Second, integrated service digital network (ISDN) is not so much a product as a guideline for offerings that permit a single network to handle simultaneous voice, data, video, and other services, in contrast with the separate arrangements now required for such simultaneous transmission. ISDN, thus, can greatly facilitate communications between local area networks, on-line business transactions, desktop conferencing, work at home, and a host of other applications. The intelligent network (IN)—the most advanced of these network services—involves moving the software housed in every switch to fewer centralized databases. INs facilitate the rapid creation of new services because software modifications are made only to the centralized databases, rather than to every switch in the network. In addition, IN promises the eventual adoption of personalized communications—a personal telephone number wherever one happens to be located—rather than the current system of terminal-assigned telephone numbers.[38]

While the F.C.C. has been occupied with proceedings focused on unbundling and ONA issues with respect to these and other technologies, it has also been involved in court proceedings aimed at untracking the *Computer III* program and reverting to the *Computer II* separate-subsidiary rules. An appeal of the *Computer III* rules was made to the Court of Appeals for the Ninth Circuit by the California PUC and others. The court held in 1990 that the F.C.C. abused its discretion in abandoning structural separation by failing to show that (1) its new program adequately protected against cross-subsidization of enhanced services by the RBOCs, and (2) the sweeping preemption of state regulation was necessary to achieve F.C.C. goals. The preemption, in short, was too broad.[39] *Computer III* was, therefore, remanded to the agency for future proceedings consistent with the court's conclusion. After additional F.C.C. and court proceedings, revising the original *Computer III* order, the commission modified but still retained the basic ONA/CEI system that it originally devised. In April 1994 the agency decided to apply the framework to the GTE Corporation. But the commission received another court of appeals rebuff in the 1994 *California III* decision.[40] Eight years after the *Computer III* rules were announced, the court of appeals accepted the F.C.C.'s preemption language but faulted the agency for failing to adjust its cost-benefit analysis. The court held that the agency still had not sufficiently explained its conclusion that "totally removing structural separation requirements was in the public interest given that . . . ONA requirements no longer called for 'fundamental unbundling' of the BOC networks."[41] The Ninth Circuit court, one might add, is the most interventionist one in the federal system.

And so the *Computer III* proceedings drag on to the benefit of the innumerable lawyers involved in the proceedings. But in the period from the end of the *Computer II* proceedings in 1980 to the present day, technology has not stood still. Developments would further integrate telecommunications and computing in ways then undreamed. The microprocessor would spawn the personal computer (PC) revolution, which in turn would spawn the Internet, the World Wide Web, and the multimedia revolution.

The Microprocessor and the PC

How important was the invention of the microprocessor in 1971? Clearly it is one of the most important inventions of the twentieth century. Netscape Communications vice president Marc Andreessen asserts, "When we add human vision, innovation, insight, knowledge and wisdom in the form of software to the microprocessor, we can see that [the impact has been] so much more than even the wheel. And we've only begun to scratch the surface of what the microprocessor makes possible."[42] Perhaps this is an overstatement; only time will tell. Nevertheless, there is no question that the telecommunications-computer interface has changed dramatically since its invention. When Intel launched the 4004, the first commercial microprocessor, in 1971, only three years after the company's founding, it boasted that the invention would usher in a new age in microelectronics. The boast, even at that primitive stage of microprocessor development, was fully justified. The 4004, costing about two hundred dollars and occupying twelve square millimeters, offered approximately the same performance that the ENIAC did in 1946. The extraordinary achievement involved incorporating two remarkable innovations. First, most of the transistors in a computer's logic circuits were placed on a single chip. Second, the chip was programmable: it could be controlled by software and could, therefore, perform numerous functions. In the words of Intel CEO Andrew S. Grove, "Microprocessors are the brains of the computer; they calculate while memory chips merely store."[43] Microprocessors (the central processing units, or CPUs, of personal computers) have been frequently analogized to brains, the functions of which include receiving input from one's senses through nerve connections (buses, in the case of microprocessors) and then determining a response based on the information stored in one's memory. In the case of the microprocessor, the response is based on the control software stored in the main memory.

The road from the invention of the microprocessor to its use in the personal computer and the subsequent dramatic transformation in telecommunications is a long and fascinating one.[44] Every observer agrees that these developments changed the world, but from the perspective of this book, the most important focus is on how they changed telecommunications by both enlarging the uses of conventional channels and creating new ones—most significantly, the various components of the Internet. In the former case, greatly increased use of fax machines, dial-up information services, modems, telemedicine devices, and so on have dramatically increased the use of conventional telephone lines. On the other hand, the explosion of communication through electronic mail, wireless modems, and more recently Internet telephones poses a long-term revenue threat to telephone carriers. One should appreciate, however, that the microprocessor's impact on modern products is hardly limited to the realms of telecommunications and computing. New cars use microprocessors that monitor and control engine operations, antilock brakes, air bags, and other facets of automobile travel. Cameras, ovens, air conditioners, watches, VCRs, video games, and a host of other devices also employ microprocessors (often called microcontrollers when they are designed so that their primary function is to manage ongoing physical events rather than provide intelligence).

Considering how microprocessors have found their most important use in computers, it is surprising how long it took for that application to come to fruition. The story begins when Busicom, a Japanese calculator company, in 1969 approached Intel, then a small start-up firm, to design and manufacture a customized chip that would put all of the calculator's functions on a single chip using the new metal-on-silicon (MOS) manufacturing technology. Instead Ted Hoff, Intel's twelfth employee, began working on a new general-purpose calculator chip architecture. The principal difficulty was in translating the architecture into a working chip design. By October 1970 Intel's Federico Faggin had resolved the problems, and the 4000 family of microprocessors went into prototype fabrication. In March 1971, Intel shipped the first 4000 chip sets to Busicom, and the microprocessor revolution had begun. But Intel would not have clear sailing, for in the same year Texas Instruments would also develop a single chip microprocessor, dubbed "the calculator on a chip."[45] The showdown would occur not so much in technological innovation but in envisioning the market possibilities—with a little bit of luck thrown in.

By the middle of 1972, the electronics industry was cognizant of the microprocessor's potential. During the 1970s, Intel and a number of competitors sold microprocessors for many embedded applications, including calculators, digital watches, home appliances, and machine tools. In the face of competition Intel developed improved models, most importantly in 1972 the 8008, the first eight-bit microprocessor. This model, in turn, was improved and simplified to create the 8080 in 1974, a microprocessor capable of addressing 64 kilobytes of memory. Intel did not then know it, but the 8080 planted the seeds of the forthcoming PC revolution. That event began quietly when Ed Roberts, an electronic hobbyist, built a PC in early 1975 using the 8080, a primitive PC by today's standards, but one with slots for additional memory and devices. That PC, termed the Altair, sold well in the electronic hobbyist community and created a market for add-on devices. Within months competitors entered the market, and Gary Kildall had written CP/M, the first important operating system, triggering considerable applications software. Altair's success spurred a vision among some firms that the market could reach beyond hobbyists, and in 1977 the new machines included the Apple II, using Motorola microprocessors. While Apple Computer was one of the fastest-growing American companies in 1978, cofounder Steve Jobs's vision became greater than satisfying business, scientific, and enthusiast markets. In 1979 Jobs conceived the PC as a household device that could be used by the average person.

Jobs's ambitious project was based on a visit he had made to Xerox's PARC research center in Palo Alto. On that visit and subsequent ones, Jobs observed graphics-oriented computers with sharp display images, on-screen icon controls, and a hand-operated mouse. Overcoming opposition within the Apple organization, Jobs was intent on creating a PC incorporating the Xerox research group's innovations with a powerful Motorola microprocessor. Continuing to release PCs without these features, Apple prepared the ground for the eventual introduction of the Macintosh on Super Sunday 1984 through earlier moves, including the introduction of a printer in 1979; the establishment of a school educational program to overcome computer fear; the supplying of applications software (made by other firms) for people who could not write their own programs; the use of interface cards allowing the computer to be linked to scientific and technical instruments; the addition of a hard disk; and the production of various peripheral devices, including modems for the transmission of computer-generated information. This last was in response to a 1979 F.C.C. announcement encouraging the use of PCs for electronic mail.[46]

As important as Apple's innovations were, in some ways they were overshadowed by IBM's introduction of the 5150 PC in August 1981. Featuring a 4.77 MHz Intel 8088 microprocessor, 64 kilobytes of random access memory, and Microsoft's MS-DOS operating system, it sold for approximately three thousand dollars.[47] More importantly, the entry of IBM, which dominated the world mainframe market, into the PC arena legitimized the new industry for much of the world. Many observers confidently expected IBM to soon dominate the new market as it had dominated most other markets that it had entered since the company's founding. IBM, it should be noted, had failed in earlier attempts in the 1960s and 1970s to sell low-end computers, but Apple's successes persuaded IBM executives that the time was now ripe. IBM selected the Intel over other microprocessors, not only because the 8088 was perceived to be the superior microprocessor, but also because Intel produced support chips and made a long-term commitment to the 8086 microprocessor family (of which the 8088 was a version). Notwithstanding the enormous introductory success of the IBM PC, IBM made a strategic error from its perspective, although not from the consumer's. IBM decided that its PC should be open, allowing anyone to design hardware or software for it. Its purpose was to encourage hardware and software competition that would provide the best possible products. This led to the development of an enormous clone market, and it allowed Intel and Microsoft to become economic powerhouses as these firms supplied the microprocessors and operating systems for the exploding PC market.

From the perspective of telecommunications, the competition expanded the developments in which Apple led the way. Since almost any kind of information could be transformed into digital form, computers and peripherals could generate, transmit through translation channels, modulate (convert digital signals to analog form), and demodulate (the reverse process). The information content could be not only data—the traditional one—but also voice, still pictures, motion images, music, text, and so on. The computer, in a word, was on its way to transforming discrete markets into a single one, the product of which is information. Telecommunications was in the process of being transformed into hypercommunications, as any digital device or source convertible into digital information could create a market for a computer peripheral. Thus, photo, audio, and video discs, or any other information-storage device, and sound and television broadcasts could theoretically be inputted and transformed in a PC. Moreover, two or more of these media could be brought into play at once—the so-called multimedia revolution. Lighting, mechanical animation, and sound could also be added. Thus, the PC was not simply a smaller computer but was the vehicle of a revolutionary transformation in telecommunications.[48]

All of these developments, of course, took time to unfold; indeed, they are still unfolding. Two significant steps were required to point the way: networking and perfecting the modem. Xerox once again led the way in the early 1970s in networking, allowing local resources to be linked together to serve work groups by connecting machines together more reliably and faster than before. The development of such networking would obviously have wider implications for communications outside the local area network. In 1980 Intel, Digital Equipment Corporation (DEC), and Xerox joined hands to create Ethernet, which would become the dominant PC networking technology. In this way PCs within a limited area can exchange information, share expensive peripherals, and draw on the resources of a vast storage unit called a file server. The first Ethernet standard, and subsequent ones designed for faster communication, received the imprimatur of the prestigious Institute of Electrical and Electronics Engineers (IEEE) and have become widely used in large organizations. Networking through Ethernet and its competitors, in short, not only encouraged the wider deployment of PCs, but also fostered the development of communications between computers.[49]

The second important device that enlarged the use of computer communications was the modem. In the early 1960s, Bell Labs engineers invented a method to convert the computer's digital data into a form that could be carried over ordinary telephone lines. Their device, the modem (modulator-demodulator), converted data into a series of tones that travel over telephone lines to another modem where they are reconverted into digital data. The modem allowed businesses to avoid expensive, specialized leased lines to carry data—they could now use ordinary telephone lines. But several entrepreneurs saw the modem in a new way—the device that would permit PC users to communicate with each other and bring a vast amount of information into the home through the PC. "Communications will break open the home market," said Michael Preston, a New York microcomputer securities analyst.[50] As database services such as CompuServe, The Source, and Dow Jones News Retrieval sprang up in the early 1980s, they encouraged start-up modem manufacturers, most importantly Hayes Microcomputer Products, to fashion faster, more accurate, and cheaper modems for the PC market.[51] But it was once again IBM's endorsement of the information-service market through a joint venture with Sears in 1988 called Prodigy that marked the arrival of the modem. Prodigy, unlike its predecessors, would use colorful graphics that required faster modems than the 300 bits per second then prevalent for text-only services. Prodigy teamed up with Hayes, which then produced the Hayes Personal Modem 1200, designed specifically for the home market.[52] Prodigy and Hayes would eventually fall on hard times, but the launching of the new service would forever reshape the marriage of computers and telecommunications. A little-known government agency, the Advanced Research Projects Agency (ARPA), would trigger the next phase.

The Internet

In contrast to the telephone network, the structure of which was framed largely by commercial considerations, the Internet network (hereafter the Internet) initially developed largely because of defense considerations and the efforts of the United States Defense Department. Later, universities came to play a major role in shaping civilian Internet applications, but even then the initial defense phase stamped the shape of the Internet. Only since the development of information services such as CompuServe and, more recently, the growth of the World Wide Web have commercial considerations played a considerable role. But to this day the defense phase determines the basic structure, which is far more decentralized than the telephone network. Because of this decentralization, the Internet is composed of a variety of very different services—electronic mail, Gopher, UseNet, the World Wide Web, and so on. Many people are content to use but one of these services (usually electronic mail), while others will use several. Because of its variety of services, the Internet is difficult to define. Perhaps the best definition of the Internet is "a worldwide network of computer networks."[53] Another definition is, "It's a network of networks, all freely exchanging information."[54]

The origins and underlying purpose provide a better sense of what became the Internet than these definitions.[55] In 1957 the Soviet Union launched Sputnik, the first artificial earth satellite. In panicked response, the government established ARPA within the Defense Department to work on highly sophisticated defense-related projects. One of the key problems on which ARPA focused was maintaining the defense communications system in the event of hostilities. The great fear was that the telecommunications network (essentially the AT&T network) could easily be disabled in case of an enemy strategic attack. The network was based on a hierarchical system of centralized switches, so that a concerted attack on high-level switches would completely disable the network. Unless a substitute telecommunications system could be found, the entire command and control system that a modern military establishment requires would collapse. The development of such a system, therefore, became a high priority, not only within ARPA but also among military contractors such as the Rand Corporation, where Paul Baran, who more than anyone else was responsible for the eventual shape of the Internet, became interested in the survivability of communications systems under nuclear attack.

Baran, basing his ideas on the ability of the human brain to bypass dysfunctional regions to send messages, proposed in 1962 a twofold solution to the problem. First, he proposed a distributed network instead of a centralized one. Under this concept the network would be composed of many nodes without central command points but in which all surviving points would be able to reestablish contact in the event of attack on any one or several points (see Figure 1). He devised the notion of redundancy—the number of interconnections between neighboring nodes. A redundancy of one meant that there was only a single link to a node, implying a low probability of survival in case of an attack. The concept of redundancy,

Figure 8.1 **Network Types**

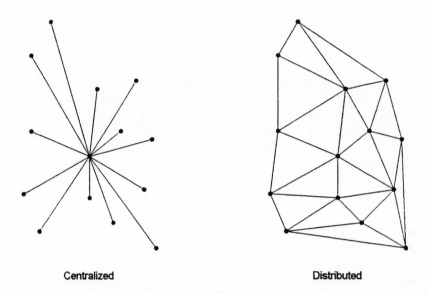

Centralized   Distributed

therefore, sharply focused on the issue of comparing redundancy levels with probability of survival. From our contemporary perspective, however, the distributed network idea was the germ of the highly fragmented nature of the Internet and its architecture providing many paths to obtaining information when one is occupied. It is also one of the reasons that there is no huge international firm providing connections to the various Internet users throughout the world. As the Internet has grown and the issue of survival has receded in importance, there are, of course, hierarchy and backbones (networks through which other networks are connected), but the distributed network idea is still the heart of the Internet.

Baran's second extraordinary idea was packet switching. In packet switching a digital or digitized analog message is broken into smaller packets. Each packet is appended with the destination address of the entire message as well as the sequence number of each packet so that it can be reassembled at the destination in the same sequence in which it was sent. In this way each packet can be sent over a different route, depending on availability. The destination computer holds the packets until all arrive. The sequence in which they arrive, thus, becomes irrelevant. Packet switching also allows the receiving computer to send a message back so that lost packets can be identified and re-sent. Notwithstanding AT&T's skepticism about the feasibility of packet switching, ARPA produced a design paper in

1967 on a proposed Arpanet. By 1969 the Defense Department was prepared to establish a network linking university sites that were engaged in defense-contract work. By 1971 fifteen nodes (with twenty-three hosts) were connected to the Arpanet. In this way, the forerunner to the Internet was born. At this stage no one saw these networks as a threat to traditional telephone networks.

The next important step taken, the development of electronic mail (E-mail), which now does constitute a major threat to telephone company revenues, came about almost casually as a minor byproduct of the scientific and technical work of the few persons with ready access to the Arpanet.[56] J.C.R. Licklider, one of ARPA's top officials, had been an advocate of humanizing the computer since he became associated with the project in 1962. Ray Tomlinson, an engineer at an ARPA contractor, sent the first E-mail in 1971 to himself. The second message, sent out to others, announced E-mail's availability and provided instructions on how to address users on other machines. In July 1972 Abhay Bhushan, a programmer, suggested a way of getting E-mail to run on the ARPA network by using file transfer protocol (the rules defining program and data files to be transmitted error free). That was only the beginning, as later programmers developed software that allowed subject indexing, deleting, message forwarding, and so on. Because E-mail rapidly became popular among the members of the Arpanet community, other researchers wrote programs that made it more and more user-friendly. Comparisons to the telephone were inevitable, and E-mail's advocates argued that "among the advantages of the network message services over the telephone were . . . the message services produced a preservable record, and that the sender and receiver did not have to be available at the same time."[57]

The inevitable next step was the development of mailing lists directed to persons on the Arpanet with similar interests. Most of the early subjects were, of course, scientific in nature. But as E-mail's popularity increased, topics such as wine tasting, science fiction, and so on proliferated. At first system administrators cautioned against the overuse of such lists, but they were overwhelmed by the flood. This eventually led to the development of the UseNet in 1979 when two Duke University graduate students came up with the idea of distributing information of interest to UNIX operating system users. In 1981 a Berkeley graduate student and a nearby high school student added more features that were able to handle a large number of postings in comparison to the small-scale plan envisioned by the Duke students. The idea spread like wildfire, eventually leading to the thousands of newsgroups that flourish today.

The necessary prelude to the proliferation and enlargement of networks

beyond the limited community of defense-related researchers was the establishment of protocols that linked the various machines and networks. The
problem was acute in the military itself because the army, air force, and
navy had accepted bids on very different computers. How could the army's
DEC computers speak to the air force's IBMs and the navy's Unisys? The
Defense Department commissioned a project that would link different networks designed by different suppliers into a network of networks—an Internet. Work begun in the 1970s resulted in the transmission control protocol
(TCP) and the Internet protocol (IP), commonly known as TCP/IP, becoming established in 1982. TCP is responsible for verifying the correct delivery of data from client to server and retransmitting until the correct data is
completely received. IP moves packets of data from node to node based on
a destination address.[58] TCP/IP thus permitted the creation of the Internet
from the variety of networks created in the wake of Arpanet, the most
important of which were UseNet, CSnet, and Bitnet. Bitnet, established in
1981, was a network of cooperating universities that provided E-mail between persons associated with the universities. CSnet (computer science
network), established in the same year through seed money provided by the
National Science Foundation, provided networking services to scientists
with no Arpanet access.

Slowly, then, the Internet was being formed, expanding from a small
community of defense scientists and engineers to the larger university community. Numerous other nets were formed in the 1980s, the most important
of which was NSFnet, created in 1986 with five supercomputer centers to
provide widespread high computing power.

The next significant development requires us to shift focus to Switzer-
land. This was the 1992 release of the World Wide Web (WWW) by
CERN, the European particle physics laboratory located near Geneva, Swit-
zerland. Prior to the WWW, there had been few commercial Internet activities, the most important of which were the 1990 relay between MCI Mail
and the Internet through the clearinghouse for Networked Information, and
the 1991 establishment of the Commercial Internet Exchange to facilitate
packet exchange among commercial service providers. To appreciate the
enormous role the WWW has played in spawning commercial use of the
Internet, consider only that the number of hosts grew from approximately
376,000 in January 1991, the year before the WWW release, to almost
thirteen million in 1996.[59] Much of that explosive growth has been spurred
by the attractiveness of the WWW. Innumerable companies and other organizations have created Web sites, in many cases very complex ones, and
that Netscape and Microsoft have created Web browsers while DEC, Sun
Microsystems, and others have established search engines that offer great

facility to look for information. By 1994 the WWW had become the second most popular service, after E-mail, on the Internet.

The heart of the WWW is hypertext, by which information is organized as a series of documents with links for search and retrieval of text, images, sound, and video.[60] Thus, hypertext incorporates multimedia as part of its basic conception. Hypertext is also nonsequential. In contrast to a book, where page three is necessarily read after page two, hypertext allows the reader to choose his or her own options in the sequence desired. For example, you may choose option D, then B, skipping C and E entirely. Another person's options and sequence may be different. The central idea of hypertext can be traced to Vannevar Bush, who feared in 1945 we would be drowned in an explosion of information and sought ways in which to make it more accessible. One answer was hypertext, which Bush called "associative trails." In the early 1980s, physicist Tim Berners-Lee, working at CERN, began his project on hypertext links. In 1989 he proposed such a program, but it was initially met with skepticism on the ground that a hypertext program would be too complicated. Gradually he won converts, and in 1990, he wrote the first Web browser and Web server programs. By the end of 1990 the CERN phone book became the first hypertext file. When MIT and CERN signed a pact in July 1994 to further develop and standardize WWW software, the credentials of the new service attained the respectability that would gain it worldwide success.

The WWW, unlike the other Internet services, has become a commercial success. Web-masters have proliferated to design extraordinarily attractive Web sites for small and large companies to not only provide information but sell products and services as well. In every city and town, large and small firms have become Internet providers, allowing a user paying a monthly fee to access the Web and enjoy a sophisticated E-mail service like Qualcomm's Eudora. Software and hardware manufacturers have produced innumerable products, including high-quality graphics cards and sound cards. Nevertheless, one company above all others stands out for making the WWW as popular as it has become. That is Netscape Communications, which provides the Navigator, the most popular family of browsers, and the Netsite Commerce Server, a purportedly secure method of paying for goods and services. Founded in April 1994, the company provided the earlier versions of Navigator free in order to become the industry leader. While it has been challenged by Microsoft's Explorer browser, there is no question that its ease of use has been a valuable instrument in making large numbers of people comfortable in searching the WWW. The combination of easy-to-use browsers and inexpensive access through the fierce competition among Internet providers has been instrumental in the vast expansion of Internet use.

This same expansion has in one way benefited the telephone companies through vastly increased use, as many people will not uncommonly access the WWW all evening. But lurking in the background is a threat, perhaps more serious than E-mail. For not only are text, data, and attractive graphics among the multimedia features of the WWW, so potentially is the voice-grade telephone, especially for long-distance calls. Internet technology readily permits voice transmission.[61] Users must have a microphone, speakers, a plug-in card that converts speech to data and back, and phone software stored in their PCs, and they must agree to make the call at the same time. The voice is encoded to a file using software developed for this purpose and then decoded back to sound at the other end. Often the software is provided free over the WWW or by file transfer protocol. Since the call is almost free, Internet telephony, although in its infancy, is viewed by telephone companies as a very serious threat. One estimate is that there will be sixteen million Internet telephone users by 1999. Accordingly, the American Carriers Telecommunications Association (ACTA) filed a petition with the F.C.C. seeking to ban the sale of Internet telephone software. Local telephone companies are also seeking to make Internet providers, now exempt from paying access charges under F.C.C. rules, begin paying.[62] While it is not clear from the present perspective whether Paul Baran's or Alexander Graham Bell's and Theodore Vail's network vision—or both— will prevail, the impact of the computer on communications is only beginning. From the perspective of any firm, this provides one more reason to cover all bases, either through internal expansion, or through links with others.

9

Telecommunications Turbulence

The Future as History

Telecommunications history has consisted of the interactions between government intervention, entrepreneurial and corporate innovation, and technological and scientific invention. This book has sought to trace the complex relationships among these factors, and to show that reductionist arguments purporting to explain the progress and development of the United States telecommunications system are misplaced. Certainly, as the experience of the communist countries has shown, publicly owned and operated enterprises have been found wanting. But there is surely enough experience to show that private ownership coupled with some degree of public involvement can yield good economic and social results. As the last chapter indicated, the Internet would probably not have been constructed without government and then university dominance. Yet in the most recent phase of the World Wide Web, government has quite properly retreated into the background.

No one would deny that private enterprise, relatively unhindered by public regulation, has contributed mightily to technological progress, but the view that state intervention can only impede the deployment of the technological fruits of private enterprise is grossly overstated. The close relationships between the state and private enterprise in Japan, in several Western European states, and most recently in such newly industrializing nations as South Korea have shown that government may play a positive role in technological advancement. Most of the recent complaints about government involvement have been concerned about its welfare role, broadly defined, not its role in technological advancement. The state can adopt a variety of postures toward new technologies extending from benign neglect to active participation, and the impact of public intervention can range from destructive to helpful. Each case must be considered separately.

American historical examples illustrate the diverse ways that government can act upon and affect technological and economic development. Consider first the American industry that is the envy of the rest of the world—agriculture. Not only is American agriculture extraordinarily technologically progressive and efficient, it has had a remarkable record in contracting the period between technological discoveries and their actual deployment. Wayne Rasmussen's important study of agricultural innovation has shown that the exemplary record of American agriculture is directly related to the agricultural extension stations, land-grant colleges, and other programs fostered by the Department of Agriculture and such statutes as the post–Civil War Morrill Act.[1] Government intervention is most intense during periods of war, and it is precisely during such periods that government has accelerated the pace of technological deployment, as many examples in this book have shown.

Of course, government intervention does not *necessarily* lead to a more rapid deployment of new technologies than a free market would. Indeed, as Paul MacAvoy and James Sloss have shown, the deployment of the unit train (a train devoted to shipping only one commodity between two points) was adopted very slowly because the Interstate Commerce Commission instituted inconsistent and wrong-headed policies that discouraged the progressive new service. Again, a governmental authority can foster an inferior and unnecessarily costly technological option, as Congress did when it enacted a law forcing manufacturers of television sets sold in the United States to include UHF reception capacity.[2] Notwithstanding these cases of misguided government intervention at the administrative and legislative levels, one can point to many counterexamples of successful government intervention, as we have seen.

The relationship between government intervention, entrepreneurship, and technological innovation is a complex one. Shibboleths, like faith in free and open competition, are too simplistic and reductionist to enable us to understand the interface between government and the private sector in advancing new technologies. Nor, of course, is government intervention, no matter how it is applied, the only important variable in understanding the pace of new inventions, their importance, or the rate at which they are commercially deployed. One must concur in Jacob Schmookler's conclusions that potential profits, the state of science and technology, risk of failure and the type of invention are among the crucial variables.[3] Government policies (or nonpolicies) may be appropriate under one set of conditions but wrong in others. Telecommunications, during most of this century, was a homogeneous product—plain old telephone service—carried over a single kind of pipe—copper wires—in which the primary goal was to attain universal coverage as rapidly as feasible, because the positive externalities on business and residential subscribers would be very high. The solution, after the failure of a competitive interlude, was the AT&T-dominated regulated network manager system, involving substantial cross-subsidies from business to residential subscribers, urban to rural ones, and so on. Open interconnection of devices could impair the system and even be dangerous with few compensating benefits. The private firms were regulated by the F.C.C. and state commissions, which, overall, did their jobs well. The system worked. For example, in the period between 1972 and 1977, the Bell system's labor productivity growth (closely related to the deployment of newer technologies) exceeded that of all industries but one (hosiery) that the Labor Department studied. Again, while the consumer price index between 1960 and 1973 increased by 44.4 percentage points, the residential telephone service component of the index increased by only 14.6 percentage points.[4] Moreover, it is universally accepted that Bell Telephone Laboratories was one of the—if not *the* preeminent research institution—in the world.

Conditions began to change slowly in the 1960s. Hindsight is wonderful, but regulators unfortunately do not have crystal balls. Nevertheless, the agencies began to grope and feel their ways toward new policies that would respond to would-be entrepreneurs who wanted to challenge the Bell system with their new technologies, most importantly the computer. Quite significantly, as the unknowns multiplied, the agencies more and more moved in the direction of allowing markets to reach solutions. Markets can offer a variety of alternatives and let consumers decide on the basis of quality and price—a preferable solution when conditions are in flux and the future is unclear. Accordingly, AT&T was less and less able to protect its monopoly positions before the regulatory agencies as they moved toward adopting procompetition positions. If this sounds like a naïve argument that regulators seek to reach the best results that will advance the public interest, so be it. But there are sound reasons for holding that regulators are compelled to behave in just that way, as this book has attempted to show.

Our administrative system has to a considerable extent been patterned on our judicial system. That is, it is based on an adversary system (often involving many more than two sides) in which skilled advocates forcefully present the factual and legal arguments of their clients. Agencies cannot ignore such arguments and, indeed, are compelled to rationally explain what they reject. In contrast, legislators can babble away, act as demagogues, or ignore what is inconvenient. Agencies are also bound by most of the formal mechanisms concerning evidence, precedent, and so on that characterize the Anglo-American legal system. Consequently, an agency proceeding almost always contains: (1) the position and arguments advanced by the various sides to a controversy, (2) agency consideration of the arguments, and (3) a reasoned basis for the adoption of one policy rather than others. This is not to suggest that agencies are "above politics" or that there cannot be "hidden agendas." Rather, they are severely constrained to make decisions on policy grounds. Notions that large corporate interests routinely "capture" agencies are belied by the facts and by the crucial importance of procedure in their proceedings. AT&T, for example, was routinely thwarted by the F.C.C. after 1968, losing important markets to much smaller competitors. And in cable television the F.C.C. began to render decisions favorable to the upstart cable industry and against the interests of the three giant over-the-air networks.

In the present era the imponderables in telecommunications have reached an unprecedented state. CPE now includes everything from computer workstations to traditional "dumb" telephones. The distribution systems include copper wire, coaxial cable, microwave, optical fiber, different kinds of satellites, and a wide variety of other wireless technologies. Transporters of information include local and long-distance companies, cable television firms, Internet providers, and a variety of other interests. Thanks to the digital revolution, computing and telecommunications architectures are more open than ever before. At the same time digital compression technologies have made it possible to transport data in smaller packages so that virtually any kind of medium can move any kind of information. And we are only at the beginning of compression technology (through encoding, reducing redundant information, and other techniques), the mirror effect of which is to greatly enlarge the transmission capacities of each telecommunications sector.[5] The inevitable tendency of these trends is to converge markets. Information is information, and if there is sufficient capacity to carry it and there is a profit to be made, the type and content are unimportant. Of course, we should underestimate neither the technological and business difficulties in entering a new business nor the cumulative benefit of experience in each market. But these barriers can be overcome by entering into the right alliance. Congress, as we will see later in this chapter, recognizing the inexorable trend of market convergence, enacted the Telecommunications Act of 1996, the basic purpose of which was to open up each telecommunications sector to the competition of other sectors. Cable companies can enter local telephone markets and vice versa; local companies can enter into long distance and vice versa, and so on.

But who will the winners be? What technologies will prevail? In attempting not to guess incorrectly and to hedge their bets, firms have a strong incentive to enter into alliances with others emphasizing different technologies or operating in a different region of the country or a different part of the world. But will this inexorable incentive lead to the creation of a few colossal "telesauri"?

Telesaurus Rex?

In 1995 alone the telecommunications sector witnessed 126 deals, merging assets of $39.1 billion. Entertainment, media, computer software, and other sectors impinging on telecommunications also saw numerous combinations.[6] Of course, many other sectors were involved in alliances, mergers, and acquisitions. Nevertheless, the turbulence in telecommunications requires investigation. And mergers and acquisitions were just part of the structural activity in telecommunications and its related sectors. There were joint ventures, divestments, the formation of new units, and so on. Consider just the major Internet-related activities that occurred in the first twenty-three days of the single month of January 1996: Sun Microsystems formed Java Soft to promote the Java programming language; Microsoft bought Vermeer Technologies, a Web page maker; Sears-Roebuck made clear that it was going to sell its interest in Prodigy; Netscape and Verifone announced a joint venture to develop software that would make it easier for banks and merchants to accept credit-card payments over the Internet; Sun Microsystems was engaged in (eventually unsuccessful) talks to take over Apple Computer; General Electric agreed to sell GEnie, its on-line service, to Yovelle Renaissance Corporation. And this occurred in only one sector of the vast number of activities embraced within modern hypercommunications.[7]

The Sun-Apple deal was never consummated. But from our perspective of understanding the nonstop turbulence, that is relatively unimportant; after all, you are still shopping for a new car even if you walk away from twenty dealerships. Consider the labyrinth of deals, some of which were successfully concluded while others were not, in which the RBOC spin-off companies were involved, even before the 1996 Nynex–Bell Atlantic and SBC–Pacific Telesis mergers, reducing the number of such companies to five. Nynex has made major telecommunications investments overseas, joined with Philips, the electronics giant, to develop voice and text information services for residential subscribers using visual display telephones, and invested $1.2 billion in Viacom, the huge entertainment and cable firm. SBC (formerly Southwestern Bell) acquired two cable systems in the Washington, D.C., area; together with Cox Communications (with which it had discussed a merger) it operates the fourth largest cable television system in the United Kingdom; and it purchased a substantial interest in Telmex, the Mexican telephone company. Bell Atlantic, in addition to its failed merger with Tele-Communications, Inc. (TCI), the largest cable television provider, and its successful one with Nynex, owns shares in telephone companies in New Zealand and Mexico and has worked with Oracle Systems, a leading maker of database management systems, to create an interactive shopping, entertainment, and information service.

One could go on and illustrate that every other player has engaged in a bewildering variety of ventures. The theme, however, is evident. Traditional telephone companies have sought international ventures and other opportunities outside the narrow range of plain old telephone service. A look at the failed Bell Atlantic–TCI merger can provide important data on the dynamics at work. The deal fell apart when Bell Atlantic rejected the $32 million price tag.[8] International opportunities and perceived market convergence are among the principal factors that have driven most of the structural moves in telecommunications, including the Bell Atlantic–TCI one. Bell Atlantic chairman Raymond W. Smith, one of the most articulate telecommunications executives, clearly described the incentives on both sides of the proposed merger:

> It also became clear that digital technology was causing a convergence of markets and industries. . . . "Convergence" means that the three principal consumer communications devices—computer, TV and telephone—are merging into one, and as they do, so too are the distinctions among once-separate businesses. . . . As the pace of change in our industry began to pick up, we started looking for the best way to put together all the capabilities we need—distribution, programming and packaging—in the shortest possible time.[9]

The media construed the attempted merger in much the same way. *Business Week,* for example, asserted, "With their deal, Bell Atlantic and TCI plan to bring their communications expertise to new markets—challenging local phone monopolies by providing video-on-demand, home shopping and even local phone service."[10] The *San Jose Mercury-News,* one of the leading sources of information on technology topics, summarized: "Bell Atlantic and TCI join a growing list of telecommunications and technology companies bent on being major players in building and operating the information highway. Early this year another huge phone company, U.S. West, bought a major stake in Time-Warner, the second largest cable operator in the country. . . . On Wednesday, BellSouth bought a 22.5 percent stake in Prime Management, a Texas-based cable operator."[11] The article then pointed to the enormous hardware expenses, including fiber-optic cables, switches, computers, terminals in homes, and so on necessary to create the information superhighway—a colorful term that essentially means an expanded network that can carry every kind of information to every kind of terminal device—PC, television set, telephone, or some combination of all of these. The risks in guessing wrong on any component of the network, the *Mercury-News* added, are very high, as are the risks in failing to patch together the complex technologies required to transmit the different kinds of information on demand to a multitude of customers with varying requirements. Acting as a disincentive to market convergence is whether a sufficient number of people want everything from voice, video, and data to sophisticated interactive services, such as home shopping and videoconferencing, at the rates requisite to return a sufficient profit on the enormous investment required.

The Bell Atlantic–TCI merger failed; but many have succeeded, and the pace of intercorporate linkups remains dizzying. The lessons of the Bell Atlantic–TCI failed engagement are as valid as the deals that resulted in a marriage—or, at least, the partners living together in a less formal arrangement. The trend is clear and compels us to ask why.

We begin with Moore's law, an observation first uttered by Intel cofounder Gordon Moore in 1964. The number of transistors on a given area of silicon had roughly doubled every year. The relation held until the late 1970s, at which time the doubling period slowed to eighteen months. These ratios have persisted at least until late 1995. While Moore has predicted that his law "will continue for a couple of more generations," he concedes that "Beyond that things look difficult."[12] Whether his prophecy will be right is almost beside the point. The microchip, whether in the form of microprocessor, microcontroller, DRAM chip, or whatever, is the fundamental technology that has moved telecommunications at its amazing pace. Chip advances not only determine the speed of devices and networks, but also lead to better performance, new applications, new devices, and "smarter" equipment. As hundreds of firms undertake the application tasks for new generations of chips, telecommunications company risks in guessing wrong on a new technology or holding on to one in danger of rapidly becoming obsolete are very high. For example, how can a firm heavily invested in fiber-optic transmission guard against the possibility that a new wireless technology (for example, CDMA, mentioned in Chapter 7) will make its current technology backward, or even obsolete?

The solution to the risk posed is hedging. Make bets on other existing technologies or new ones that may come on line. You can do this in one of three ways: (1) incurring the development costs, (2) purchasing a new technology after it comes on line, or (3) entering into an alliance or merger with another firm that has superior expertise in the new technological area. While all three options are possible, there are often significant shortcomings in the first and second. The first alternative does nothing to reduce risk, and can be very costly, and the possibility of failing to develop a technology new to the company's scientists and engineers can be high. Second, while purchasing a new technology reduces development risks, it may not be available at the earlier marketing stages. This is a crucial drawback in telecommunications because of the lightning speed with which older technologies are upgraded and new ones introduced. In such a situation even a short delay in coming on line with a new technology can have a serious adverse effect on a company's profits and, perhaps more importantly, its reputation for being a technological leader. There is no danger more serious in modern telecommunications than being viewed as a laggard. Accordingly, the third option is frequently the most attractive one. It can resolve the issues raised in the first two options, and while one must share the potential profits, risks are reduced. Sanjay Kumar, president of the software giant Computer Associates International, observed: "It's much more acceptable for companies that have good technology to supplement their own products." A managing director at the investment firm Lazard-Freres put the same thought in a different way: "Entrepreneurialism is giving way to basic economic trends of consolidation."[13] In summary, one can guard against imperfect knowledge about future trends in technology by engaging in mergers, joint ventures, and alliances.

There are other reasons driving the same trend. Some are, of course, financial. High-technology industries flourished in the stock market boom, and firms engaging in alliances and mergers frequently enjoyed an especially large spurt in stock values—to the delight of the executives involved. Second, vertical integration *can*, but does not necessarily, lead to economies of scope stemming from technological complementarity of the two or more firms, improved coordination of output through successive stages, and elimination of transaction costs (purchasing and selling). Third, a firm that does business in many geographical markets and has a variety of product offerings in the increasingly heterogeneous hypercommunications sector satisfies the desire of large buyers for one-stop shopping. This helps to drive combinations that enlarge both geographical markets and the diversity of product offerings.

Fourth, the promise of digital compression technologies effectively enlarges the transmission capacity of telecommunications carriers. In turn this provides a major incentive to utilize the enlarged capacity. One way of doing this is to transmit types of information that a firm traditionally has not carried. For cable systems this means carrying not only video information, but also data and voice telephone. It also provides an incentive to offer newer services such as interactive video and voice-over-data. But the problems that cable confronts to meet such challenges virtually call out for such firms to seek partners. Cable companies have traditionally been the technological laggards in the telecommunications area. Facing the daunting technological challenges as well as the detailed market information requisite to offering data, telephone, and advanced services virtually compels them to seek out loose-knit or tight-knit partnerships. Additionally, cable transmission has traditionally been a downstream business transmitting entertainment. The contemplated expansion of services requires solving the problems associated with moving information upstream to the cable system head-end *and* switching and interconnecting into other networks. Resolving these problems as well as expanding upstream bandwidth also provides incentives to undertake combination with firms in other telecommunications sectors. Similar technological and marketing problems also face telephone companies, Internet providers, and others who, therefore, also are provided with similar incentives, especially if they wish to provide entertainment over networks.[14]

Fifth, the concept of product differentiation provides still another reason for alliances. Product differentiation refers to the question of whether the products of competing sellers in a market are viewed as identical or different. What matters is consumers' subjective judgments about quality, design, packaging, reputation, variety of offerings, and so on, not objective criteria. For example, gasoline of a certain octane rating produced by different petroleum refiners is objectively very much the same. Yet each corporation in that industry spends vast sums every year to create in consumers' minds the impression that its brand is superior to the others. If firms in the emerging telecommunications industry largely deploy the same menu of technologies and kinds of offerings, the content of offerings looms as one major method of achieving a high degree of product differentiation. The disadvantages to a firm of failing to achieve a reasonable degree of product differentiation are, first, that it cannot increase rates and hold customers if competitors do not follow suit; sellers are even forced to match the rate reductions of competitors in order to hold customers. Second, sales promotion will be ineffective in attracting customers or in securing higher rates since buyers already view the competing outputs as perfect substitutes for each other. The inexorable trend, then, without product differentiation, is for profit margins in such industries to be thin, since any rate movement upward can be viewed as a rival's only opportunity to increase market share by not following suit.[15]

When one introduces a reasonable degree of product differentiation, all of this changes. Advertising and promotion become important in attracting customers. Sellers are no longer bound to sell at a single rate, and they may elevate rates if consumers are led to believe that a particular offering is superior to competitors' (even if the belief is objectively false). There are, of course, a variety of ways in which one firm can differentiate its products from others, including advertising and promotion. But from the perspective of any hypercommunications firm, one of the most effective can be to offer content different from that of its rivals. It is from this perspective that close links between information-transmission firms and those in industries that have traditionally specialized in the generation of content aids product differentiation. I refer, of course, to the Hollywood film factories and their distributors as well as their counterparts in television program production and distribution. Their great invention—the star system—is the most successful example of product differentiation ever seen. Entertainment companies, after initial periods of resisting such advances as VCRs and cable television, now take full advantage of them to their enormous profit. Potential new outlets, such as full motion video on the Internet, can only be a mouthwatering prospect to the dream merchants. Large entertainment firms are already deeply involved in other information sectors.[16] From the perspective of the information-transmission firms, such links go a long way in solving the problem of product differentiation.

It is conceivable that any of the dominant telecommunications firms can go it alone in two or more of the submarkets, but it is unlikely that they can do so in all of the submarkets. Consider, for example, Sprint, which began as a long-distance provider but is entering the local telephone market, constructing a digital wireless and paging network, has giant international partners in Deutsche Telekom and France Télécom, is building high-speed connections to the Internet, and is selling movies and other entertainment programs with cable partners. Like other large telecommunications firms, Sprint sees a significant advantage in providing one-stop shopping and a seamless network. In the succinct words of G. Christian Hill, a *Wall Street Journal* analyst, the emerging hypercommunications firms "want to sell you the bundle."[17] For this reason, close links have been established between Time Warner, US West, PCS Prime, and BellSouth. In summary, because of the risks and incentives set forth in this section, the twenty-first century portends the emergence of hypercommunications groups embracing local-loop service, international long distance, national long distance, cable television, Internet provision, satellite, wireless (cellular, PCS and other technologies), and entertainment components with selected equipment vendors linked to the group.

AT&T's split into three corporations—NCR, Lucent, and AT&T—announced in September 1995, does not negate the central trend in hypercommunications. AT&T conceded that NCR was a bad acquisition, never fitting into the larger firm and never becoming a major factor in most parts of the computer business. AT&T's equipment arm, according to telecommunications analyst Jack Grubman, "makes the world's best network technology. They never have sold one dollar's worth of equipment to MCI,

British Telecom, France Telecom, or other operators around the world who fear AT&T on the service side."[18] Obviously, AT&T's strategic consideration in spinning off Lucent was that the world's best network technology manufacturer would continue to sell to AT&T and pick up many other large buyers as well. But, as we have seen, AT&T has also entered the other key submarkets directly or through purchase, such as wireless provider McCaw Cellular. AT&T has also invested in Direct TV, a direct broadcast satellite (DBS) firm that competes with cable television. It, too, intends to cover all bases.

Cable Television

The history of cable television, a communications medium not yet discussed in detail, illustrates the risks and tendencies described in the last section. Cable television began modestly, gradually changing its structure, and is now on the road to sharing in the new hypercommunications market. At the same time, it is being challenged on its home turf by other technologies, such as DBS. Finally, its strategies have been shaped by F.C.C. actions, judicial decisions, and legislation, most importantly the Telecommunications Act of 1996. Cable television has been defined as a medium that distributes television signals through wires (at first coaxial cables, more recently optical fibers in many systems). In its early days cable television was able to serve several complementary functions that aided the new over-the-air television networks. First, during the period in which the F.C.C. imposed a freeze on television licenses that ended in the early 1950s, cable television was able to bring television to small and medium-sized communities. Second, even after the freeze was ended, cable television was able to provide reception to areas that could not be reached by over-the-air television. Third, it often provided improved clarity compared to over-the-air TV. This included not just rural areas and television sets distant from local television station antennae, but urban areas as well, in which tall buildings and other sources of distortion interfered with good reception. Thus, in the early stages cable television was not conceived as a threat to over-the-air television but, rather, as a beneficial supplement. Because of its rural roots, the service was at first known as community antenna television (CATV).

John Walson, Sr., of Mahanoy City, Pennsylvania, has received public distinction as "the father of cable television." He was a line serviceman for the Pennsylvania Power and Light Company who also owned an appliance store at the time that television sets were first being mass marketed. Having found that video signals could not be received in his area due to the surrounding Appalachian Mountains acting as a barrier; in 1948 Walson erected a large antenna on top of a seventy-foot utility pole and strung flat wire from the antenna down the mountain to a warehouse. With the help of amplifiers positioned along the wire route, he was able to provide reasonable reception of television programs in order not only to sell television sets but also to obtain subscribers to his cable connection. For this service he charged a one-hundred-dollar installation fee plus monthly subscriber fees of two dollars.

Other students of CATV history recognize a system constructed by Jerrold Electronic Corporation in Lansford, Pennsylvania, as the first community antenna television system specifically designed to earn a profit. Early in 1950, Jerrold offered three amplified television signals to subscribers in Lansford who paid an installation charge and agreed to pay monthly service charges.

Another system was constructed by a store owner wishing to dispose of a backlog of television sets in Pottsville, Pennsylvania, about twenty miles from Lansford. The owner obtained permission from the town council, negotiated a contract with the local telephone company to attach cables to their poles, and within a year enlisted a thousand subscribers to his service. Originally, this system offered only two channels, but later service was expanded to five channels, including an independent station and an educational one.[19]

Most cable companies in the earlier days of cable television conveyed their signals to the subscriber by running their wires on poles belonging to existing utilities. The utility companies reserved space on poles to be specifically used for cable television transmission. Because cable systems arrived many years after telephone and electric service, there was not a regulatory agency to require entrenched telephone and power utilities to share their poles with the cable systems; cable operators could gain access to the utility poles only by contract with telephone companies for pole attachment space. Initially, telephone companies attempted to gain ownership or control of the broadband cable used to provide cable television service. However, their attempts were thwarted by a number of F.C.C. decisions. Unable to maintain their own CATV channel services, the telephone companies began demanding vastly increased cable television pole attachment rates. Problems relating to the cost of erecting poles and pole attachment surfaced in the early 1950s. In 1951, the F.C.C. attempted to remedy the problem and decided that a pole attachment agreement was required as a condition for the procurement of a municipal franchise. However, the commission later decided that the resolution of the problem should be in the hands of legislators. A number of bills regarding pole attachments were introduced in Congress, and eventually the Communications Act was amended to resolve this issue. Under the statute's provisions, the F.C.C. was granted jurisdiction to set the rates, terms, and conditions for pole attachments unless a given state already had its own pole attachment regulations.[20]

From its inception in the late 1940s until the enactment of the 1984

Cable Communications Policy Act, the cable television industry experienced three major developmental phases. Initially, cable systems were constructed to bring conventional broadcast programming to remote areas that were unable to receive over-the-air television signals. From 1948 until 1961, cable systems were able to operate in an environment relatively free from governmental intervention. CATV did not require special regulation because cable was merely doing what the television system would otherwise be unable to accomplish. However, as cable became more advanced, it began importing distant signals by microwave to supplement local broadcast programming, and governmental oversight began. Following a landmark 1962 Supreme Court decision, cable television, particularly in respect to the importation of distant signals, became subject to F.C.C. regulation.[21] The principal reason that the F.C.C. moved to regulate CATV was that the service was becoming not just a supplement to over-the-air television but a competitor as well. The battle between the two groups, in an early example of the process of market convergence, came to a head before the agency in 1958. A complaint had been filed under the Communications Act of 1934 by over-the-air television licensees against 288 CATV operators in thirty-six states. The commission was asked by a group of Western broadcasters to enjoin cable systems from carrying their programs and to declare the cable systems to be interstate common carriers.

The primary reason for the complainants' interest in subjecting CATV to the commission's common-carrier jurisdiction was the alleged adverse economic impact of such systems on local television broadcast stations.[22] The independent cable programming that disturbed the over-the-air systems was very modest by contemporary standards; cable systems began carrying FM radio stations and weather scans in which local advertising messages were printed on the screens containing weather information. Nevertheless, over-the-air stations saw the danger to their interests that could be imposed in the future and decided to act early before the CATV interests became powerful. In 1966, deluged with over-the-air broadcast complaints against the industry that was now becoming known as cable, the F.C.C. issued regulations requiring cable systems to carry all local television channels, and prohibiting the importation of distant signals duplicating local over-the-air television stations' offerings. The Supreme Court in 1968 again upheld the F.C.C.'s authority to issue such rules, even though they would retard the new industry's development.[23]

In 1969 the F.C.C. began to do an about-face, recognizing the increasing importance of independent cable origination. In that year 2,260 cable systems served more than 3.6 million homes. Earlier in the decade, entrepreneurial Tele Promp Ter introduced pay television in a world-championship boxing match. Technical quality of reception had improved dramatically through the introduction of aluminum-shielded distribution cable with foam dielectric. Most importantly, a set-top converter was introduced in 1967 that broke the previous twelve-channel barrier for home television sets. In short, entrepreneurial activity in the cable industry was compelling regulators to see cable television in a new way. The F.C.C. now allowed cable companies to carry advertising in connection with programs, but in a major restriction and concession to localism, it ruled (later modified) that no cable system with more that thirty-five hundred subscribers could carry any broadcasting signal unless it made facilities available for local program production and transmission.[24]

Then in 1976 the F.C.C. went too far, requiring cable systems with more than thirty-five hundred subscribers to develop a minimum twenty-channel capacity by 1986, to make channels available to third parties, and to furnish equipment and facilities for access purposes. The Supreme Court in 1979 held that these requirements were beyond the agency's powers. The Court invited Congress to clarify the agency's jurisdiction over cable.[25] During the period of uncertainty between the 1979 Supreme Court decision and the new federal law enacted in 1984, local governments, covetous of protecting their powers, franchise fees, and leverage over cable television operators, moved aggressively to assert more authority over the medium. The myth of localism, in which cable franchises were expected to be owned by local interests and a number of valuable channels allocated to municipal and local programming (which accounts for the continuing presence of such channels that virtually no one watches), was an invaluable ideological tool to the powerful combination of local governments who have played a major role in shaping federal policy.

The reality was different. Many (perhaps most) of the franchise awards were tainted. For example, Mayor Marion Barry of Washington appointed the two top executives in the city's cable TV franchise as consultants. In Washington, the partners in the winning franchise included Barry's media adviser, several of his close confidants, and his reelection treasurer. While overt bribery was not the predominant method in franchising—at least not the discovered preferred method—the "rent-a-citizen" approach typifies most awards in large communities. In Omaha, for example, Cox Cable won the local franchise and included eight prominent Omahans as shareholders in the local subsidiary. These persons made investments in the range of $20 to $40; at the time a $40 investment was expected to yield $1.9 million. The Houston example also illustrates the dynamics. According to the U.S. Court of Appeals for the Fifth Circuit, in 1978 Jim McConn, then mayor, divided the city's franchises among four applicants, each backed by local political influentials. Later these "local" franchisees sold their valuable franchises to national firms for enormous profits.[26]

Cities were exploiting the myth of localism in the very period that the cable TV industry was undergoing a dramatic transformation. In 1977 annual cable TV revenues exceeded $1 billion, and giants, such as American Express, came into the industry. TCI, formed in 1968 from smaller cable companies, had twelve employees in that year. By 1975 it was the nation's second largest cable operator with more than 651,000 customers from 149 systems in thirty-two states. By 1982 TCI passed the two-million subscriber mark.[27] Cox Enterprises, a broadcasting company, entered cable in 1962 when it bought a small system in Lewistown, Pennsylvania; by 1972 it had 500,000 subscribers in nine states. Time, Inc., entered the cable business in 1972 with the purchase of Home Box Office (HBO). By 1975 HBO was offering uncut, uninterrupted, relatively new Hollywood movies and special events. One could go on, but the point is eminently clear. By the time of the 1984 Cable Communications Policy Act, cable television had become big business, dominated by a relatively few large firms, which in some cases had become vertically integrated backward into the production of entertainment. By the 1990s the cutting-edge model of a cable company had become Time Warner, Inc., formed in 1989 by a merger of Time, Inc. and Warner Communications. It was in both film and television production and cablecasting, ran cable networks, wireless and paging operations, and data services. Time Warner had an international presence and was linked to a number of other firms in the various telecommunications submarkets. In short, Time Warner had become a quintessential hypercommunications firm. We are a long way from the localism myth.

These trends were clear in 1984 when Congress enacted the first comprehensive statute on cable television. The most important change the act sought was to deregulate cable rates. Congress based its decision on three factors. First, it feared that without a check on franchise fees, local governments would be tempted to solve their fiscal problems by levying a burdensome tax on the cable industry. Second, the legislators believed that the cable industry had matured and was capable of competing with over-the-air television. Consequently, rate regulation at the local level was no longer a necessity. Finally, they concluded that cable services, unlike electricity or gas, were nonessential and did not possess any of the characteristics of public utilities. In short, legislative feeling was that cable deregulation was an idea whose time had come because the benefits of cable technology, which could finally be offered in a competitive market environment, were being impeded by local regulation.

As enacted by Congress, the legislation largely deregulated the cable communications industry and removed most of the ability of municipal, state, or federal franchising authorities to regulate the rates charged by franchisees for the provision of cable service where there was "effective competition." However, it recognized the power of cities to grant and renew franchises and outlined standard franchise procedures that made cable companies less vulnerable to capricious and harmful decisions.

A sharp increase in cable rates, much greater than the rate of inflation, in the period following enactment of the new statute inevitably led to consumer resentment. A few weeks before the 1992 presidential election, Congress handed President George Bush the sole override of a veto during his presidency. The new statute, since modified by the Telecommunications Act of 1996, compelled cable companies to renegotiate licenses from over-the-air stations for the right to carry the latters' programming, allowed small over-the-air stations to demand that cable systems carry their programs (the "must carry" provision), and required cable operators who produce popular programming to make it available to direct broadcast satellite (DBS) and other competing technologies. Significantly, the law required the F.C.C. to provide guidelines for local government cable rate making on the "basic tier of services" (consisting of local and network over-the-air and public access stations) and to provide rate guidelines for "expanded services," such as cable news or sports channels. In the latter instance, consumers and local governments could appeal "unreasonable" rates.[28] The statute, needless to say, set off a flurry of F.C.C. rule-making proceedings, some rate freezing, and cable company appeals.

On to the Future

While in broad outline the statute and the F.C.C. actions under it were largely (although not entirely) upheld, the 1992 statute was mainly a sideshow next to the basic changes taking place in telecommunications. By 1992 cable companies were investing heavily in fiber-optic lines that would greatly enlarge capacity. As it is, coaxial cables, which carry less information than fiber, can carry up to nine hundred times the information that copper wires, still widely employed by local telephone companies, can.[29] Optical fiber has still other major advantages and important business implications. First, transmission costs will drop because signals can be carried much greater distances without the use of amplifiers, which degrade signal quality. Amplifiers incur high maintenance costs as well. Moreover, fiber optics offers the promise of two-way communications, high-quality voice, data, and video, and more channels. At the same time fiber-optic technology has been improving so that the channel capacity for each fiber has increased from eighteen to eighty video channels.

However, the cable giants are not betting entirely on fiber-optics. Coaxial cable and hybrid fiber-coaxial (HFC) may support a new family of cable modems that promise to operate at speeds up to one thousand times faster than the current family of 28.8 or 33.6 kilobits per second (Kbps) telephone modems used for Internet access, and ten times faster than the telephone companies' 128 Kbps ISDN line limit. Cable systems, thus, are adding Internet access to their other offerings. Instead of going through an Internet provider, one simply turns on his or her computer with the cable company connecting to the Internet. Of course, the cable companies must reconfigure architecture and dramatically increase the system's ability to handle upstream traffic. As 1997 began, only 7 percent of the United States's cable systems could handle two-way traffic, even though more than 70 percent of households had the ability to access cable. The capital requirements to upgrade are obviously enormous. Already @Home and TCI have launched such an experimental service in California, while other major cable companies and partners have begun similar efforts using cable modems in other parts of the country. But like all advanced technologies, cable modems may not work as well as planned, reinforcing the hedging strategy and its implications discussed earlier. Intel president Andrew Grove, for example, after initial enthusiasm and backing, concluded that the cable modem system is "awfully difficult to implement," endorsing other technologies instead that are closely associated with telephone companies.[30]

Telephone companies have not sat idly by in the face of the cable threat. During the 1990s, as we noted earlier, they began a series of cable acquisitions, culminating in US West's 1996 acquisition of Continental Cablevision. After winning court battles against cable systems in the 1990s, US West and other telephone companies launched video dial tone, a system that delivers voice, data, and video signals. Under that system voice signals are split off from video signals with voice sent to the home through copper wires and video carried into the home through coaxial cables.[31] While the legal status of video dial tone has been in doubt, the telephone companies are now banking on a technology called asynchronous digital subscriber lines (ADSL) to compete with cable modems. ADSL uses filters to split existing copper-wire phone lines into three frequency channels carrying, respectively, telephone signals, data transfers, and either video on demand or WWW information. ADSL's enormous advantage is that it can use existing phone lines rather than requiring the enormous upgrading cable modems require. But serious questions exist about technological problems, the cost of the special equipment required at consumers' premises, and the cost of the service. In addition, ADSL requires new transformers, analog filters, and analog-digital converters. Moreover, there are technological problems concerning the dynamic range of sound and noise. Nevertheless, ADSL has been tested successfully. But the road from tests to market is often a difficult one. If that were not enough competition for cable modems, there is also wireless cable, in which a dish is placed on one's roof that can receive data and pass it down to a modem through coaxial cable. Further, there are various satellite services. On the horizon are local multipoint distribution service (LMDS) and multichannel multipoint distribution service (MMDS), two cutting-edge wireless technologies that use small antennae mounted on window sills. Telephone companies and other players are involved in these new technologies as well.[32]

As if this bewildering stew of proven and experimental technologies and the large number of actors were not enough, 1995 and 1996 saw another submarket suddenly grow in prominence. Old and new telecommunications firms, new alliances, and the hedging strategy all played a role in the revival of direct broadcast satellite (DBS) after years of foundering. Prices for the satellite dish, which is now the size of a pizza pan, dropped to two hundred dollars by late 1996. The technology then had four million subscribers and boasted picture quality that put typical cable quality to shame. Moreover, it offered more than two hundred channels. Internet access through DBS was in the offing, as well. DBS's major problem was that, while it could bring video from around the world, it could not show local TV channels. Symptomatic of the converging nature of communications, cable companies, while competing against DBS, also formed a consortium, called Primestar Partners, to enter the DBS market as a hedge. AT&T, GTE, and other telecommunications companies have also moved into the industry through acquisition or strategic alliances. Thus, from cables below the ground to satellites in the sky, hypercommunications has replaced the separated markets of the past.[33]

The Telecommunications Act of 1996

In February 1996 President Clinton signed into law the Telecommunications Act of 1996, the law that recognized the dramatic changes taking place in the telecommunications marketplace. While every player in hypercommunications saw the need for a new statute that would reflect the enormous changes since the enactment of the 1934 basic law, working out the details was an enormously difficult and time-consuming process. Every player agreed to allow entry into its markets. But the issues of when, how, and under what conditions required intense and complex negotiations and lobbying. Of course, those people who thought that regulation would come to an end under the new statute, or that litigation in this highly litigious sector of the economy would disappear, were laboring under an illusion. Indeed, the F.C.C. and state regulators have been very active, and the litigation began on the day President Clinton signed the act into law. Nevertheless, even at the signing ceremony, attended by virtually every player in hypercommunications, executives were discussing mergers, alliances, and entering new markets.[34] Access-charge issues and a host of others were continuing to be debated within the F.C.C. and state agencies notwithstanding the new law.

Even though the 1996 act will hardly end regulation and disputes, the statute has been widely viewed as a great leap forward. Perhaps the most important aspect of the statute is the recognition that telecommunications has become a converged market and not a set of discrete ones. Television, cable TV, entertainment, computers, wireline telephone and wireless, and other sectors were conceived as a single hypermedia market, the combined revenues of which approached $1 trillion at the time President Clinton signed the bill into law.[35] While the general thrust of the law is clearly in the direction of allowing more open competition, restrictions nonetheless remain. Cable companies are forbidden to purchase telephone companies except in rural areas, but they may purchase up to 10 percent of a telephone company elsewhere. Large cable company rates for extended basic service will not be deregulated until 1999, except where a telephone company delivers a comparable cable service. Cable companies may provide telephone service, and local telephone carriers are required to assist *any* new competitors, including cable companies, in the areas of interconnection, access, and number parity. Restrictions on over-the-air television stations have been liberalized, although any television station owner may reach no more than 35 percent of United States homes. Broadcast companies may own cable stations. A network may not purchase a competing network, but may create new ones.

Telephone companies are bound with rules that parallel those of cable companies. They may not own more than 10 percent of a cable company and are prevented from buying cable systems, except in areas with fewer than thirty-five thousand people. They may, however, provide video programming. If they do so, they may choose to be regulated as a cable system, common carrier, or "open video system." If they choose the third classification, they must offer independent programmers the right to telecast over their systems without discrimination and are generally bound by the local and national rules covering cable systems. Local telephone companies are permitted to offer long-distance service, while long-distance carriers can offer local service. Each will be bound by the applicable F.C.C. and state rules covering the service they enter. Local carriers enjoying a de facto monopoly must show that there is effective competition for both residential and business subscribers before they are allowed to enter equipment manufacture and long distance (which, of course, has had effective competition). Finally, all telecommunications companies must contribute to a universal service fund that assures that everyone will have access to the system.

The statute also contained provisions concerning transmission of "indecent" material over the Internet—provisions rapidly declared unconstitutional by lower courts—and using the Internet to inflame people. The Internet, in short, remains largely a free, open, and competitive structure. Television set manufacturers are required to include a "violence microprocessor" (V-chip) that will read a rating signal accompanying each program and block those considered undesirable by the viewer. This requirement does not go into effect until V-chip technology is developed and proven. Television broadcasters were required to develop a rating system indicating the degrees of violence, sexual content, and vulgarity in each program and assign the rating to each program. There is much more in the 280–page law, but the broad contours are generally in the direction of more openness and competition, as the foregoing description indicates. Lurking in the background is the advent of high definition television (HDTV), soon to come on line. What its impact will be on the hypercommunications stew remains to be seen.

What Hath God Wrought!

In 1832, during a leisurely ocean voyage returning to the United States from Europe, Samuel F.B. Morse conceived the idea of transmitting letters, and therefore words, by an electromagnetic device. Benefiting from the advice of the great scientist Joseph Henry, Morse gave a demonstration of his new device, the telegraph, in 1837 before a group of scientists at New York University. In 1843 Congress appropriated $30,000 to demonstrate the device on a line between Washington, D.C., and Baltimore. On May 24, 1844, Morse tapped out his famous message—"What hath God wrought!"—and set in motion a revolution, the effects of which continue to be experienced into the foreseeable future. Morse and Henry, as brilliant as they were, could have no sense of the enormous social, economic, and technological changes that would be wrought only a few years after the telegraph's invention. Similarly, one would be foolhardy today to predict what the future of telecommunications holds in ten, twenty-five, or fifty years' time. But the past does hold lessons, the most important of which can be summarized in two words: Don't overgeneralize.

Bearing this caution in mind, there are several persisting themes in this examination of what is now one-sixth of the United States economy. Almost from its beginnings telecommunications became a major factor in the process of control. In 1851 the New York and Erie Railroad installed a telegraph line that allowed the company to coordinate and control its operations as never before. Today, a global economy is possible only because the speed of communications allows any company to control operations and dealings throughout the globe from a central facility. At the same time, the ability of telecommunications to control implies an important note of caution. A surfeit of information does not imply that the information is accurate or beneficial; one can only recall Adolf Hitler's remarkable use of the radio during the 1930s to poison the minds of the German people. In less dramatic fashion the United States Congress's insistence that future television sets include a V-chip attests to the negative impact that powerful telecommunications can have. But this is only to suggest that technologies bear costs as well as benefits. The technology itself cannot be blamed; all other things being equal, technological progress should be welcomed. Telecommunications technology has, on balance, made our lives immeasurably better, both in overcoming solitude for individuals and through its innumerable business applications.

We, therefore, owe a debt of gratitude to the many engineers, scientists, and innovators who have been mentioned in these pages. From the innovators who formed and guided Western Union in 1855 through those at Sun Microsystems who, in 1995, gave us the Java programming language for the WWW, a continuing theme in this book has been the central role of innovators in advancing telecommunications. But note, an innovator is not an inventor. Invention alone has no economic or social effects. An innovator is one who combines invention and investment. Steve Jobs, as we saw in the last chapter, visited Xerox's research facilities, observed many inventions, invested in developing them, and radically transformed the PC from a scientific tool to a consumer product. Innovators are often entrepreneurs who, in Joseph Schumpeter's words, "reform or revolutionize the pattern of production by exploiting an invention or, more generally, an untried technological possibility for producing a new commodity or producing an old one in a new way, by opening up a new source of supply . . . or a new outlet for products, by reorganizing an industry and so on."[36] Yet the very risky activity of bringing new services to market, as we have seen, has been undertaken not just by small start-up companies, but by such giants as IBM and AT&T as well. Indeed, AT&T, while still a monopolist, probably compiled the finest record of innovation that the world has ever seen.

And just as one must be wary about facile generalizations concerning the size of firms or the extent of competition that leads to innovation, one must also be careful about the role of government. In what is perhaps his most widely quoted statement, Adam Smith observed:

> Every individual necessarily labours to render the annual revenue of the society as great as he can. He generally, indeed, neither intends to promote the public interest, nor knows how much he is promoting it. . . . By directing that industry in such a manner as its produce may be of the greatest value, he intends only his own gain, and he is in this, as in many other cases, led by an invisible hand to promote an end which was no part of his intention. Nor is it always the worse for the society that it was no part of it. By pursuing his own interest he frequently promotes that of the society more effectually than when he really intends to promote it.[37]

But while extolling self-interest as the underlying source of wealth, Smith recognized in many places a role for government. We will never know whether or not the Internet would have been constructed if the United States government had not been involved. We do, however, know that government organized the effort that led to the remarkable commercial and social benefits that take place on the Internet. Indeed, Adam Smith recognized the important role of government in subsidizing very large scale projects, especially if they relate to national defense or some other great public good that the market will not readily undertake. The experience of socialism has rightly made us very wary of government control. But this in no way supports the reductionist argument that government can serve no role (other than central banking) in the economic arena. Government has subsidized and supported many important economic developments and, as portions of this book have sought to show, it has often regulated industries and disputes effectively. Certainly we should be very wary of government intervention, with its long record of oppression throughout history in most of the world. But there are always situations in which desirable results "cannot be attained at all or attained only in inappropriate amounts if left to the free market."[38]

We must, in short, be wary of overconfident judgments, not only about the future of telecommunications technology but about such other factors as business structure and government involvement. Our watchword should be, "It all depends."

Notes

Chapter 1. From the Telegraph to Hypercommunications

1. U.S. Bureau of the Census, *Historical Statistics of the United States, Colonial Times to 1970* (Washington, D.C.: Government Printing Office, 1975), 2:716.
2. See Paul A. Baran and Paul M. Sweezy, *Monopoly Capital* (New York: Monthly Review Press, 1966), 219, 220; Alfred D. Chandler, *Giant Enterprise: Ford, General Motors, and the American Automobile Industry* (New York: Harcourt, Brace and World, 1964), 3–20; Charles H. Hession and Hyman Sardy, *Ascent to Affluence* (Boston: Allyn and Bacon, 1969), 520–23.
3. Daniel Bell, "The Disunited States of America," *TLS,* June 9, 1995, 17.
4. James R. Beniger, *The Control Revolution* (Cambridge: Harvard University Press, 1986), 7, 8.
5. Alfred D. Chandler, *The Visible Hand* (Cambridge: Harvard University Press, 1977), 18.
6. The best discussion of information costs remains George J. Stigler, *The Organization of Industry* (Homewood, Ill.: Richard D. Irwin, 1968), 171–88.
7. Richard B. Duboff, "The Telegraph and the Structure of Markets in the United States, 1845–1890," in *Research in Economic History,* vol. 8, ed. Paul Uselding (Greenwich, Conn.: JAI Press, 1982), 257–65.
8. See Beniger, *Control Revolution,* 278–87; James H. Madison, "Communications," in *Encyclopedia of American Economic History,* ed. Glenn Porter (New York: Charles Scribner's Sons, 1980), 1:335–43; Richard N. Current, *The Typewriter and the Men Who Made It* (Urbana: University of Illinois Press, 1954).
9. See Richard Schmalensee, *The Control of Natural Monopolies* (Lexington, Mass.: Lexington Books, 1979); Leonard Waverman, "The Regulation of Intercity Telecommunications," in *Promoting Competition in Regulated Markets,* ed. Almarin Phillips (Washington, D.C.: Brookings Institution, 1975), 232, 233.
10. Peter W. Huber, Michael K. Kellogg, and John Thorne, *The Geodesic Network II: 1993 Report on Competition in the Telephone Industry* (Washington, D.C.: Geodesic Company, 1992), p. 3.44.
11. Details are provided in Charles H. Ferguson and Charles R. Morris, *Computer Wars* (New York: Times Books, 1993), 17, 18; "The Third Age," *Economist,* September 17, 1994, Survey, 3, 4.
12. Friedrich A. Hayek, *Law, Legislation, and Liberty* (Chicago: University of Chicago Press, 1973), 1:15.
13. Walter Lippmann, *The Public Philosophy* (Boston: Little, Brown, 1955), 101.

14. The concept I am advancing is different from but similar to the idea of social learning advanced in Peter A. Hall, "Policy Paradigms, Social Learning, and the State," *Comparative Politics,* April 1993, 275–96.

15. John Maynard Keynes, *The General Theory of Employment, Interest, and Money* (London: Macmillan, 1936), 383.

16. Thomas S. Kuhn, *The Structure of Scientific Revolutions,* 2d ed. (Chicago: University of Chicago Press, 1970), 92.

17. On the path to such changes in public philosophy, see Margaret Thatcher, *The Path to Power* (New York: HarperCollins, 1995), 50–52; and Margaret Thatcher, *The Downing Street Years* (New York: HarperCollins, 1993), 7, 680–87.

18. See Michael E. Porter and Victor E. Millar, "How Information Gives You Competitive Advantage," *Harvard Business Review,* July-August, 1980, 149–60.

19. See Richard S. Rosenbloom and Michael A. Cusumano, "Technological Pioneering and Competitive Advantage: The Birth of the VCR Industry," *California Management Review,* Summer 1987, 51–76.

20. Kim B. Clark and Takahiro Fujimoto, *Product Development Performance* (Boston: Harvard Business School Press, 1991) 35.

21. Joseph Schumpeter, *Capitalism, Socialism, and Democracy,* 3d ed. (New York: Harper & Row, 1950), 132.

22. See R.H. Coase, "The Nature of the Firm," *Economica* 4 (New Series, November 1937): 404.

23. Joe Bain, *Price Theory* (New York: John Wiley, 1952), 50–53; *United States v. E.I. du Pont de Nemours,* 351 U.S. 377 (1956).

24. David Hume, *A Treatise of Human Nature* (1739; reprint, London: Penguin Books, 1969), 553.

25. R.H. Coase, "The Federal Communications Commission," *Journal of Law & Economics* 2 (October 1959): 1–40. See also R.H. Coase and Nicholas Johnson, "Should the Federal Communications Commission Be Abolished?" in *Regulation, Economics, and the Law,* ed. Bernard H. Siegan (Lexington, Mass.: D.C. Heath, 1979), 41–56.

26. *United States v American Telephone and Telegraph,* Civil Action 74–1698, Defendants' Third Statement of Contentions and Proof (1980): 1:60, 61.

27. Simon Nora and Alain Minc, *The Computerization of Society* (Cambridge: MIT Press, 1980), 19, 20.

28. Fritz Machlup, *The Production and Distribution of Knowledge in the United States* (Princeton: Princeton University Press, 1962).

29. Beniger, *Control Revolution,* 25.

30. See Robert Britt Horwitz, *The Irony of Regulatory Reform: The Deregulation of American Telecommunications* (New York: Oxford University Press, 1989); and Alan Stone, *Wrong Number: The Breakup of AT&T* (New York: Basic Books, 1989).

Chapter 2. The Rise of AT&T

1. There is an enormous literature on the disputes concerning the invention of the telephone. The most important sources upon which I rely are David A. Hounshell, "Elisha Gray and the Telephone: On the Disadvantages of Being an Expert," *Technology and Culture* 16 (April 1975): 133–61; Lloyd W. Taylor, "The Untold Story of the Telephone," *American Physics Teacher* 5 (1937): 250; Fred De Land, *The Invention of the Electric Speaking Telephone,* in AT&T Archives, Box 1098; William Aitken, *Who Invented the Telephone?* (London: Blackie and Son, 1939), chaps. 1–14; George B. Prescott, *Bell's Electric Speaking Telephone* (New York: D. Appleton & Co., 1884);

Robert V. Bruce, *Bell: Alexander Graham Bell and the Conquest of Solitude* (Boston: Little, Brown, 1973); and W. James King, "The Telegraph and the Telephone," in *The Development of Electrical Technology in the Nineteenth Century*, Paper 29, Bulletin 228 (Washington, D.C.: United States National Museum, 1962), 312–18.

2. The most important legal materials are *Telephone Cases*, 126 U.S. 863 (1887), and *The Deposition of Alexander Graham Bell in the Suit Brought by the United States to Annul the Bell Patents* (Boston: American Bell Telephone Co., 1908); John E. Kingsbury, *The Telephone and Telephone Exchanges: Their Invention and Development* (New York: Longmans, Green, 1915), Chap. 5; Charles H. Swan, *Narrative History of the Litigation on the Bell Patents, 1878–1896*, in AT&T Archives, Box 1098. See also *American Bell Tel. Co. v. American Cushman Tel. Co.*, 35 F. 734 (N.D., Ill., 1888), and *American Bell Tel. Co. v. People's Tel. Co.*, 22 F. 309 (S.D., N.Y., 1884).

3. Details on the Western Union battle are based on Rosario Joseph Tosiello, *The Birth and Early Years of the Bell Telephone System, 1876–1880* (New York: Arno Press, 1979), 81–83, 484–91; Alvin F. Harlow, *Old Wires and New Waves* (1936; reprint, New York: Arno Press, 1971), 409–11; Robert W. Garnet, *The Telephone Enterprise* (Baltimore: Johns Hopkins University Press, 1985), Chap. 4; and Federal Communications Commission, Special Investigation, Dkt. 1, Exhibit 2096F, *Financial Control of the Telephone Industry* (1937), 13–29.

Gifford's views are recorded in Affidavit of George Gifford, September 19, 1882, in AT&T Archives, Box 1006.

Details on Gould's involvement are found in Maury Klein, *The Life and Legend of Jay Gould* (Baltimore: Johns Hopkins University Press, 1986), 276–82.

4. R.H. Coase, "The Nature of the Firm," *Economica* 4 (New Series, November 1937): 404.

5. See Leonard S. Reich, *The Making of American Industrial Research* (Cambridge: Cambridge University Press, 1985), 144.

6. Biographical material on Vail is based primarily on Albert Bigelow Paine, *In One Man's Life* (New York: Harper & Row, 1921); although an example of the "hero worship" genre, it contains much factual information. On the business details, see Alan Stone, *Public Service Liberalism* (Princeton: Princeton University Press, 1991), 89–96.

7. See Stone, *Public Service Liberalism*, 96–103; Garnet, *Telephone Enterprise*, 76–80.

8. Harold C. Livesay and Patrick G. Porter, "Vertical Integration in American Manufacturing, 1899–1948," *Journal of Economic History* 29 (September 1969): 495–96.

9. See Garnet, *Telephone Enterprise*, 14–17, 138; Stone, *Public Service Liberalism*, 103–21.

10. *Johnson County Home Telephone Co.*, 8 Mo. P.S.C.R. 637 (1919).

11. On patent policies, see F.C.C., Special Investigation, Dkt. 1, Exhibit 1989, *Patent Structure of the Bell System, Its History and Policies and Practices Relative Thereto* (1936).

The conclusion on franchise battles is based on an examination of every issue of *Telephony*, then the leading independents' trade journal, before 1920.

12. AT&T, *1907 Annual Report*, 18.

13. AT&T, *1910 Annual Report*, 32, 33.

14. As examples of the view of merchants on the undesirability of telephone competition, see the reports of the Merchants Association of New York opposing the grant of competing franchises. *Telephone Competition from the Standpoint of the Public* (New York: New York Telephone Co., 1906), in AT&T Archives, Box 1082; Special Telephone Committee, Merchants Association of New York, *Supplemental Telephone Report, Further Inquiry into Effect of Competition* (1905).

15. Stuart Daggert, "Telephone Consolidation under the Act of 1921," *Journal of Land & Public Utility Economics,* 7: 27.

16. Stipulation/Contention Package, Episode 5, paragraphs 580–82, 615–73, *United States v. AT&T.*

17. R.H. Coase, "Discussion," in *A Critique of Administrative Regulation of Public Utilities,* ed. Warren J. Samuels and Harry Trebing (East Lansing: Institute of Public Utilities, Michigan State University, 1972): 311–16.

18. James Q. Wilson, "The Politics of Regulation," in *The Politics of Regulation* (New York: Basic Books, 1980), 370.

19. *Pacific Telephone & Telegraph Co.,* 15 Cal. R.C.R. 993, 994 (1918).

20. See, for example, a leading scholarly work during the 1920s, Ellsworth Nichols, *Public Utility Service and Discrimination* (Rochester, N.Y.: Public Utility Reports, 1928), 479.

21. See Stipulation/Contention Package, Episode 4, paragraphs 31, 32, 39, 412, and Episode 5, paragraphs 505–10, 534–36, *United States v. AT&T.*

22. See A.H. Griswold, "The Radio Telephone Situation," *Bell Telephone Quarterly* 1 (April 1922): 6–8; AT&T, *1918 Annual Report,* 28.

23. The principal sources utilized for the discussion of the early history of radio are Hugh G.J. Aitken, *Syntony and Spark-The Origins of Radio* (New York: John Wiley, 1976); Hugh G.J. Aitken, *The Continuous Wave: Technology and American Radio* (Princeton: Princeton University Press, 1985); W. Rupert MacLaurin, *Invention to Innovation in the Radio Industry* (New York: Macmillan, 1949); Gleason Archer, *History of Radio to 1926* (New York: American Historical Society, 1938); Hiram L. Jome, *Economics of the Radio Industry* (Chicago: A.W. Shaw, 1925); Federal Trade Commission, *Report on the Radio Industry* (Washington, D.C.: Government Printing Office, 1924); and Erik Barnouw, *A Tower of Babel* (New York: Oxford University Press, 1966).

24. William Peck Banning, *Commercial Broadcasting Pioneer* (Cambridge: Harvard University Press, 1946), 68.

25. The principal materials on the creation of the F.C.C. and the background are U. S. Senate, *A Study of Communications by an Interdepartmental Committee* (Washington, D.C.: Government Printing Office, 1934), known as the Roper Report; U.S. House of Representatives, *Preliminary Report on Communications Companies* (Washington, D.C.: Government Printing Office, 1934), known as the Splawn Report; U.S. House of Representatives, Committee on Interstate and Foreign Commerce, *Federal Communications Commission, Hearings* (Washington, D.C.: Government Printing Office, 1934); U.S. Senate, Committee on Interstate Commerce, *Commission on Communications, Hearings* (Washington, D.C.: Government Printing Office, 1929); Philip T. Rosen, *The Modern Stentors* (Westport, Conn.: Greenwood Press, 1980); G. Hamilton Loeb, *The Communications Act Policy toward Competition: A Failure to Communicate* (Cambridge: Harvard University Center for Information Policy Research, 1977).

Chapter 3. The Assault Begins

1. 47 U.S.C., Para. 151 (1970).

2. See Ellis W. Hawley, *The New Deal and the Problem of Monopoly* (Princeton: Princeton University Press, 1966), part 4; David W. Lynch, *The Concentration of Economic Power* (New York: Columbia University Press, 1946), chaps. 1, 2, 7, and 9.

3. The F.C.C.'s final report is Federal Communications Commission, *Investigation of the Telephone Industry in the United States* (Washington, D.C.: Government Printing Office, 1939). Other sources on which my summary is based are Arthur W. Page, *The Bell Telephone System* (New York: Harper & Row, 1941), 143–48; and AT&T, Brief of

Bell System Companies on Commissioner Walker's Report on the *Telephone Investigation* (1938), 248–56.

4. "Wrong Number," *Business Week,* March 28, 1936, 11.

5. Hawley, *The New Deal,* 387–88.

6. *United States v. Paramount Pictures,* 334 U.S. 131 (1948).

7. *United States v. Pullman Co.,* 50 F. Supp. 123, 134 (E.D., Pa., 1943).

8. For details of AT&T's World War II effort, see M.D. Fagen, ed., *A History of Engineering and Science in the Bell System: National Service in War and Peace, 1925–1975* (Murray Hill, N.J.: Bell Telephone Laboratories, 1978), part I. On postwar plans see "Item: Twelve Million New Telephones," *Fortune,* June 1950, 81–86, 139–46.

9. "Washington Outlook," *Business Week,* December 18, 1948, 16.

10. Charles Zerner, "U.S. Sues to Force AT&T to Drop Western Electric Co.," *New York Times,* January 14, 1949, 1, 3.

11. Complaint, *United States of America v. Western Electric Co.,* Civil Action No. 17–49 (January 14, 1949), 68–72.

12. Answer, *United States of America v. Western Electric Co.,* Civil Action No. 17–49 (April 24, 1949), paragraph 3.

13. See, generally, Alvin H. Hansen, *The Postwar American Economy* (New York: W.W. Norton, 1964).

14. U.S. House Committee on the Judiciary, Antitrust Subcommittee, *Consent Decree Program of the Department of Justice Report* (Washington, D.C.: Government Printing Office, 1959).

15. See, for example, *International Salt Co. v. United States,* 332 U.S. 392 (1947).

16. Some advertisements for such devices are found in "Foreign Attachments—1892–1894," in AT&T Archives, Box 1212.

17. American Bell Telephone Co. to G.F. Hudson, June 19 1894, memorandum no. 249047, in AT&T Archives, Box 1212.

18. "Something Up to Date for All Telephone Receivers" (n.d.), in AT&T Archives, Box 1353.

19. "Danger Lurks in the Telephone," in AT&T Archives, Box 1353.

20. See, for example, correspondence, H.K. McCann to J.D. Ellsworth, January 7, 1909, in AT&T Archives, Box 1353; and H.K. McCann to J.D. Ellsworth, February 27, 1909, in AT&T Archives, Box 1353.

21. See correspondence, L.G. Richardson to George V. Leverett, June 24, 1911, in AT&T Archives, Box 1353.

22. See, for example, *Hush-A-Phone Corp.,* 20 F.C.C. 391, 413 (1955), and *Cammen v. American Tel & Tel Co.,* 2 F.C.C. 351 (1936).

23. *Pennsylvania PUC v. Bell Telephone Co. of Pa.,* 20 Pa. PUC 702, 706–7 (1940).

24. See, for details, Alan Stone, *Wrong Number* (New York: Basic Books, 1989), 94–100.

25. Ibid., pp. 101–18.

26. *Hush-A-Phone Corp.,* 20 F.C.C. 391, 398 (1955).

27. *Telecommunications Reports,* May 20, 1949, 11, 12.

28. *Hush-A-Phone Corp.,* 20 F.C.C. 391, 424 (1955).

29. *Hush-A-Phone Corp. v. United States,* 238 F. 2d 266 (D.C. Cir., 1956).

30. Ibid., 269.

31. For details on early microwave, see H.T. Friis, "Microwave Repeater Research," *Bell Systems Technological Journal,* April 1948: 183–246.

32. For details, see *Philco Corporation v. American Telephone & Telegraph Co.,* 80 F. Supp. 397 (E.D., Pa., 1948).

33. *Television Charges and Regulations,* 42 F.C.C. 1 (1949)

34. See *Telecommunications Reports,* December 5, 1947, 21, 22.

35. *Telecommunications Reports,* August 3, 1953, 24, 25.

36. *Allocation of Microwave Frequencies Above 890 Mc,* 27 F.C.C. 359, 412 (1959).

37. *Telecommunications Reports,* March 7, 1960, 13, 14; *Allocation in Frequencies in Bands above 890 Mc,* 29 F.C.C. 825 (1960).

38. See Stone, *Wrong Number,* 134–40.

39. Jonathan F. Galloway, *The Politics and Technology of Satellite Communications* (Lexington, Mass.: D.C. Heath, 1972), 23.

40. See *Domestic Communications-Satellite Facilities,* 22 F.C.C. 2d 86 (1970). "Domestic Communications Satellite Fight Opens. Ford Fund Offers Play," *Wall Street Journal,* August 2, 1966, 9; "AT&T Drops Opposition to TV Networks Operating Own Communications Satellite," *Wall Street Journal,* October 16, 1969, 9.

41. See *Telecommunications Reports,* September 26, 1966, 22, 23; *Allocation of Microwave Frequencies above 890 Mc,* 27 F.C.C. 359, 414 (1959).

42. See, for example, *Electronic Detectors Inc. v. New Jersey Telephone Co.,* 62 PUR 3d 186 (1965).

43. Patti Hartigan, "At Home with Tom Carter," *On Communications,* February 1985, 24; *United States v. AT&T,* Stipulation/Contention Package, Episode 42A, paragraph 177; and M.A. Adelman, *The World Petroleum Market* (Baltimore: Resources for the Future, 1972), 30, 31, 201. This summary is drawn from the Record, vol. 2, *Use of the Carterfone Device in Message Toll Telephone Service,* F.C.C. Dkt. 16942 and 17073.

44. *Carterfone,* 14 F.C.C. 2d 571 (1968).

45. Ibid., 420, 423–24.

46. Ibid.

Chapter 4. MCI and the Long-Distance Challenge

1. U.S. Bureau of the Census, *Statistical Abstract of the United States: 1986* (Washington, D.C.: Government Printing Office, 1985), 547, 548.

2. *United States v. AT&T,* Civil Action no. 74–1698, D.D.C. (1974), Stipulation/Contention Package, Episode 5, paragraph 507, 509, 535, 536.

3. U.S. Senate Committee on the Judiciary, Subcommittee on Antitrust and Monopoly, *The Industrial Reorganization Act,* part 6 (Washington, D.C.: Government Printing Office, 1974), 4423.

4. Roland Mueser, ed., *Bell Laboratories Innovation in Telecommunications, 1925–1977* (Murray Hill, N.J.: Bell Telephone Laboratories, 1979), 39–41, 95–104, 125–29, 162–66.

5. Bell Telephone Laboratories, *1971 Annual Report,* 14.

6. For details of the advances that Bell Labs made in the physical sciences, see S. Millman, ed., *A History of Engineering and Science in the Bell System: Physical Sciences, 1925–1980* (New York: Bell Telephone Laboratories, 1983).

7. See Bernard Schwartz, ed., *The Economic Regulation of Business and Industry,* vol. 4 (New York: Chelsea House, 1973), 2500.

8. *Illinois State Telephone Co. v. Illinois Commerce Commission,* 73 PUR 3d 525, 527, 528 (1968).

9. *United States v. AT&T,* Stipulation/Contention Package, Episode 21, paragraph 2.

10. William J. Baumol, Otto Eckstein, and Alfred E. Kahn, "Competition and Monopoly in Telecommunications Services," in *The Industrial Reorganization Act,* part 2, 1342.

11. *Microwave Communications,* 18 F.C.C. 2d 979, 986, 991, 994 (1986).

12. Larry Kahaner, *On the Line* (New York: Warner Books, 1986), chaps. 3, 4. Although this book is an unabashed laud of MCI and completely undocumented, it does contain useful background information on the early development of MCI.

13. See Richard Vietor, *Contrived Competition* (Cambridge: Harvard University Press, 1994), 223–28.

14. Peter Huber, Michael Kellogg, and John Thorne, *The Geodesic Network II* (Washington, D.C.: Geodesic Company, 1992), p. 3.44.

15. MCI's statement on Series 11000 is reprinted in *Telecommunications Reports,* June 23, 1969, 14, 15. See generally Alan Stone, *Wrong Number* (New York: Basic Books, 1989), chap. 6, for more details.

16. Kahaner, *On the Line,* 40.

17. *Microwave Communications,* 18 F.C.C. 2d 953, 954 (1969).

18. Ibid., 959.

19. Ibid., p. 978.

20. See *F.C.C. v. RCA Communications, Inc.,* 346 U.S. 86 (1952).

21. See *Allocation of Frequencies above 890 Mc,* 27 F.C.C. 359, 370 (1959).

22. *Specialized Common Carrier Services,* 29 F.C.C. 2d 870 (1971).

23. *United States v. AT&T,* Trial Record, 3713; Kahaner, *On the Line,* 67, 68.

24. *United States v. AT&T,* Stipulation/Contention Package, Episode 23, paragraph 52.

25. Ibid., paragraph 69.

26. Ibid., Episode 24, paragraph 22.

27. Ibid., paragraph 28.

28. *AT&T—"Foreign Attachments" Tariff Revisions,* 15 F.C.C. 2d 605, 609, 610 (1968)

29. Ibid., 608.

30. See Stone, *Wrong Number,* 184–94 and notes, for more details.

31. Ibid.

32. *MCI Communications Corp. v. American Telephone & Telegraph Co.,* 369 F. Supp. 1004, 1029 (E.D., Pa., 1973).

33. *MCI Communications Corp. v. American Telephone & Telegraph Co.,* 496 F. 2d 214, 221 (3d Cir., 1974).

34. *Bell System Tariff Offerings,* 46 F.C.C. 2d 413, 427 (1974).

35. Jimmy Carter, "Remarks on Signing S.1946 (Staggers Rail Act of 1980) into Law," *Weekly Presidential Documents,* October 14, 1980, 2226.

36. *United States v. AT&T,* Stipulation/Contention Package, Episode 24B, AT&T Stipulation 75A.

37. See *United States v. AT&T,* Transcript of Testimony, 4006 and 4007; Stone, *Wrong Number,* 241–43.

38. *Telecommunications Reports,* June 23, 1980, 14.

39. *MCI Communications Corp v. American Telephone & Telegraph Co.,* 708 F. 2d 1081 (7th Cir., 1983).

40. *MCI Telecommunications Corporation,* 60 F.C.C. 2d 25, 26 (1976).

41 See Steve Coll, *The Deal of the Century* (New York: Atheneum, 1986), 88, 89; *United States v. AT&T,* Defendants Third Statement of Contentions and Proof, vol. 1, 694.

42. *MCI Telecommunications Corporation,* 60 F.C.C. 2d 25, 36 (1976).

43. *MCI Telecommunications Corp v. F.C.C.,* 561 F.2d 365, 378 (D.C. Cir., 1977).

44. *MCI Telecommunications Corp v. F.C.C.,* 580 F.2d 590 (D.C. Cir., 1978).

45. See, for example, *Competitive Carrier Rulemaking,* 85 F.C.C. 2d 1, 22–24 (1980).

46. See Vietor, *Contrived Competition,* 219–23.

220 NOTES TO CHAPTER 5

Chapter 5. The Biggest Case in History

1. R.H. Coase, "The Nature of the Firm," *Economica* 4 (New Series, November 1937): 404.

2. On the complex issues raised by Coase's theory of the firm, see Oliver E. Williamson and Sidney G. Winter, eds., *The Nature of the Firm* (New York: Oxford University Press, 1993).

3. "Media Gets a Message from Justice," *Business Week,* June 8, 1968, 110, 112.

4. For an excellent description of the antitrust views, see Suzanne Weaver, *Decision to Prosecute* (Cambridge: MIT Press, 1977), 169, 170.

5. Leslie Wayne, "AT&T's New Challenge," *New York Times,* February 4, 1982, D1, D8.

6. Weaver, *Decision to Prosecute,* 170.

7. "Trustbuster Hart Tilts with AT&T," *Business Week,* August 4, 1973, 15, 16.

8. Paul Weaver, "Unlocking the Gilded Cage of Regulatory Reform," *Fortune,* February 1977, 180.

9. *International T&T Corp. v. General T&E Corp.,* 351 F. Supp. 1153, 1185–86 (D. Hawaii, 1972).

10. *International T&T Corp. v. General T&E Corp.,* 518 F. 2d 913 (9th Cir., 1975).

11. Mitchell C. Lynch et al., "Fighting Bell," *Wall Street Journal,* November 21, 1974, 1.

12. *Telecommunications Reports,* December 9, 1974, 8.

13. "Why the Justice Department Took AT&T to Court," *Business Week,* November 30, 1974, 70.

14. "The Antitrust Lawyers Roll Up Their Sleeves," *Business Week,* November 30, 1974, 69.

15. "The Potential Fallout from AT&T's Defeat," *Business Week,* June 30, 1980, 45.

16. Lawrence A. Sullivan, *Handbook of the Law of Antitrust* (St. Paul, Minn.: West Publishing Co., 1977), 77.

17. *United States v. AT&T,* Plaintiff's First Statement of Contentions and Proof, 515, 516.

18. *United States v. AT&T,* Complaint, 14, 15.

19. Editorial, "The Largest Antitrust Suit," *Wall Street Journal,* November 22, 1974, 18.

20. "Statement by AT&T Chairman on Suit," *New York Times,* November 21, 1974, 68.

21. *United States v. AT&T,* Answer, 12.

22. *U.S. v. AT&T,* 1976–2 Trade Cases, paragraph 61,163, p. 70, 248 (D.D.C., 1976).

23. Peter M. Gerhart, "Report on the Empirical Case Studies Project," in *Report to the President and Attorney General,* vol. 2, National Commission for the Review of Antitrust Laws and Procedures (Washington, D.C.: Government Printing Office, 1979), 22.

24. *United States v. American Telephone & Telegraph Co.,* 416 F. Supp. 1314 (D.D.C., 1978).

25. *U.S. v. AT&T Co.,* 1980–2 Trade Cases, paragraph 63,533, p. 76,859 (D.C. Cir., 1980).

26. *MCI Communications Corp. v. American Telephone & Telegraph Co.,* 708 F. 2d 1081 (7th Cir., 1983).

27. See Alan Stone, *Wrong Number* (New York: Basic Books, 1989), 308–10, for more details.

28. Robert E. Taylor, "Activist Judge," *Wall Street Journal,* December 30, 1983, 12. The decision is reported at *United States v. American Telephone & Telegraph Co.,* 524 F. Supp. 1336 (D.D.C., 1981). For an analysis see Stone, *Wrong Number,* 310–13.

29. Information on AT&T's changing strategy is based to some extent on Peter Temin and Louis Galambos, *The Fall of the Bell System* (Cambridge: Cambridge University Press, 1987), chaps. 6 and 7.

30. AT&T, *1978 Annual Report,* p. 24.

31. *U.S. v. American Telephone & Telegraph Co.,* 1980–81 Trade Cases, paragraph 63,711, p. 77,795 (D.D.C., 1981).

32. *Telecommunications Reports,* April 13, 1981, 4. For more details on the settlement see Stone, *Wrong Number,* chap. 10.

33. *United States v. Western Electric,* Modification of Final Judgment, Section II, 3.

34. *United States v. American Telephone & Telegraph Co.,* 552 F. Supp. 131 (D.D.C., 1982).

35. *U.S. v. Western Electric Co., Inc.,* 1983–2 Trade Cases, paragraph 65,756, p. 69,855 (D.D.C., 1983–2).

Chapter 6. Internationalization and Competition

1. Tony Jackson, "Ringing Rapid Changes in Telecoms," *Financial Times,* February 12, 1996, 24.

2. Hugo Dixon, "Cable and Wireless Talks Collapse," *Financial Times,* January 22, 1992, 17.

3. "Scramble of the Titans," *Financial Times Survey: World Telecommunications,* October 7, 1991, 21.

4. Jack L. Hervey, "Foreign Trade and the U.S. Economy," *Chicago Fed Letter,* March 1995, 1–3.

5. John J. Keller, "A Scramble for Global Networks," *Business Week,* March 21, 1988, 141.

6. Kenichi Ohmae, "The Global Logic of Strategic Alliances," in *Collaborating to Compete,* ed. Joel Bleeke and David Ernst (New York: John Wiley, 1993), 37. The concept of a global economy was first developed by Theodore Levitt, "The Globalization of Markets," *Harvard Business Review,* May-June 1983, 92–102.

7. Stephen P. Bradley, Jerry A. Hausman, and Richard L. Nolan, "Global Competition and Technology," in *Globalization, Technology and Competition* (Boston: Harvard Business School Press, 1993), 17, 18.

8. Ibid., 12.

9. Michael Porter and Victor E. Millar, "How Information Gives You Competitive Advantage," *Harvard Business Review,* July-August 1985, 149–60.

10. See, for example, J.Y. Bakos and E. Bryn Jolfsson, "When Quality Matters: Information Technology and Buyer-Supplier Relationships," Massachusetts Institute of Technology, Center for Coordination Science Technical Report (1992).

11. "The Revolution Begins, at Last," *Economist,* September 30, 1995, 15.

12. John J. Keller, "Spanning the Globe," *Wall Street Journal,* October 4, 1991, R1.

13. See, for example, William Boston, "Newcomers Snap at Heels of Europe's Phone Companies," *Reuters World Service,* August 14, 1994; Matthias-Wolfgang Stoetzer, "New Telecommunications Services in Germany," *Telecommunications Policy* 18 (1994): 522–37.

14. For details on Sprint's early history, see *Southern Pacific Communications Co. v. AT&T,* 556 F. Supp. 825 (D.C., D.C., 1983).

15. Michael Lindemann, "Data Transmission Deal," *Financial Times,* May 28, 1994, 2; William Boston, "Germany Takes New Steps to Open Telecommunications Markets," *Reuters European Community Report,* May 27, 1994.

16. John Celentano, "Who's Got the Money for Those Multimedia Networks," *Telephony,* May 29, 1995, 32.

17. Keith Bradsher, "Science Fiction Nears Reality: Pocket Phone for Global Calls," *New York Times*, June 26, 1990, 1; Edmund L. Andrews, "Motorola's Network Attracts Few Investors," *New York Times*, January 8, 1993, D3; Edmund L. Andrews, "Motorola Unit Has Funds for Sky Phone System," *New York Times*, September 22, 1994, D3.

18. Bloomberg Business News, "Iridium, A Satellite Company, Now Looks Overseas for Financing," *New York Times*, November 10, 1995, D5; George Black, "Survey of Mobile Communications," *Financial Times*, November 27, 1995, 6; William Boston, "Vebacom, Stet in Iridium Cooperation," *Reuters European Business Report*, March 26, 1996; Yumiko Okuno, "Communications Firms Reach for Stars," *Nikkei Weekly*, April 15, 1996, 10; "Iridium Taps Chase, BZW to Arrange Final Financing," *Reuters*, April 25, 1996. Peter Eistrom, "Iridium Is Crossed," *Business Week*, April 14, 1995, 40.

19. François Bar, "Information and Communications Technologies for Economic Development," note prepared for Berkeley Roundtable on the International Economy (May 1987), 1.

20. National Telecommunications and Information Administration, *Telephone Areas Serviced by Bell and Independent Companies in the United States* (Washington, D.C.: Government Printing Office, 1982), 77–114.

21. See Michael Carpentier, Sylvaine Farnoux-Toporkoff, and Christian Garric, *Telecommunications in Transition* (New York: John Wiley, 1992), 81, 82; Alfred L. Thimm, *American Stake in European Telecommunications Policies* (Westport, Conn.: Quorum Books, 1992), 16, 21.

22. On the European equipment industry, see Eli Noam, *Telecommunications in Europe* (New York: Oxford University Press, 1992).

23. On the early European history of telecommunications see, generally, A.N. Holcomb, *Public Ownership of Telephones on the Continent of Europe* (Boston: Houghton-Mifflin, 1911).

24. "Telecommunications Survey," *Economist*, November 23, 1985, 20.

25. Information on Japanese telecommunications is primarily based on Jill Hills, *Deregulating Telecoms: Competition and Control in the United States, Japan, and Britain* (New York: Quorum Books, 1986), and Douglas W. Colber, "Reform of Japanese Telecommunications Law: Panacea or Placebo?," *Journal of International Law and Business* 8 (spring 1987): 145–79.

26. Daniel I. Okimoto, *Between MITI and the Market* (Stanford: Stanford University Press, 1989), 73–76.

27. See Henry Scott Stokes, "Breakup? The View from Inside a Besieged NTT," *Scientific American*, April 1990, 78; "Deregulation Lets Nippon Telephone Off the Hook," *Economist*, August 6, 1983, 56; Robert Cottrell, "Competitive Forces Gather for Pickings," *Financial Times*, October 23, 1984, 4.

28. European Commission, *Growth, Competitiveness, Employment: The Challenges and Ways Forward into the Twenty-First Century* (Luxembourg: Office for Official Publications of the European Communities, 1994), 9.

29. Ibid., 13.

30. Bangemann Group, *Europe and the Global Information Society: Recommendations to the European Council* (Brussels, May 26, 1994).

31. Commission of the European Communities, *Europe's Way to the Information Society: An Action Plan* (Brussels, July 19, 1994).

32. Ibid., Section 3. The document is not paginated.

33. European Commission, *Communication to the Council and the European Parliament: Green Paper on the Liberalization of Telecommunications Infrastructure and Cable Television Networks, Part One* (October 25, 1994), 3.

34. The primary source for the history of international telecommunications is

George A. Codding, Jr., and Anthony M. Rutkowski, *The International Telecommunications Union in a Changing World* (Dedham, Mass.: Artech House, 1982).

35. Paul A. David, "Some New Standards for the Economics of Standardization in the Information Age," in *The Economic Theory of Technological Policy,* ed. P. Dasgulpa and P.L. Stoneman (London: Cambridge University Press, 1987).

36. At about 22,300 miles high, a satellite orbits the Earth in twenty-four hours, which corresponds to the Earth's rotational period. "Thus a satellite at this distance on an orbit going East to West above the equator will revolve about the Earth at the same speed as the Earth turns. Consequently the satellite is referred to as being in 'geosynchronous' orbit so that it appears relatively motionless from the Earth." U.S. Department of Commerce, *NTIA Telecom 2000: Charting the Course for a New Century* (Washington, D.C.: Government Printing Office, 1988), 272.

37. The best source for the early history of communications satellites is Heather Hudson, *Communications Satellites, Their Development and Impact* (New York: Free Press, 1990).

38. See Stuart Z. Chiron and Lise A. Rehberg, "Fostering Competition in International Telecommunications," *Federal Communications Law Journal* 38 (March 1986): 29–32.

39. Lawrence A. Adashek, "Public and Private Developments in the Communications Industry, 1991–1992," *Commlaw Conspectus* 1 (1993): 145–47.

40. Monica Horten, "Backbone of the Worldwide Corporate Structure—Private Networks," *Financial Times,* October 7, 1991, 17; Elisabeth Horwitt, "Undersea Fiber Link Up," *Computerworld,* December 19, 1988, 14; Department of Commerce, *NTIA Telcom 2000,* 262, 263.

41. Michael Kenward, "Light Relief for Today's Long Distance Telephone Links," *Financial Times,* October 3, 1995, 28.

42. Irving Goldstein, "INTELSAT Transforming a Market Leader to Meet Changing Global Telecommunications," *Federal Communications Law Journal* 39 (December 1994): 243.

43. Mention should be made of Inmarsat, the third of the international organizations devoted to telecommunications. It was created in 1979 to provide worldwide mobile satellite communications for the maritime community. Its activities have been uncontroversial.

44. Mary E. Thyfault, "Global Communications Get Real," *Information Week,* November 13, 1995, 34.

45. Michael Y. Yoshino and U. Srinivasa Rangan, *Strategic Alliances* (Boston: Harvard Business School Press, 1995), 4.

46. Peter Lorange and Johan Roos, *Strategic Alliances* (Cambridge, Mass.: Blackwell, 1992), 17, 18.

47. "A Collect Call from Olivetti," *Financial Times,* December 22, 1983, 12; Paul Betts, "AT&T Continuing Olivetti Talks," *Financial Times,* October 7, 1983, 21; Guy de Jonquieres, "Moves toward Wider Collaboration," *Financial Times,* January 14, 1985, 11.

48. Hudson Janisch, "Regulation and Competition: Foreign Ownership and Participation," Seminar Paper, University of Toronto, May 16–20, 1995, 23, 24.

49. Mary Fagan, "BT Paying $4.3 Bn for Stake in US Operator," *Independent,* June 3, 1993, 29; Lawrence Malkin, "Phone Firms' Link Is Only a First Move," *International Herald Tribune,* June 3, 1993; Carla Lazzareschi, "British Telecom to Buy 20% of MCI; Global System Seen," *Los Angeles Times,* June 3, 1993, A1; Kevin Maney and John Schneidawind, "MCI Builds Global Alliance," *USA Today,* June 3, 1993, 1B; James Vicini, "Justice Agrees to British Telecommunications/MCI Deal," *Reuters World Ser-*

vice, June 15, 1994; Steven Lipin, "British Telecom and MCI Unveil $20.88 Billion Merger Agreement," *Wall Street Journal,* Interactive Edition, November 4, 1996.

50. Eric Auchard, "AT&T Unisource Still Play Catch-Up," *Reuters,* May 14, 1996.

51. "Experts Cast Doubt on Marriage of Unlikely International Partners," *Telecom Markets,* June 23, 1994; "Sprint Sells 20% Stake in German-French Alliance for $4.2 Billion," *Common Carrier Week,* June 20, 1994; Dan O'Shea, "French and German Telcos Answer Sprint's Plea for Help," *Telephony,* June 20, 1994, 6.

Chapter 7. The Wireless Revolution

1. See generally Hugh G. Aitken, *Syntony and Spark* (New York: John Wiley, 1976).

2. W.J. Baker, *A History of the Marconi Company* (New York: St. Martin's, 1971); Susan J. Douglas, *Inventing American Broadcasting* (Baltimore: Johns Hopkins University Press, 1987), chaps. 1–3.

3. Hugh G. Aitken, *The Continuous Wave: Technology and American Radio, 1900–1932* (Princeton: Princeton University Press, 1985), 12; Leonard Reich, *The Making of Industrial Research* (Cambridge: Cambridge University Press, 1985), 160–64.

4. Gleason L. Archer, *Big Business and Radio* (New York: American Historical Co., 1939), 198–205; Erik Barnouw, *A Tower in Babel* (New York: Oxford University Press, 1966), 64–68.

5. Tom Lewis, *Empire of the Air* (New York: HarperCollins, 1991), 89–107.

6. Archer, *Big Business and Radio,* 112.

7. On AT&T's role in broadcasting, see Alan Stone, *Public Service Liberalism* (Princeton: Princeton University Press, 1991), chap. 8.

8. See Christopher H. Sterling and John M. Kittross, *Stay Tuned,* 2d ed. (Belmont, Calif.: Wadsworth, 1978), 70, 71, 112–14; Lewis, *Empire of the Air,* 183, 184; Erik Barnouw, *The Golden Web* (New York: Oxford University Press, 1968), 55–69; William S. Paley, *As It Happened* (Garden City, N.Y.: Doubleday, 1979).

9. The best source of information on the AT&T toll system is William Peck Benning, *Commercial Broadcasting Pioneer* (Cambridge: Harvard University Press, 1946).

10. The story of television's growth is nicely told in Andrew F. Inglis, *Behind the Tube* (Stoneham, Mass.: Butterworth, 1990), chaps. 4 and 5. See also Joseph H. Udelson, *The Great Television Race* (University: University of Alabama Press, 1982).

11. The best source of information on FM's development is D.H.V. Erickson, *Armstrong's Fight for FM Broadcasting* (University: University of Alabama Press, 1973).

12. Erickson, *Armstrong's Fight for FM Broadcasting,* 113–54, 204–11.

13. M.D. Fagen, ed., *A History of Engineering and Science in the Bell System* (New York: Bell Telephone Laboratories, 1975), chap. 5.

14. Details on the origins of the Federal Radio Commission are found in Laurence R. Schmeckebier, *The Federal Radio Commission* (Washington, D.C.: Brookings Institution, 1932).

15. See Stone, *Public Service Liberalism,* 275–83; Philip T. Rosen, *The Modern Stentors* (Westport, Conn.: Greenwood Press, 1980).

16. R.H. Coase, "The Federal Communications Commission," *Journal of Law & Economics* 2 (October 1959): 1–40.

17. *Ashbacker Radio Corp v. F.C.C.,* 326 U.S. 327 (1945); *Johnston Broadcasting Co. v. F.C.C.,* 175 F. 2d 351 (D.C. Cir., 1949).

18. Federal Communications Commission, *Annual Report to Congress,* fiscal year ended June 30, 1954 (Washington, D.C.: Government Printing Office, 1955), 5. On the

early history of fixed services, see Dallas W. Smythe, *The Structure and Policy of Electronic Communication* (Urbana: University of Illinois Press, 1957), chap. 4.

19. Statement of Evidence of Automobile Manufacturers Association, Box 2227, p. 850 in F.C.C. Docket 11866, *Above 890Mc.*

20. D.L. Guill and P.R. Hartmann, "Matching Microwave to the Digital Network," *Telephone Engineer and Management,* July 1, 1983, 50. See also Alan C. Walker, "Microwave Aims at the Local Loop," *Telephone Engineer and Management,* July 1, 1983, 47.

21. *Establishment of Policies and Procedures for the Use of Digital Modulation Techniques in Microwave Radio,* 40 F.C.C. 2d 938 (1973). See also R.W. Sanders, "Microwave Keeps Up with the Times," *Telephone Engineer and Management,* October 1, 1983, 72.

22. Alan Stewart, "Spectrum Based Communications," *Telephone Engineer and Management,* October 15, 1984, 76.

23. Leonard Waverman, "The Regulation of Intercity Telecommunications," in *Promoting Competition in Regulated Markets,* ed. Almarin Phillips (Washington, D.C.: Brookings Institution, 1975), 201–39.

24. Steven Flax, "The Latest Way to Foil the Phone Monopoly," *Fortune,* April 16, 1984, 108. See also Bruce C. Netschert, "The Bypass Threat—and What to Do about It," *Telephony,* July 18, 1983, 112–21.

25. Jim Brown, "RHBCs Cite Big Losses from Bypass," *Network World,* May 9, 1988, 1.

26. Lisa Warner, "Wireless Technologies Creating Competition in the Local Exchange Market, *Comm Law Conspectus,* winter 1996, 69; Edmund L. Andrews, "Bell Units' Rivals Gain at F.C.C.," *New York Times,* May 10, 1991, D1; Gary Slutsker, "Divestiture Revisited," *Forbes,* March 18, 1991, 118; Robert S. Murray, "Local Carrier Access: The Battleground of the 1990s," *Telephony,* January 8, 1990, 32.

27. Peter Huber, Michael K. Kellogg, and John Thorne, *The Geodesic Network II* (Washington, D.C.: Geodesic Company, 1992), pp. 2.40, 2.41.

28. Steve Creedy, "Mandl Says Wireless Has Lucrative Future," *Pittsburgh Post-Gazette,* August 21, 1996, C12; Andrew Kupfer, "Can Cable Win Its Phone Bet?" *Fortune,* September 18, 1995, 175; Paula Roesler, "Microwave Mushrooms in the Cellular Network," *Telephony,* December 2, 1991, 533; James E. Innes, "The Microwave Factor in Disaster Recovery," *Telephony,* October 9, 1989, 38; Doug Docherty, "The Short Haul," *America's Network,* September 15, 1996, 1–4.

29. Mark D. Schneider, "Cellular Communications Service: Wireline Delivery or Delay," *Georgetown Law Journal,* February 1984, 1183.

30. S. Millman, *A History of Engineering and Science in the Bell System: Communications Sciences* (AT&T Bell Laboratories, 1984), 234, 235.

31. Details on mobile radio history are found in "The ABCs of Cellular Radio," *Telephone Engineer and Management,* May 15, 1983, 76.

32. Colin Leinster, "Mobile Phones: Hot New Industry," *Fortune,* August 6, 1984, 108.

33. Stephen Booth, "Cellular Technology Strives to Keep Pace with Market Growth," *Consumer Electronics,* November 1989, 35.

34. Leslie Brennan, "Say Hello to Car Phones," *Sales & Marketing Management,* October 1986, 97; "A Survey of the Technologies, the Players, and the Prospects," *Cook Report* (n.d.), 1; PCIA, *1994 PCS Market Demand Forecast,* January 30, 1995, 2.

35. John J. Keller, "Will Cheaper Cellular Put a Phone in Every Pocket?" *Business Week,* December 5, 1988, 142.

36. *F.C.C. v. Sanders Brothers Radio Station,* 309 U.S. 470 (1940).

37. *Land Mobile Service. Use of 806–90 MHz Band*, 14 F.C.C. 2d 311, 312 (1968).
38. *Land Mobile Service, Second Report*, 46 F.C.C. 2d 752 (1974). A good study of the early history of cellular is John W. Berresford, "The Impact of Law and Regulation on Technology: The Case History of Cellular Radio," *Business Lawyer*, May 1989.
39. John Oetting, "Cellular Mobile Radio—An Emerging Technology," *IEEE Communications Magazine*, November 1983, 11.
40. *Cellular Communications Systems*, 86 F.C.C. 2d 469 (1981).
41. See, for example, *United States v. Western Electric Co.*, 1986–1 Trade Cases, p. 166,987 (D.D.C., 1986); and most importantly, *United States v. Western Electric Co.*, 797 F. 2d 1082 (D.C. Cir. 1982).
42. *Cellular Lottery Rulemaking*, 98 F.C.C. 2d 175 (1984).
43. Details on McCaw's career are found in Fleming Meeks, "Would You Believe It—Craig McCaw Says He Is Risk Averse," *Forbes*, March 1993, 78.
44. Robert Hof and Peter Coy, "Step One for Craig McCaw's National Cellular Network." *Business Week*, October 22, 1990, 108.
45. KLR Consulting, Inc., "Cellular Digital Packet (PCD): What Makes it Reliable," vks@doc.ic.ac.uk, pp. 1–5; Brian Washburn, "CDPD—The Tower of Power," *America's Network*, August 15, 1996, 1–6.
46. Reshma Memon Yabub, "Flight Control: Airphones Lifting Communications to New Heights," *Chicago Tribune*, April 25, 1994, C1; Michael Fitzgerald, "Document Faxing Goes Airborne—But Will It Fly?" *Computerworld*, February 7, 1994, 62.
47. On the newer cordless phones, see Chris O'Malley, "The Wireless World," *Popular Science*, November 1995, 56; Mark Fleischmann, "Digital Cordless Phones Go Further," *Popular Science*, January 1995, 48.
48. Thomas McCarroll, "Betting on the Sky," *Time*, November 22, 1963, 57; Duane Stoltzfus, "Nextel Betting on Wireless Future," *Bergen Record*, November 22, 1963, D1.
49. John Anderson, Director, Transportation and Telecommunications Issues, General Accounting Office, before U.S. House Commerce Committee, October 12, 1995.
50. Louis Kehoe, "MCI Invests $1.3 bn in Nextel," *Financial Times*, March 1, 1994, 23; Laura Evenson, "Wireless Venture by MCI," *San Francisco Chronicle*, March 1, 1994, B1.
51. See, for example, Fred Dawson, "Analysts Praise Nextel's New Wireless Technology," *Multichannel News*, September 12, 1994, 55; Barbara De Pompa, "It's Quits for Carriers," *Information Week*, September 12, 1994, 20.
52. "AT&T and McCaw Cellular Complete Largest Ever Telecom Merger," *AT&T News Release*, September 20, 1994.
53. John J. Keller, "AT&T Wireless Raises the Bar in Battle for New PCS Market," *Wall Street Journal*, Interactive Edition, October 3, 1996, 1, 2; John J. Keller, "AT&T Steps Up Its Fight for Local Phone Markets," *Wall Street Journal*, Interactive Edition, February 24, 1997, 1.
54. Ron Schneiderman, *Wireless Personal Communications* (Piscataway, N.J.: IEEE Press, 1994), 5.
55. Thomas A. Monheim, "Personal Communications Services: The Wireless Future of Telecommunications," *Federal Communications Law Journal* 44 (March 1992): 336.
56. *Amendment of the Commission's Rules to Establish New Personal Communications Services, Notice of Inquiry*, 5 F.C.C. Rcd. 3995 (1990).
57. *Amendment of the Commission's Rules to Establish New Personal Communications Services, Notice of Proposed Rule Making and Tentative Decision*, 7 F.C.C. Rcd. 5676 (1992), n. 1.
58. See *In the Matter of Implementation of Section 309J of the Communications Act—Competitive Bidding, Second Report and Order*, 9 F.C.C. Rcd. 2348 (1994). An

excellent history of the proceedings is Jennifer Pia Brovey, "Crossing the Line from Regulation to Implementation," *Comm Law Prospectus* 2 (1994): 67.

59. Liza McDonald, "Bidding War for Wireless Tops $1 Billion," *Rocky Mountain News,* September 25, 1996, 8B.

60. See Tom Nolle, "Overcoming Cellular Deja Vu," *America's Network,* September 15, 1996, 1–8; Patrick Flanagan, "Personal Communications Services: The Long Road Ahead," *Telecommunications On-Line,* February 1996, 1–5.

61. See Chris Kraul, "The Cutting Edge: Down to the Wireless," *Los Angeles Times,* May 20, 1996, D1; Alan Cane, "Survey of Mobile Communications," *Financial Times,* November 27, 1995, 1; Qualcomm, *CDMA Bulletin,* winter/spring 1996; Qualcomm, *The Complete CDMA Solution,* 1996; Schneiderman, *Wireless Personal Communications,* 19–25.

Chapter 8. A Marriage Made in Heaven: Computers and Communications

1. Excellent histories of computers and computing are too numerous to mention. Among others on which I have relied are Michael R. Williams, *A History of Computing Technology* (Englewood Cliffs, N.J.: Prentice-Hall, 1985); William Aspray, *Computing before Computers* (Ames: Iowa State University Press, 1990); Herman H. Goldstine, *The Computer from Pascal to von Neumann* (Princeton: Princeton University Press, 1972); and James W. Cortada, *The Computer in the United States* (Armonk, N.Y.: M.E. Sharpe, 1993).

2. Thomas P. Hughes, *Elmer Sperry: Inventor and Engineer* (Baltimore: Johns Hopkins University Press, 1971), 146–47, 232–33.

3. Details on Hollerith are found in Geoffrey D. Austrian, *Herman Hollerith: Forgotten Giant of Information Processing* (New York: Columbia University Press, 1982).

4. In addition to the materials cited in note 1, see also S. Millman, ed., *A History of Engineering and Science in the Bell System: Communications Sciences, 1925–1980* (New York: AT&T Bell Laboratories, 1984), chap. 9; Harry Wulforst, *Breaking Through to the Computer Age* (New York: Charles Scribner's, 1982), 43–48.

5. Stan Augarten, *Bit by Bit: An Illustrated History of Computers* (New York: Ticknor and Fields, 1984), 101.

6. Kenneth Flamm, *Creating the Computer* (Washington, D.C.: Brookings Institution, 1988), 33.

7. See Texas Instruments, "First Commercial Silicon Transistor," Industrial News Release, May 10, 1954, 1–3.

8. Cortada, *Computer in the United States,* 76.

9. Although written by consultants for IBM in legal matters, a good examination of IBM's market share over time is Franklin M. Fisher, John J. McGowan, and Joan Greenwood, *Folded, Spindled, and Mutilated* (Cambridge: MIT Press, 1983), chap. 4.

10. Alvin J. Harman, *The International Computer Industry* (Cambridge: Harvard University Press, 1971), 9–13; Saul Rosen, "Electronic Computers: A Historical Survey," *Computer Surveys,* March 1969, 7–36.

11. David Farber and Paul Baran, "The Convergence of Computing and Telecommunications Systems," *Science,* March 18, 1977, 1169.

12. See *United States v. AT&T,* Defendants' Third Statement of Contentions and Proof, vol. 2, 1276–89, and Plaintiff's Third Statement of Contentions and Proof, vol. 2, 1500–1505.

13. The principal source for the early history of the computer-communications inter-

face is "Computer Services and the Federal Regulation of Communications," *University of Pennsylvania Law Review,* December 16, 1967, 328–46.

14. *New York Telephone Co.,* 44 PUR (NS) 265, 269–70 (1942).

15. R.M. Fano and F.J. Corbato, "Time Sharing on Computers," *Scientific American,* September 1966, 129–40.

16. *Computer Use of Communications Facilities, Tentative Decision,* 28 F.C.C. 2d 291, 297 (1970).

17. *GTE Service Corporation v. F.C.C.,* 474 F. 2d 724 (7th Cir., 1973).

18. *United States v. AT&T,* Stipulation/Contention Package, Episode 42B, paragraphs 327, 330, 332.

19. *Interstate and Foreign Message Toll Telephone Service et al, Recommended First Report and Order,* 56 F.C.C. 2d 593, 597 (1975).

20. Details on the development of the integrated circuit are found in T.R. Reid, *The Chip: How Two Americans Invented the Microchip and Launched a Revolution* (New York: Simon and Schuster, 1984); and Robert Noyce, "Microelectronics," *Scientific American,* September 1977, 63–69.

21. See Kathleen K. Wiegner, "The Micro War Heats Up," *Forbes,* November 26, 1979, 49.

22. "A Grab at Ma Bell's Market," *Business Week,* June 19, 1978, 92B.

23. N.R. Bradley Lambert, "The Effect of the Second Computer Inquiry on Telecommunications and Data Processing," *Wayne Law Review* 27 (1981): 1543.

24. See, for example, "Who Will Supply the Office of the Future?" *Business Week,* July 27, 1974, 42.

25. *AT&T Revisions to Tariff 260 and 267 Relating to Dataspeed 40,* 62 F.C.C. 2d 21 (1977).

26. *Computer Inquiry, Tentative Decision,* 72 F.C.C. 2d 358, 393 (1979).

27. Ibid., 394.

28. Ibid., 430

29. *Second Computer Inquiry, Final Decision,* 77 F.C.C. 2d 384, 419–20 (1980).

30. Mark L. Goldstein, "Letting the Phone Company Off the Hook," *Industry Week,* February 17, 1986, 29. See also Herbert E. Marks and James L. Casserly, "An Introduction to the F.C.C.'s Third Computer Inquiry," in *Telecommunications and the Law,* ed. Walter Sapronov (Rockville, Md.: Computer Science Press, 1988), 309–32.

31. See, for example, Bryan Wilkins, "CBEMA vs. Deregulation," *Computerworld,* December 30, 1985/January 6, 1986, 105.

32. Mitch Betts, "Users and Vendors Blast F.C.C. Protocol Conversion," *Computerworld,* November 24, 1986, 13.

33. *Computer III Further Remand Proceedings,* 10 F.C.C. Rcd. 8360 (1995).

34. *Amendment of Sections 64.702 of the Commission's Rules and Regulations (Third Computer Inquiry, Report and Order),* 104 F.C.C. 2d 958 (1986).

35. Ibid., 988, 1008.

36. The chronological development of *Computer III* is detailed in Chris L. Kelley, "The Contestability of the Local Network: The F.C.C.'s Open Network Architecture Policy," *Federal Communications Law Journal* 45 (December 1992): 89–147.

37. See the excellent Gary K. Nitzberg, "Open Network Architecture (ONA)," http://www.nitzspace.com/gary/papers/tmona.html.

38. Details are provided in *Computer III Remand Proceedings: Bell Operating Company Provision of Enhanced Services,* 10 F.C.C. Rcd. 8360 (1995). See also Kelley, "Contestability of the Local Network," 141–45.

39. *California v. F.C.C.,* 905 F. 2d 1217 (9th Cir., 1990).

40. *California v. F.C.C.,* 39 F. 3d 919 (9th Cir., 1994).

41. *Computer III Remand,* 8360.

42. Robert L. Hummel, "Eight Ways to the Future," *Byte,* December 1996, 85.

43. Andrew S. Grove, *Only the Paranoid Survive* (New York: Currency Books, 1996), 87.

44. The two principal sources on which I rely for much of my summary are Richard N. Langlois, "External Economies and Economic Progress: The Case of the Microcomputer Industry," *Business History Review,* spring 1992, 1–50; and Michael S. Malone, *The Microprocessor: A Biography* (New York: Springer-Verlag, 1995).

45. Texas Instruments, Press Release, "Standard Calculator on a Chip Announced by Texas Instruments," September 17, 1971.

46. In addition to the sources in note 44, see also "The Personal Computer Strives to Come of Age," *Economist,* May 19, 1979, 101; Apple Computer, "Corporate Timeline —January 1976 to May 1995," http://product.info.apple.com/pcbackground/1995/.

47. On Microsoft's role in the development of the IBM PC, see Daniel Ichbiah, *The Making of Microsoft* (Rocklin, Calif.: Prima, 1993), chap. 9.

48. See Tim Frost, "Multimedia and the Information Superhighway," *Gramophone,* July 1996, 158–66.

49. See James Martin, *Telecommunications and the Computer* (Englewood Cliffs, N.J.: Prentice-Hall, 1990), chap. 32.

50. Joel Dreyfuss, "What Will Send Computers Home," *Fortune,* April 2, 1984, 71.

51. Stan Veit, "Helpful Hints on How to Use the Various Communication Networks That Are Available on Your Microcomputer: The Computer Network Maze," *Computers & Electronics,* March 1983, 60.

52. Jim Duffy, "Trintex Hatch Plan to Revive Videotex," *MIS Week,* March 7, 1988, 20.

53. Harley Hahn and Rick Stout, *The Internet Complete Reference* (Berkeley, Calif.: McGraw-Hill, 1994), 2.

54. John R. Levine and Carol Baroudi, *The Internet for Dummies* (San Mateo, Calif.: IDG Books, 1993), 7.

55. For the early history I rely primarily on Katie Hafner and Matthew Lyon, *Where Wizards Stay Up Late* (New York: Simon and Schuster, 1996).

56. An excellent source on the history of electronic mail is Ian R. Hardy, "The Evolution of ARPAnet email," History Thesis Paper, University of California, Berkeley (spring 1996).

57. J.C.R. Licklider and Albert Vezza, "Applications of Information Networks, *Proceedings of the IEEE* 66 (November 1978): 1331.

58. See H. Gilbert, "Introduction to TCP/IP," http://pelt.cis.yale.edu.

59. Robert H. Zakon, "Hobbes Internet Timeline V.2.5," http://info.isoc.org/guest/zakon/internet/history/hit.html.

60. The discussion of hypertext is based on Jakob Nielsen, *Multimedia and Hypertext* (Cambridge, Mass.: Academic Press, 1995), chaps. 1–3; Steven Baker, "Hypertext Browsing on the Internet," *UNIX Review,* September 1994, 21; Tim Berners-Lee et al., "The World Wide Web," *Communications of the ACM,* August 1994, 76.

61. See Jon Hill, Jan Ozer, and Thomas Mace, "Real Time Communication," *PC Magazine,* October 8, 1996, 102–5; Joint Opposition of Netscape Communications Corp., Voxware Inc., and Insoft Inc., *Provision of Interstate and International Interexchange Telecommunications Service via the Internet,* F.C.C. Docket, RM 8775, May 8, 1996.

62. George Cole, "World on a Local Line," *Financial Times,* November 13, 1996, 21; Norm Alster, "Intel Flexes Its Muscles to Deter Net Access Fees," *Investor's Business Daily,* January 2, 1997, A2; Christopher Libertelli, "Internet Telephony Architecture and Federal Access Charge Reform," *Boston University Journal of Science and Technology Law* 2 (May 2, 1996): 13–25.

Chapter 9. Telecommunications Turbulence

1. Wayne Rasmussen, "The Impact of Technological Change on American Agriculture, 1862–1962," *Journal of Economic History* 22 (1962): 578–91.

2. Paul MacAvoy and James Sloss, *Regulation of Transport Innovation* (New York: Random House, 1967); Douglas W. Webbink, "The Impact of UHF Promotion: The All-Channel Television Receiver Law," *Law and Contemporary Problems,* summer 1969.

3. Jacob Schmookler, *Invention and Economic Growth* (Cambridge: Harvard University Press, 1966).

4. *United States v. AT&T,* Stipulation/Contention Package, Episode 5, paragraphs 507, 509, 535, 536.

5. See Ron Goldberg, "The Big Squeeze," *Popular Science,* November 1993), 100–103.

6. "The Spectrum of 1995 Dealmaking," *Mergers & Acquisitions,* March/April 1996, 43.

7. "The Year on the Net," *Wall Street Journal,* Interactive Edition, December 9, 1996.

8. Details on the breakdown of the Bell Atlantic–TCI deal are provided in Paul Wiseman and James Cox, "Information Highway Under Construction," *USA Today,* February 25, 1994, 1B; Anthony Ramirez, "Partners in a Failed Merger," *New York Times,* February 24, 1994, D6; Dennis K. Neale, Johnnie L. Roberts, and Leslie Cauley, "Why Mega-Merger Collapsed," *Wall Street Journal,* February 25, 1994, A1.

9. Raymond Smith, Speech at Harvard University Business School, March 7, 1994.

10. Peter Coy, "There'll Be a Heaven for Couch Potatoes, By and By," *Business Week,* November 1, 1993, 38.

11. Mike Antonucci, "Bell-TCI Merger Offers a Peek into the Future," *San Jose Mercury-News,* October 14, 1993, 1A.

12. David P. Hamilton and Dean Takahashi, "Fearing End of Moore's Law, Labs Push Chips to the Limit," *Wall Street Journal,* December 10, 1996, A1.

13. Steven Lipin and Don Clark, "More High Tech Firms Tying the Knot, Spurred by a Buy-Not-Build Strategy," *Wall Street Journal,* May 3, 1996, A3.

14. See "Cable TV: Advanced Technology," *Jones Telecommunications and Multimedia Encyclopedia,* http://www.digitalcentury.com/encyclo/.

15. See Joe S. Bain, *Industrial Organization* (New York: John Wiley, 1959), 210–18.

16. See generally Janet Wasko, *Hollywood in the Information Age* (Austin: University of Texas Press, 1994).

17. G. Christian Hill, "Telecom Providers Scramble as Battle of the Bundle Begins," *Wall Street Journal,* Interactive Edition, September 16, 1996.

18. John J. Keller, "Why AT&T Takeover of NCR Hasn't Been a Real Bell Ringer," *Wall Street Journal,* September 19, 1995, A1, A5; "Analysts Applaud AT&T's Move, Suggest Market Overreacted," *CNN,* News, September 21, 1995, 6:21 A.M., Transcript no. 1183–3.

19. Details on CATV history are provided in Don R. Le Duc, *Cable Television and the F.C.C.: A Crisis in Media Control* (Philadelphia: Temple University Press, 1973), 68, 69.

20. 47 U.S.C. 224.

21. *Carter Mountain Transmission Corp. v. F.C.C.,* 375 U.S. 951 (1963).

22. *Frontier Broadcasting v. Collier,* 24 F.C.C. 251 (1958); Mary Alice Mayer Phillips, *CATV: A History of Community Antenna Television* (Evanston, Ill.: Northwestern University Press, 1972), 57.

23. *United States v. Southwestern Cable Co.*, 392 U.S. 157, 178 (1968).

24. *First Report and Order (Cablecasting)*, 20 F.C.C. 2d 201 (1969). See also *Memorandum Order and Opinion (Cablecasting)*, 23 F.C.C. 2d 825 (1970). The local-content rules were upheld in *United States v. Midwest Video Corp.*, 406 U.S. 649 (1972).

25. *Report and Order in Docket 20528*, 59 F.C.C. 2d 294 (1976), and *F.C.C. v. Midwest Video Corp.*, 440 U.S. 689 (1979). This case is known as "Midwest Video II," to distinguish it from the one cited in note 24.

26. Thomas W. Hazlett, "Wired," *New Republic*, May 28, 1989, 11–13; James W. Roman, *Cable Mania* (Englewood Cliffs, N.J.: Prentice-Hall, 1983), 142; John Cooney, "Cable TV's Costly Trip to the Big Cities," *Fortune*, April 18, 1983, 82–88; "Judge Rules Houston Cable Awards Violate Antitrust Law," *Broadcasting*, August 13, 1984, 66, 67.

27. TCI, *History of TCI*, http://www.tci.com:80/.

28. See the excellent analysis of the law in Donald J. Boudreaux and Robert B. Ekelund, Jr., "The Cable Television Consumer Protection and Competition Act of 1992: The Triumph of Private Over Public Interest," *Alabama Law Review*, winter 1993, 355.

29. *Continental Cablevision*, "How a Cable System Works," http://www.continental.com.

30. Brooke Crothers, "Grove Casts Doubts on Cable Modems," *C/NET*, May 31, 1996, 1. See also Katie Barnes, "Cable Modems: Fast Pipe or Pipe Dream," *C/NET*, http://www.cnet.com; Rose Aguilar and Jeff Pelline, "The Cable Era Begins," *C/NET*, September 5, 1996, 1–3; Alex Lash, "Big Bandwidth Finally Here, Sort Of," *C/NET*, August 14, 1996, 1–3; Alex Lash, "Cable Service to Hit the Road," *C/NET*, August 13, 1996, 1, 2; Jim Connors, "The Evolution of Cable Television to Interactive Communications Service Provider," http://www.catv.org:80/modem/sun.html.

31. See Peter Krasilovsky, *Interactive Television Testbeds*, Benton Foundation Working Paper 7 (n.d.).

32. "The Competition," *C/NET*, http://www.cnet.com; "ADSL Tutorial," http://198.93.24.23/adsl; Debbie Sallee, "Motorola's Copper Gold ADSL Transceiver Delivers: More, Better, Faster," http://www.mot.com/sps/mctg/mdad; Doug Lakin, "An Alternative to ADSL and DBS: LMDS," *Silicon Investor*, May 11, 1996, 1; Fred Dawson, "LMDS Poised to Make Significant Inroads," *Interactive Week*, January 15, 1996, 1–5.

33. Mark Robichaux, "The Pizza Pan Dishes Fly off the Shelves; Prices Plunge," *Wall Street Journal*, November 7, 1996, A1.

34. Edmund L. Andrews, "Communications Bill Signed, and the Battles Begin Anew," *New York Times*, February 9, 1996, A1.

35. An excellent discussion of the statute is Peter W. Huber, Michael K. Kellogg, and John Thorne, *The Telecommunications Act of 1996* (Boston: Little, Brown, 1996).

36. Joseph A. Schumpeter, *Capitalism, Socialism, and Democracy*, 3d ed. (New York: Harper & Brothers, 1950), 132.

37. Adam Smith, *The Wealth of Nations* (1776; reprint, New York: Random House Modern Library, 1937), 423.

38. Aaron Director, "The Parity of the Economic Market Place," *Journal of Law & Economics* 7 (October 1964): 2.

Index

UHF television, 137, 192
Unisource, 129
Unisys Corp., 157
United Fruit, 38
United Independent Broadcasters, 135
United Kingdom, 119
United Nations, 122–123
United States v. AT&T,
  Judge Greene's first decision, 92–93
  beginning of the case, 82–86
  the complaint, 86–88
  reaction to suit, 88–91
  settlement factors, 96–105
United States v. IBM, 91
United States v. Pullman Company, 44
United States v. Western Electric Case,
  44–46
  Modification of Final Judgment, 86, 96,
    100, 142, 178
  purpose of suit, 45
  settlement of (1956), 46–48, 83
United Telecommunications, 112
Unitel, 128–129
Universal Automatic Computer (Univac),
  161
University of Pennsylvania, 159
University of Pittsburgh, 132
UNIX operating system, 62, 163, 175, 187
U.S. Army Signal Corps., 137
U.S. Rubber, 43
US West, Inc., 102, 196, 200, 207
UseNet, 185, 187, 188

Vail, Theodore J., 14, 26–33, 149, 190
Valley Telephone Company, 116
VEBA, 114
Verifone, Inc., 111, 195
Vermeer Technologies, 195
Vertical integration, 44–45, 82, 88, 94, 103
Verveer, Philip, 85
Viacom, 195
Videocassette recorder (VCR), 13
Videoconferencing, 112, 124
Videotex, 112

Violence microprocessor (V-chip), 210
Vodafone, 113
Voice services, 172–173, 177
Von Neumann, John, 160

Waddy, Joseph C., 91
Wal-Mart, 109
Walker, Paul A., 42
Walson, John, Sr., 201
WATS (wide area telephone service), 70,
  76, 79
Watson, Thomas, 132
Waverman, Leonard, 141
Weaver, Suzanne, 83
Western Electric, 26, 28, 40, 96, 170
  AT&T case codefendant, 87–88, 90, 101
  aviation radio and, 137–138
  1949 case, 44–46
  prelude to 1949 case, 42–44
  settlement of (1956), 46–48, 83, 85,
    98–99, 163
Western Union, 22–23, 27, 71, 73, 211
  Bunker-Ramo case, 164–166
Westinghouse, 38, 133–134
Westrex Corporation, 47
Willis-Graham Act, 33
Wilson administration, 134
Wilson, James Q., 35
Wire pairs, 8
Wireless transmission, 131–133, 143
  allocation, 16–17
  AM broadcasting, 135
  development of industry, 133–137, 143
  personal communications services (PCS)
    and, 153–155
World Partners, 129
World Wide Web (WWW), 105, 180, 185,
  188–200, 211
Wright, Skelly, 80

Xerox, 182–183, 211

Yellow Pages, 101, 103
Yovelle Renaissance Corporation, 195

Alan Stone is professor of political science at the University of Houston. Educated at Columbia Law School (J.D.) and the University of Chicago (M.A., Ph.D.), he has been a senior trial attorney with the Federal Trade Commission. He is the author of many books, including *Wrong Number: The Breakup of AT&T* and *Public Service Liberalism: Telecommunications and Transitions in Public Policy,* and is a past president of the Policy Studies Organization.